A JEW

A MIRACLE

AND A MISSION

A JEW
A MIRACLE
AND A MISSION

By

WILHELM BAUM

A division of Squire Publishers, Inc.
4500 College Blvd.
Leawood, KS 66211
Phone: 1/888/888-7696

COVER PHOTO:
I used an extreme wide angle (fish eye) lens which made it look as though my arms were far apart. Having my back toward the students and holding the camera over my head, it took various tries since I couldn't look through the viewfinder.

ISBN: 1-58597-047-6

Library of Congress Catalog Card No. 00-135029

A division of Squire Publishers, Inc.
4500 College Blvd.
Leawood, KS 66211
Phone: 1/888/888-7696

TABLE OF CONTENTS

PREFACE

SOMEWHAT OVER A YEAR AGO, during one of my many visits to my homeland, Germany, I was encouraged by a dear and long-time friend to write "my story." He thought it would be a challenge and a blessing especially to those living in America, since many of my Jewish acquaintances who have been fortunate enough to escape the Holocaust have sworn never to set foot on German soil again. I, however, though Jewish, find myself repeatedly drawn back to the land of my birth with the story of the great transformation in my thinking and in my entire outlook on life.

At present my manuscript, in German, lies on the desk of the editor, awaiting the next bi-yearly meeting with the publisher.

Thus, ere it be too late, I have decided to tell "my story" for my English-speaking friends as well: the story of my youth in Germany until the time of Hitler; my immigration to America including my five years of service in the U.S. Army Air Corps in World War II — during which time I came to hear about and to trust Him of Whom "Moses and the prophets did write." My story also includes Bible school days, my experiences as a missionary in Japan for 28 years, and finally my far-reaching "post-retirement mission" travels which thus far have encompassed 26 countries.

W.B.

Shawnee, Kansas

June 1994

ACKNOWLEDGMENTS

"He who has found a wife has found a good thing and has obtained from the Lord something that pleases him well."

(German translation of Proverbs 18:22)

Our Lord surely knew whereof he spoke, and I want to again express my gratitude to Him for his direction which enabled me to find this "good thing," Augusta, my dear wife who never voiced a word of complaint, but for many months put up with a husband who spent practically every hour of those days behind the type-writer in his study.

I sensed this so keenly that I would interrupt my work periodically to go to her to tell her I loved her and how much I appreciated her understanding. I am also well aware of and therefore most grateful to my dear wife, who, throughout my many trips abroad, had to look after the affairs of our home all by herself and who had to spend many lonely hours; yet did so most happily and without complaining, knowing that her dear husband was about our Father's business.

My thankfulness to our Lord indeed extends especially to my good friends Alice and John Russie who, after I had finished my rough draft, invited me to their home in California, where Alice, a retired English teacher, spent many weeks and even months at her work processor revising, reorganizing and chronologically rearranging my manuscript.

Without her loving suggestions and her tireless efforts, this, "my story," might never have come into print.

DEDICATION

SINCE IT SEEMS to be the custom to dedicate one's writings, I would like to do this herewith to you, our children, Mary Esther and Timothy, and to our grandchildren, for in the accounts contained in this book I'm endeavoring to leave you somewhat of a record to look back upon.

Perhaps you will see or recall some of those things which you may not have known, or might have forgotten.

Yet this account is primarily and foremost dedicated to and in honor of my blessed Lord, who very early in my life — yes, even before I was fully aware of it — must have had His guiding and protecting hand upon me.

To Him do I devote this book, and to Him do I look for guidance as I write each page, even to the very last line — and into all eternity.

PART ONE

Life Begins

The "G.I. Gospel Team" through whose testimonies I came under the sound of the Gospel. Rev. David Morken at the extreme right, Bob Wesley (head only) next to him, and I stand at the extreme left (September 1944).

1

The Issues of Life

FROM THE MOMENT I entered the church, camera in hand, I felt apprehensive. I looked around, hoping no one was there who knew I was Jewish, wondering what I was doing at a gathering of "Goyim" (Hebr.: Gentiles) on a Sunday morning.

Then the singing started, clear and joyous and enthusiastically. What goes on here? I thought. Do they really believe what they are singing about? I distinctly heard them worshipping this Jesus, referring to Him also as Saviour and even Lord. Their heartiness irritated me. Couldn't they sing more slowly and reverently, as I was used to hearing it in our synagogue?

Besides, it seemed to me they were ascribing to this Jesus the attributes belonging only to God. While yet a youth, I learned the Hebrew phrase that is deeply ingrained in the heart of every Jew: **Sh'ma Yisroel, Adonai, Elohenu, Adonai, Echod** — Hear, O Israel, the Lord our God, the Lord is One. How, then, could this Jesus be worshipped as God? I was wrestling with the very basic issue of Judaism, the absolute One-ness of God, the Creator.

Then they came marching onto the platform, a group of soldiers, sailors and marines singing with radiant expressions, and I felt that they were convinced about the message of their song. But what were they doing here on their day off? Why wouldn't they go and have a "good time" in town?

One of the group then stepped up to the mike, and I was wondering what he was doing there. I didn't expect a Rabbi, but at least a preacher of some sort.

He told of the clean life which he thought he was living until he was shown the verse in the Bible which said that: *"All have sinned and fallen*

3

short of the glory of God.” Why did he have to say that? Then I heard him say: — *“The heart is deceitful above all things, and desperately wicked”* — and that — *“Man looks on the outward appearance, but the Lord looks upon the heart.”*

I hoped that nobody saw me cringe as a full-scale war began to erupt between my traditional Jewish upbringing and my newly awakened conscience as this eternal truth began to make inroads into my soul.

I tried to defend, to justify myself, to reason, to argue — do these people, who appear to be rather intelligent, actually believe all this? Isn't the one they call Jesus just a substitute for the One we Jews know to be Jehovah, the only true and eternally living Creator?

"It is appointed unto man once to die and after that the judgment — he that hears my word and believes on Him that sent Me has everlasting life and shall not come into judgment, but is passed from death unto life.”

Wasn't this Jesus a blasphemer, and besides that, an illegitimate child?

“God so loved the world, that He gave His only begotten Son, that whosoever believes in Him should not perish, but have life which lasts forever and ever.”

I felt myself ensnared by such love which I had not known before; yet I wanted to get away, out of that church to shake off those words which convicted me of what I knew was in my heart.

Am I not a Jew? God's Chosen? Besides, I don't belong to this church; I've come here only to photograph this “Gospel Team” for my buddy. If these things were really true, surely my parents, or at least our Rabbi, would have told us about them.

“... that at the name of Jesus every knee should bow, of things in heaven and things in earth and things under the earth ...” and at the same time, **Hear, O Israel, the Lord our God, the Lord is one.**

The battle of my heart raged on, intensifying with every new Scripture that pounded into my ears. I forgot all about taking those pictures, and the leader of the group had to remind me — how miserable I was.

“He that hath the son hath life and he that hath not the son of God hath not life.”

I was smitten with the conviction that what I had heard might actually be eternal truths, and I was jealous that these Gentiles had the joy, the peace and the assurance that their sins were forgiven, and how I longed for the same, but I was a Jew — and that left me out.

At that time, I had no knowledge that Jesus Christ is our Jews' promised Messiah, the Anointed One of God, of whom Moses and the prophets did write, the son of David, the son of Abraham. Had I known, no doubt, my struggles would have been over; I was fully persuaded of my need of a Savior. As it was, I was battling with the one conviction that is so deeply ingrained in us Jews, our total psychological and emotional pillar and stay, the one proclamation that we Jews have scrupulously guarded and tena-

4

ciously clung to with every available ounce of our being, the final authority which we believe God has entrusted unto us, the very last words uttered by thousands of our people as they were being led to their deaths in
the concentration camps, as an expression of their unshakable trust:
namely, the absolute ONE-ness of God, their Creator. I simply could not
comprehend the TRINITY, the TRI-UNITY of God.

Thou shalt have no other gods before me.

According to Jewish law, anyone who would transgress this command
was to be put to death by stoning:

*If there be found among you ... man or woman, that hath wrought
wickedness ... in transgressing his covenant, and hath gone and served
other gods, and worshipped them ... then shalt thou ... stone them with
stones till they die. So thou shalt put the evil away from among you (Deuteronomy 17:2-7).*

Even those who would secretly try to persuade someone to worship
other gods could expect the same punishment:

*If thy brother, the son of thy mother, or thy son, or thy daughter, or the
wife of thy bosom, or thy friend ... entice thee secretly, saying, Let us go
and serve other gods ... thou shalt surely kill him ... because he has sought
to thrust thee away from the Lord thy God ... (Deuteronomy 13:6-10).*

These verses echoed and re-echoed in my mind. I was feeling sorry I
had been born a Jew. For as a Jew, I did not dare to trust this Jesus; **yet I
knew of no Jewish way to be assured of Heaven.** At the same time,
I was filled with great fear to not trust this Gentile Savior, for I was convinced that God saw my sinful self, and that without a Savior I would be
under His wrath, just as I had heard, and I'd be forever banned from His
presence.

I knew I needed forgiveness of sin, and peace with my Creator. But
somehow I had to obtain it without having anything to do with the name
of Jesus or with Christianity.

Then there were my friends, and my family. I agonized especially over
the reaction of my family if I should make such a momentous decision. I
was not so much concerned with what they would do or say to me — we
were, after all, reformed Jews — but I knew they would feel I was reject-
ing Judaism.

I was in anguish for the grief I was sure it would bring to their hearts.
The gratitude I felt to them for getting me and my brother out of Germany only compounded my torment.

I spent a week of restless, mostly sleepless, nights, trying to reason
that all this didn't really concern me, since I didn't belong to that church
and only went there to take pictures. I stuck my fingers in my ears in the
vain attempt to block out all that had already entered into them.

*All have sinned ... the wages ... death ... the gift of God ... eternal
life ... but that only through Jesus Christ.*

If only I had not gone — if only I had not accepted the invitation of my barracks' buddy, Bob Wesley. After all, he was to blame, for he was the one who had asked me to go with him to photograph the gospel team.

I really didn't want to give him the satisfaction of finding out that I was under such conviction of sin, so I decided to go once again with the gospel team and asked the leader, the Rev. David Morken, to help me solve my problem. Following the sermon I said to him, "What you have proclaimed today and also what I heard last week makes good sense, and in some way or other I would like to have a part in it. Please fix me up."

He knew instantly what I wanted and needed. He asked me straight out, "So, you would like to receive the Lord Jesus into your life?"

I knew exactly that this was my need, but I was not quite ready yet to surrender to this Gentile Savior. Trying to evade the issue, I told him how "good" I was, justifying myself as best I could, bargaining, so to speak.

Very tenderly this dear man put his hand on my shoulder and said, "Yes, Wilhelm, but you see, I'm not God, nor your judge who, as the Bible says *'searches the heart and tries the reins to give every man according to his ways and according to the fruit of his doings.'* And since it is so, how would you make out? Maybe you should tell God yourself how good you really are."

His words stung. I was still proud and didn't like to have these truths confront me, so I said: "All right, I'll do that," and walked out.

For a while I sauntered around in the small park next to the church, thinking about what Rev. Morken had told me. Then, looking up, I ventured forth with, "Look, God, my name is Wilhelm Baum, I ..." I couldn't go on. Why was I so proud? I realized that Rev. Morken knew my spiritual dilemma exactly and that I had not been able to fool him. Now I stood, alone — whom was I trying to impress? No need to justify myself before another human being, yet trying to do just that before the Creator of heaven and earth, whom I knew I couldn't fool.

Now I was the only one that was left, and what sense would there be in deceiving myself. I was undone and bare before Him who knew all about me, even the things I had long since forgotten.

It was much later that I learned the verse which at the time perfectly described my condition:

"Because you say, I am rich, and increased with goods, and have need of nothing; and know not that you are wretched, and miserable, and poor and blind, and naked ..." (Revelation 3:17).

At last, tired of pretending and arguing, and in desperation, I admitted my great need of a Savior. I was no longer concerned — I no longer really cared what people might say or think about me, that I, a Jew, would take this "despised God of the Gentiles" into my heart and life. I was convinced that the Lord Jesus Christ had born my sins in His own body on the cross forever and ever.

I bowed my head and simply said, "Lord Jesus, I take YOU." That was all, and that was all that was necessary. In that moment I experienced a deep peace in my heart and the absolute assurance that He had heard me, and that I belonged to Him from then on and forevermore.

It was not from any theological insight that I made my decision, but entirely from the realization that I saw myself a hopeless, helpless sinner before a holy, righteous yet loving God, and I accepted His gift, the salvation of my soul, through the substitutionary death of His son, the Lord Jesus Christ. There was no other way.

It was around one o'clock on August 26, 1944, and I was 29 at that time. Great joy filled my heart as I hurried back into the church were some of the team members, including my friend Bob Wesley, were still talking to Rev. Morken. I felt like shouting or leaping with joy as I said, "It's okay now!" He asked me outright whether I meant that I had indeed trusted the Lord Jesus for salvation. I answered him without hesitation, and with a clear "Yes."

Some of the team members hugged me, and we thanked my new Lord together. Brother Morken put his arm around me in a fatherly gesture and said: "Now, my dear son and brother in Christ, I have a further important task for you."

I wondered what was coming next as he continued, "I want you to be on the platform with the team next Sunday and tell everyone of the decision you've just made and what the Lord has done for you ."

That was almost too much for me all at once, and I involuntarily stepped back a little. "Now wait a minute," I blurted out. "Do I have to do that?"

"Oh, no," he answered, "you don't have to, but I thought you really meant what you told us just now about having committed your life to the Lord. Because in the Bible we read that *if we confess with our mouth Jesus as Lord and Savior and believe in our heart that God has raised him from the dead, we will be saved. It is with the heart that man believes unto righteousness and with the mouth that we confess unto salvation.*" (Romans 10:9, 10)

While I was considering this new idea, he added that God also said, *"Whosoever shall be ashamed of me and of my words, of him shall the Son of man be ashamed, when He shall come in his own glory and in his Father's and of the holy angels."* (Luke 9:26)

So I had to ask myself: Did I really mean it when I asked Him to come into my heart? Or was it just a one-time emotional and superficial impulse? The answer was completely clear to me. I knew that the greatest, most important transaction in my life had just taken place. I happily agreed to join the team the following Sunday.

I hurried back to my barracks and immediately went to the washroom and stood in front of the long mirror. I actually expected to look different. The transformation which had just taken place was so startling, so real and amazing, that I was eager to see what I now looked like. I was a little disappointed when I still looked the same. As yet I did not know

7

the scripture I had unknowingly manifested, namely that, "... *if any man be in Christ, he is a new creation; old things are passed away; behold, all things are become new.*" (2 Corinthians 5:17)

When I told my buddies in the barracks, they called me "Rabbi Baum," both because of my being a Jew and because, to them, I had suddenly become very religious.

I wrote home right away, searching for the right words to tell my Jewish family what had transpired. I thought it was very important to mention the name of my Lord, Jesus Christ, who had brought this miracle to pass, because sooner or later I would want to tell them the details anyway.

Mother answered immediately. She was very upset. She wrote, "How can you change your religion as simply as a woman changes her dress?" and added that I had always been "a good Jew, so why then switch over to another religion?" My heart ached. How would I ever be able to explain my newfound life and joy to all my dear ones at home? How could I get them to believe me? Would they ever understand?

The following Sunday I could hardly trust my senses and my emotions when I found myself walking onto the platform as one of the team members to sing and to sit there with them. When it was my turn to speak, I told in simple words that I had received the Lord into my heart and how it had come about.

I looked at the pew in front of me, similar to the one I had occupied a week before in a different church. At that time I had been at variance with everything I heard, frustrated, full of doubt and absolutely miserable. And now, rejoicing and unspeakably happy. Unbelievable, I thought. What a transformation. I could hardly comprehend the miracle that had taken place.

From that time on, I went with the gospel team each Sunday when I was not on duty and told what wondrous thing the Lord had done in my life.

Where I would be heading from here on forth, I had, as yet, no idea. But I could look back with great amazement when I considered the path that had brought me this far.

PART TWO

Life Before Life

The employees of my father's bedroom-furniture and mattress manufacturing store. The ones in white coats worked at our down-and-feather sorting and disinfecting plant. Father with the four of us children is at the left. I'm standing to the left of him (about 1925).

2

My Youth

I WAS BORN in Dortmund on June 3, 1915, an industrial city of the province of Westphalia in the northwestern part of Germany. World War I was gaining momentum, and my earliest recollections were those of my mother snatching me out of my warm bed, hurriedly wrapping me into a blanket and carrying me down the back steps and across the cold yard into an equally cold cellar of the adjacent building.

She later told me that I became very jittery when I heard the droning of the approaching bombers and I became progressively more nervous since this scenario often had to be repeated several times a night.

I was also very frail and undernourished because of the scarcity of food, influencing my growth which accounts also for the slight curvature of my back, even to this day.

A few years ago I visited the place which had once been home — now completely rebuilt. The cellar, however, was still the same, and I relived that part of my childhood as I looked up at its arched and steel-reinforced ceiling. I recalled how I shivered in the cold and with fear. It still seemed to re-echo the roar of the bombers overhead, and I could yet clearly visualize the anxiety on the faces of my parents and our domestic help, huddled together in one of the corners. Amazingly, it withstood the bombardments of World War II, even the most severe one in the late spring of 1944 which destroyed 95 percent of our city.

So severe was that bombing that the Germans called it Bombenteppech (carpet bombing) because the bombs fell as closely and as systematically as the weavings of a carpet. The destruction was actually so great that for a while the city fathers contemplated rebuilding the city at another location.

Dad was the prosperous owner of one of our city's biggest bedroom furniture stores. We had a mattress manufacturing shop, a feather-sorting and disinfecting plant with over 70 employees, two delivery trucks and one of the best German-made limousines of that time, driven by a chauffeur in "livree," a special uniform.

There were four of us children: Anneliese, who was two years older than I; a brother Gerhard (Gary); two years younger, and a little sister, Charlotte, who was six years younger than I. We also had a cook, a cleaning lady, a woman to do the laundry and a governess. My parents were greatly respected in our Jewish community, and I was the only one in my class at school whose father was a store owner and rather well-to-do.

Of the four or five branches of present-day Judaism: Orthodox, Conservative, Reformed, Liberal and Zionists (which really is more a political than a religious group), we considered ourselves Reformed Jews, yes, even pretty liberal, at that. Father frequently referred to our family as Freidenker (Freethinkers), implying that we were "free from any religious or Biblical precepts." We thought of ourselves as being foremost Germans and as Jews only because of our ancestral bloodline.

Our family went to the reformed synagogue two or three times a year, that is, on the High Holidays, but even then without fully understanding their significance. It was just the social thing to do. Father met many of his business acquaintances there. For us children it meant to be excused from school, to be able to dress up, to see our Jewish friends and playmates and, of course, to have a festive meal at noon. We young folks frequently walked out during the service when it became too boring, to visit with one another.

As members of that congregation we adhered to the Jewish custom of Bar Mitzvah, so I became a "son of the covenant" or of "the commandment" at the age of 13. It meant that from that day on I would be responsible for my own actions before my creator rather than my earthly father. Again I must say, we did all this more to fall in line with what was expected of us rather than because of any religious conviction.

For a few weeks I had taken special instructions from Rabbi Goldschmidt, and in the morning on that memorable day we all went to the synagogue where I was privileged to stand up in front, a gilded pointer in hand, reading from the Torah, meaning precepts or statutes. Those big parchment scrolls, which we considered nigh unto holy, encompass the first five books of the Bible, and though I was able to pronounce the Hebrew letters that morning, I did not know their meaning, for we never read the Bible at home, not even in German.

It was the first time I wore a suit with long trousers and a white shirt with a collar so stiff it scratched every time I tried to turn my head. My parents spared no expense to make my Bar Mitzvah a most elaborate affair. It was June 1928, nearly five years before Hitler's rise to power, and National Socialism was still of little concern to us, as well as it was to most Jews.

We had a sumptuous meal in Dortmund's most prestigious hotel, the "Römischer Kaiser" to which also many relatives and acquaintances from out of town had been invited. Father and Mother gave me a gold wrist watch and my "Onkel Albert" gave me a "Parker Doufold," which at the time was one of Germany's best-known and most expensive fountain pens.

It was about a year later, when I visited my grandmother in Wittlich, a little town in the Eiffel mountains, that I became unexpectedly aware of one of the privileges that went with becoming Bar Mitzvah.

One Saturday afternoon, a young Jewish fellow who with some others planned to meet for prayer in behalf of the dead in the home of their recently deceased friend came to me and said, "Wilhelm, we heard of you visiting here and were wondering if you already had become Bar Mitzvah."

When I answered in the affirmative, he continued, "We need someone to help us make Minyan; would you be willing to help us out? It won't take very long."

I felt quite elated and "grown up," for Minyan means ten, the number of adult men needed before any Jewish service can convene. All I had to do was to be present while they prayed.

In general, "Jewishness" was for me more often a hindrance than an advantage. This I sensed especially when it came to my friendship with our employees, most of all with our private Gentile chauffeur whom I practically idolized.

The sound of his name, Walter Schmidt, still takes me back to the time he invited me to share his meat sausage with him.

He would cut a portion of it, stuck it into an old tin can filled with water and, with a set of large tongs, balanced it on the burning cinders inside our big furnace in the boiler room.

The slice he gave me tasted better than even the steaks Mother used to prepare. Our friendship was mutual, and I could hardly believe it when one day he said, "Willem," that's what he called me, "Next Sunday I'm taking my family on a picnic. Want to come along?" I could hardly believe it. What great fun that would be, but I immediately thought of what my father would say and I was wondering how I could diplomatically ask for his permission.

The next day at the noon meal I just blurted out, "Father Herr Schmidt has invited me to go on a picnic with him." Even before he spoke I could see the "thunder clouds" on his face. His voice became high-pitched, and he had great difficulty controlling his anger.

"What has gotten into your crazy head? You, a Jew and the son of his employer lowering yourself to go out with a chauffeur, and a Gentile at that!"

It was one of the times I was really sorry to have been born a Jew, and before I even thought about it, I heard myself say, "Look, Dad, Herr Schmidt earns his money as honestly as you do, maybe even a little more so."

Then the thunder broke loose! Dad jumped up from the other side of the table and with balled fists headed for me. As quickly as I could, I ran out of the room and locked myself into the "toilette" (bathroom). I was afraid he might break in the door and waited until his wrath had somewhat subsided. When he finally, slowly walked back, I heard him say, "And a son like that one has to bring into the world!"

We children feared Dad very much, and when it became necessary to talk with him, we usually did so in his office where he spent most of his time. Often Mother had to protect or defend us from his anger. Once, helping to push our big limousine (a "Horch," now an "Audi") back a little, I did so with my back against one of the headlights and broke it. When I, greatly trembling, told Mother about it, she gave me some money and said, "Take this, my dear boy, and have Herr Schmidt quickly replace it, before your father finds out about it."

The most severe punishment for me in my younger years was not to be slapped or whipped which also did happen, but to hear my father say: "No bicycle for two weeks." That was a real blow because I spent most of my free time riding it all over town, and especially to school. Now I would have to get up a whole hour earlier, because it was a long way.

It was also the time in my life when I craved real love and understanding. Anneliese, my older sister, seemed to know how "absolutely crazy" I was about her classmate, Cecilia Lorig, who came from a very poor family and whom she therefore frequently brought home for a meal. I was too hesitant to let my true feelings be known to her; also, I sensed that it was a rather one-sided affair.

By that time movies began to have sound, and they became my obsession. In them I saw real romance, adventure and exciting scenes in which mighty heroes conquered impossible situations.

3

Hitler Comes to Power

"DON'T BE OVERLY CONCERNED, the German people will never tolerate the absurd plans which this mad man Hitler proposes."

It was Father who sought to calm our fears while we were all crouched around our small radio. It was summer of 1932, I was 17, and we heard about the great street battles with the Communists.

I had completed business school and had begun an apprenticeship in one of our city's largest textile stores. One day after closing time we all were told to meet in a large room in the basement.

I didn't know the reason and thought there was a change in work assignments, but it was unusual. Then I heard a man say, "The average fire bombs can be extinguished with water or smothered with sand, but there are those which carry their oxygen right with them and will continue to burn even in water and in the sand, and there is very little you can do."

We all were puzzled about this unusual demonstration, wondering what the reason for it might be. We had no idea. On the 30th of January, 1933, President Hindenburg appointed Adolf Hitler Chancellor of Germany. A few weeks thereafter when I went to the store where I worked, I saw three men in brown shirts standing at the employees' entrance.

Their legs were spread apart in typical soldier's stance with their chin straps in place. "Halt! What business do you have here?" said the one as I walked up to the door. He stepped right in front of me.

"I'm employed here," I said and tried to walk in.

"Doing what?" was his next question.

"Well, I'm a stock clerk." Then, looking at me closely and half-questioningly, "You're a JUDE, eh?" —

"Yes, I happen to be one."

"Well, then, go on in, you won't be working here for long; we will see to it that no good German will ever buy any more from this Jewish place."

It was true indeed. We sat around all that day waiting for customers. I sensed the strained atmosphere between us Jewish employees and those who were not Jewish. There were a few shoppers, however, who were brave and bold enough to talk themselves past the guards at the entrance.

But even that ended shortly, because the local newspapers began to publish photographs of people, mainly women, as they were coming out of Jewish stores, with the comments underneath: "The Camera Doesn't Lie, Look at These Admirers of Jewish Establishments."

A few days later we all were dismissed because the store was closed. At home the atmosphere was very subdued. In early July (1933) Hitler reviewed a parade of hundreds of goose-stepping Brown-shirts not far from where we lived, with their hands raised in the Heil Hitler salute.

I tried to be as inconspicuous as possible as I walked by, for there was no telling what one of the sympathizers might do, seeing me, a Jew, watching the adulation of his "Führer."

Every day there were new restrictions for us Jews. When I came home telling my father I had just seen a sign in front of our most famous restaurant, "Café Corso," reading "Jews Are Not Desired Here," he added, "Yes, and I have seen signs saying, 'Beware of Jews' and 'Admission Only for Arians,' and in front of one Jewish store it was written, 'Germans Defend Yourself, Don't Buy from a Jew.' "

In schools even young children were challenged by their teachers to write antisemitic slogans on the blackboard such as, "The Jew is our greatest enemy" and "I now have learned to really hate the Jew."

Jews could no longer go to restaurants or theatres nor own cars, and they had to surrender their drivers' licenses. They had to turn over their radios and all electrical implements, as well as all silverware and jewelry, except their wedding rings.

They could no longer go to public bath houses, but this was later changed, allowing them to wash there just before the water was changed.

All Jewish organizations and societies as well as Jewish meetings of any kind had to be dissolved.

This would be strictly enforced, and any transgression would be punishable by imprisonment; in certain cases it would be considered treason, the punishment of which would be death.

I still belonged to a group of Boy Scouts, made up (among others) of many of my classmates. We made bicycle tours into the country, even as far as Holland, set up tents, cooked in the open, or stayed in youth hostels with other travel adventurers.

One evening after dark, "Eberhardt Deutscher," the leader of our troop, came to our home. Very hesitantly and visibly unsure of himself as he began to speak, "Dear scout Willi," then he stopped. "My good friend Wilhelm, — how can I tell you — I don't want to hurt you and yet — you see — we all have been taken over by the Hitler Youth — and they don't know that you are not like most of the other Jews (a statement I was to hear many times thereafter) — but they now have a, so to say, general rule, that no Jew can any longer attend."

Then, putting his hand on my shoulder and trying to smile in order to alleviate my great disappointment somewhat, he stammered, "We'll still be good friends though, won't we, Willi?" With that he turned to leave, then stopped once more at the door. "Oh," he said, "one more thing just to keep both of us out of trouble, it probably would be best that we don't recognize one another or exchange greetings when we see each other on the street. One can never tell who might see us. I'm sure you know what I mean!"

I went to the house of one of my best friends, who I hoped would be different and understanding. When I rang the doorbell, an upstairs window opened and the mother looked down to see who it was. When she saw me, she quickly looked first to the right, then to the left and quietly said to me, "I think it would be better for both of us if you would leave right away." With that she hurriedly closed the window.

At that time, a division of Hitler's Brownshirts, called S.A. (Sturm Abteilung), commonly known as "Storm Troopers," were appointed to be Hilfspolizei (Police Assistants). They proudly patrolled the streets together with the regular police, a white armband signifying their new authority.

Up until that time, a Jew, being unjustly mistreated, was at least heard when he complained to the police. Now, however, he was not only ignored or laughed at, but as was the case with one man who came to the police saying, "I was crossing the street in front of two patrolling policemen, one a 'Hilfspolizist' (auxiliary policeman), suddenly hauled out and knocked me to the ground. My glasses were broken and look at the wound on my head."

The policeman hearing his complaint immediately said to two of his men, "Shave his head and hang a sign around his neck reading, 'Ich werde mich nie mehr bei der Polizei beschweren' (I will never again complain to the police) and march him through the main streets of the city."

As I was coming into our living room one day, I heard Dad talk to Mother in a hushed voice. I busied myself nearby to hear what he was saying.

"Gerda (Mother's name), I just found out that Herr Nordwald, our dear business friend, hung himself. I remember him saying the last time I saw him he wouldn't be around too much longer. I thought he might have been able to obtain a visa, thus be able to leave the country. They're hauling people right out of their beds these days, in the middle of the night, and the fear of that must have driven him to commit this act."

It was well known among the Jewish community that under the pretense of being placed into "Schutzhaft" (Protective Custody), men ended up first in the already greatly overcrowded city jail, and from there as soon as possible were transferred to one of the so greatly feared concentration camps.

At that time Nazi Storm Troopers had also stood in front of Father's store with a big sign that read, "This Is a Jewish Store — Good Germans Don't Buy Here."

Dortmund's mayor, decked out in his spotless Nazi uniform, had been on the platform with Hitler on the day of the parade. A few weeks prior to it, he stood at our big market place before a crowd of 500 Nazi sympathizers witnessing the raising of the big Swastika flag on the City Hall. He proudly proclaimed, "THIS FLAG WILL NEVER AGAIN COME DOWN; BE IT THEN, THAT GERMANY CEASES TO EXIST."

There also was a large banner stretched across the wall of one of our government buildings, "GIVE ME TEN YEARS AND YOU WILL NOT RECOGNIZE GERMANY AGAIN."

In making that statement, Hitler was almost right. It was five years, eight months and seven days from the beginning of the war on September 1st, 1939, until the 7th of May, 1945, when in a little red school house in Rheims (northern France), Germany admitted total defeat and signed the documents of unconditional surrender.

During those months and years, millions of people had been mercilessly slaughtered and hundreds upon hundreds of cities, villages and smaller communities completely leveled.

In the truest sense of Hitler's once-proud proclamation, Germany was indeed "NOT RECOGNIZABLE ANY MORE."

* * * * * * * * * *

Twelve years after I had left my home town Dortmund, I went back as a soldier with the American Occupation Forces. It was a totally traumatic experience. The city had been so severely bombed, I could hardly find the street we used to live on because there were no longer any houses that bordered it. When I finally succeeded, I identified our "home" only by the piece of one wall still standing, and by Mother's old kitchen stove sticking partially out of the rubble.

I wonder what the few passersby thought of this American soldier sitting there among the ruins, crying. All the wonderful memories of having lived there so happily for 19 unforgettable years had come crashing down upon me.

My good old homeland, the once beautiful Germany, which I still love with all my heart, and which under Hitler was to have lasted 1,000 years, now resembled a nearly endless devastation. As the oldest son of the family, I was to have taken over Dad's prosperous business, and the future had once seemed very bright indeed. Now it was all over.

As I sat there that day in 1945, I recalled what Dad used to tell me about real estate, using our possession as an example. He had suggested that I would do well to consider such in the future, for it would by far be the safest and most enduring investment I could make. Was **this** the type of REAL estate Dad had been thinking about? Surely not. Strange how UN-REAL it was to me just then, and I wondered who had ever coined such an expression. I reflected upon the most far-reaching decision I had made just a few months before, when I turned my whole life over to the one who said:

"Let not your heart be troubled; you believe in God, believe also in me. In my Father's house are many mansions; if it were not so, I would have told you. I go to prepare a place for you. And if I go and prepare a place for you, I will come again, and receive you unto myself; that where I am, there you may be also." (John 14:1-3)

Think of it; here was One who made an offer to you and to me, absolutely without charge, to not only prepare a REAL estate for us in an absolutely safe place, but who promised to take upon HIMSELF the responsibility of getting us safely there as well. (1 Peter 1:3-5)

I had also heeded His advice not to lay up for myself *"treasures upon earth, where moth and rust doth corrupt, and where thieves break through and steal,"* but to lay up for myself *treasures in Heaven, where neither moth nor rust corrupts* — nor, I'm pretty sure, bombs won't explode and blow up buildings. (Matthew 6:19,20)

This "most far-reaching decision" that I made, I have already described. By faith, I had trusted the Lord Jesus Christ as the Lord of my life on the basis of His sacrificial death on the cross for my sin. I responded to His invitation and promise that, *"... whosoever comes to me, I will in no way cast out"* (John 6:37). This decision I made not just for this life, but as "far-reaching" as the life hereafter — throughout all eternity.

Though I was once a citizen of Germany by birth and became one of America by naturalization, by the new birth I could now claim to be a citizen of Heaven where wars, famine, sickness and, most of all, death no longer reigns — and where injustices and prejudices forever cease.

Above: Farewell from Dortmund

Left: With Mother on the ship

Lower left: Heading for the gang plank

Lower right: Mother and Dad (in back) leaving the ship

A New World and a New Life

I CAN NEVER THANK my dear parents enough for sending my brother and me so early to America before the extreme persecution of my people began.

They had written to relatives in Kansas City, who immediately declared themselves most happy to have me and my brother Gerhard (Gary), then 17, and me 19 come to live with them. They knew what was going on in Germany, although the German press in general kept its readers pretty much in the dark concerning the severity of the Jewish persecution. The papers, however, were full of the wonderful achievements of Hitler and his Nazi party and the great plans for the future of Germany.

It wasn't long before we received the needed sponsorship papers from our relatives, and together with Dad we went to the American Embassy in Stuttgart where we personally met the Ambassador. Only a few days later we were granted our visas, and on the 5th of June, 1934, two days after my 19th birthday, we walked to the nearby railroad station with our parents and our younger sister, Charlotte.

I shall never forget that walk. I was bidding a sorrowful farewell to an integral segment of my life, my entire youth. Sadly I looked at the many stores and buildings as we passed, and as we rounded the corner I turned once more and for the last time looked up and down our so-familiar street. The excitement of the adventure in going to "the new world" could not blot out the heaviness of my heart.

A few of our close family friends saw us off at the station. Mother and Dad went with us to Bremerhafen where we boarded the great ship, the *Bremen*. This colossus of the seas and her sister ship, the *Europa,* were the fastest, most modern ocean liners of that day. They had been awarded the much coveted *Blaue Band des Ozeans* (The Blue Band of the Ocean), for crossing the Atlantic in five and a half days.

As we settled in our very attractive cabin — I still remember the number, 508 — I could hardly contain my amazement. Never before had I seen such an elegant interior, beautiful plush carpets, brilliantly glistening chandeliers and crystal glass doors with highly polished knobs.

The menu offered the most delectable dishes, all kinds of meats, vegetables, salads and desserts. There was wild duck, brisket, venison, asparagus, artichokes, avocados, a salad made of whipped cream, pistachio, marshmallows and nuts, lemon cream pies, apple and peach cobbler and every variety of ice cream. We could eat as much as we liked of each. At the time we thought this is what paradise must be like.

Even while sitting in the sun on deck, stewards came and brought cool lemonade or orangeade and chocolate cookies or macaroons. (Later during World War II, the Bremen was sunk; however, another one was built in its honor. Though it bore its name, it was much smaller and not nearly as extravagant.

When we reached America, our "Onkel Hans" picked us up and took us through customs and then to German-speaking friends of our Kansas City relatives. They couldn't do enough in showing us New York. We rode the upper deck of the busses on Fifth Avenue, visited the Museum of Science and Industry, Macy's department store and Radio City Music Hall, which all so overwhelmed us and wore us out, that we begged them to please just let us remain at their home.

When the afternoon drew near, Gary and I went into the fancy living room which had nice draperies at the window and doilies on various small tables. The big table in the middle had a delicately embroidered table cloth in the center of which was a beautiful vase full of tulips ... they really were krisanthamams, but I didn't know how to spell that ...

Our host family was gone that afternoon when we were looking forward to the German custom of having afternoon "Kaffee" with either pie or cake or some cream tarts. Gary saw the maid come in and said to me, "See, now we are getting something good to eat." We both watched her as she took the vase off the table and then the fancy table covering.

She went to the drawer, took out another table cloth, put it on the table, replaced the flower vase, went back into the kitchen, and that is where she stayed. We could not speak English, and we were reluctant to try to make ourselves understood in "sign language."

I looked at my dear brother and said, "Do you possibly have any crackers left from our room on the ship?

He didn't, and we were mighty hungry and could hardly wait to get something to eat in the evening. What a great surprise that was!

In Germany we had only our typical German Abendbrot (evening bread), and that's about all it was, except for some cold cuts and cheese, perhaps a few tomatoes or pickles to garnish our slice, and at times even some herring. We would also have something warm to drink, like tea or coffee.

Now we were being served a regular full meal, with soup, then meat and potatoes with gravy, a vegetable and even a dessert. Though we were mighty hungry, it didn't quite fit in with the way our stomachs had been "programmed."

The train which we took to Kansas City, our new home, was called the ERIE, after an old Indian tribe. Due to the fact that it took more time to reach its destination than any of the other railroads, it became the butt for denoting lethargy through the well-known proverb at the time, "As slow as the Erie."

Though we had a Pullman car, allowing us to sleep comfortably each night, it became quite boring. We looked forward to the welcome change which the mealtime would bring in the dining car. We were nearly always the first ones who would head in that direction as soon as we heard the gong while still a few cars away.

What great fun it was, sitting at a table decked with spotless white linen and starched napkins, watching the landscape pass by. The waiter soon brought a menu which, of course, neither of us could read. For some reason, one section attracted our attention, and Gary said, "This looks interesting; let's order it and see what it is." I was much in agreement and added, "How about the dish right below it?" My dear brother seemed happy about it and suggested a couple more that were written in the same part of the menu.

It was a great adventure, and we were anxious to see what those "new" dishes would taste like.

The waiter seemed amused and asked us some questions. Not understanding them, we just nodded our heads. He kept trying to tell us something, and we said, "Yes, yes," which was about all the English we knew.

We were wondering why he was shaking his head so much and mumbling to himself as he went on to the next table. When we received our order, we understood.

He set before us a bowl of mashed potatoes, a plate with baked potatoes, a dish with scalloped potatoes and one with French fries. You may guess what one of the first words was which we learned in English. We ate as much as we could, and when the waiter brought each of us a bowl of what looked like "very translucent" soup, we knew we were about ready for our next American culinary lesson.

Everything was so new to us, and I was the first to try a spoonful. "It tastes like water." My brother tried it and had the same opinion, so I suggested we ask the waiter. Gary was against it. After the potato episode he didn't want to reveal any further ignorance. I, however, really wanted to know. Just then the waiter passed by, and I gave him to understand that I was curious about the contents.

He took the bowl, stuck three of his fingers in it and swished them around. Then he dried them on his napkin.

My dear brother, with a victorious laugh, exclaimed, "See what you get, asking silly questions!"

The next surprise came after we were met by our aunt in Kansas City. We followed her to the parking lot where we expected her husband, or perhaps a chauffeur, to be waiting for us at the car. Instead, it was she who climbed behind the wheel, and we drove off to her home. In Germany it was considered quite an accomplishment for even a younger man to obtain a driver's license; for a woman it was unthinkable.

"What is this?" I asked when I saw the little instrument with buttons on the dashboard. I could hardly believe it when she told me, "It is a radio." Unbelievable, I had never seen one without a large dry cell battery and a cord to plug into the house current as we had at home. This one had no wires connected to an aerial on the roof nor a ground wire to be fastened to a down spout or to some water pipe. And it could even be heard while the car was in motion. Unbelievable!

One of my greatest surprises yet, better said, one of my greatest shocks, came soon after our arrival.

I considered the presence of a divorced woman among the household help of my aunt a great scandal and an enormous disgrace. How could my dear aunt knowingly tolerate such a person in her home? This shows how our present day society has become dulled, and I'm surprised to realize how much even my own viewpoint as well has changed throughout the intervening years.

Among my close friends are those who have gone through this trauma. It makes me conscious of our crafty and malicious adversary, who constantly goes about sowing discontent and vexation to break up families.

Nonetheless, I'm confident that healing of the heart, tranquility and peace of mind can be regained through HIM, who didn't condemn even the woman taken in adultery.

Instead, He said to her accusers, "He that is without sin among you, let him first cast a stone at her." The Scriptures continue "... they which heard it, being convicted by their own conscience, went out one by one ..."

Our relatives were financially well off. Our uncle was co-owner and president of one of the biggest envelope-manufacturing plants in the city. The family called themselves "reformed Jews," but they were the liberal variety, as were my parents, and highly esteemed by the large Jewish community.

They had a beautiful, spacious house with a large garden, well cared for by a black gardener. They also had a cleaning woman, a cook, a governess for the three small children and one more "all around" helper.

About a week after we arrived, Gary and I began working in our relatives' envelope-manufacturing plant. At first I oiled machines and pushed carts with paper, while my brother emptied waste paper baskets in the office and helped with the mailing. Neither of us spoke much English yet, so we both went to evening classes. I must confess, however, that I learned most of my English from the movies which I saw at every opportunity. I remember especially "Mr. Smith Goes to Washington," with James Stewart, and "How Green Was My Valley," with Claudette Colbert. I saw them again and again.

On weekends we usually would go with our relatives to a Jewish country club where we were introduced to young Jewish girls with whom we would then dance. Through them we met other young Jewish folk who invited us to a variety of parties, dances and other enjoyable social activities. To the synagogue we went only on special holidays, the same as we had done in Germany.

The work in the factory became a drudgery, especially when I was changed to the night shift. After two years I quit my $18-a-week job and began working in the shipping department of a local dress and millinery store for $12 a week. I wrapped suits, coats and hats and sent them out or delivered them personally to addresses in the vicinity.

Before we could become American citizens, we had to attend a weekly course on citizenship. Classes were conducted for people from various foreign countries, to acquaint them with the type of government and the Constitution of the United States, as well as with many customs and practices. Through it all we awaited the time we would "graduate," stand before a judge and be sworn in as full-fledged American citizens.

Our teacher told us that beginning that day we would have the same rights and privileges as all other American citizens in this land of "unlimited possibilities" (as it was called at that time), and that "making something of ourselves" was dependent only on our own zeal and ingenuity.

After the great event of being sworn in as a citizen, I went to our teacher, Mr. Krolik, and thanked him for his efforts in teaching us the many aspects of life in America.

Jokingly I said to him, "Mr. Krolik, now that I'm an American, maybe one day I'll be the president of these great United States." He looked at me for just a moment as though he didn't fully understand me, so I repeated what I had just said.

This time he shook his head emphatically and said, "No, not you!" That really upset me because, though I was joking, I resented his so very negative remark and tried to justify myself by saying, "Look, Mr. Krolik, I could study law, apply for a position in government and thus work myself up."

Even before I finished, he interrupted me. "Bill," he said, "you might just as well save your breath because you'll never make it." Before I could again respond he added, "I am really a little disappointed in you. You evidently didn't pay too much attention to what I taught."

Upon my quizzical look, he continued, "Don't you remember? I explained that in order to become the president of these great United States, you would have to be born in this country. You could become Secretary of State or Defense or of any of the other high positions, but not the presidency. That opportunity you missed when you were born wrong. It is nothing against you personally, Bill, for you had nothing to do with it. None of your efforts, however great or honorable they might be, can ever and will never alter the fact that you are an alien by birth. So it is not what you did or did not do, but rather what you are. You would just have to be born again."

Those were very sobering and thought-provoking words, and I had never quite forgotten them when I was confronted with an interesting biblical principle.

It was then that I understood for the first time that all humanity had inherited the "fallen nature" of Adam, the federal head of the human race, through his original sin.

In other words, we were born wrong (dead in sin). It is written, "... by one man (Adam) sin entered into the world, and death by sin; and so death passed upon all men, for that all have sinned."

The Scriptures make it very clear in saying, "... in Adam all die ... in Christ shall all be made alive."

That which is not possible in the realm of the flesh is amazingly obtainable through God's grace by receiving His Son who died for our sin, was buried and rose from the dead on the third day, granting unto us a new birth by receiving Him.

Even one of the most educated and venerated Rabbis, Nicodemus, a ruler of our people, was told by our Lord that he "must be born again."

No, I can never become President of these United States, but I have attained an unthinkably higher position, that of living eternally in the exalted, holy presence of God my Creator.

5

I Find a Career

MY PARENTS and younger sister remained in Germany hoping that conditions concerning the Jews would ease; however, restrictions became more stringent every day. After Dad's store went into "pure German hands," the family moved into a small apartment. My older sister, Anneliese, had in the meantime gone to Rio de Janeiro to marry her childhood sweetheart who had preceded her a few months earlier.

At two o'clock on the morning of the tenth of November, 1938, the Nazis launched a massive, pre-meditated reprisal for the slaying of a minor embassy official. Under orders issued by Gestapo Chief Heinrich Himmler, "spontaneous" demonstration began with waves of arson, looting, murders and arrests. The wrecking, looting and burning continued all day.*

In the issuing orgy some 200 synagogues were burned, over 800 shops destroyed and 7,500 looted. An unknown number of Jewish homes were ransacked and 20,000 Jews hauled off to concentration camps, many of them perishing even before they arrived.

The streets of Germany were so littered with the plate glass of shattered shop windows that the disaster became known as the *Night of Broken Glass,* ironically called KRISTALLNACHT (Night of Crystal).

During these hours of horror, Dad was arrested and taken to a concentration camp near Berlin.

Having heard that those over 65 with valid emigration papers could leave the country, Mother was able to obtain Dad's release on the condition he leave within ten days. Otherwise, he would be re-imprisoned. Our relatives here in America had provided sponsorship papers in time, and

---

For a more detailed account see Appendix.

he left immediately for Cuba. Mother and my sister followed a month later, where all three remained for nine months waiting for their U.S. immigration number to come up.

Meantime, I was taking very good pictures with a Leica camera Dad had sent before he left Germany. One of the saleswomen in our store asked me to take some photographs of her new baby. The result pleased her so much I was soon photographing the babies of her relatives and friends.

About that time I answered an ad for an assistant photographer of a portrait studio at $8.50 per week. From the owner I learned much about developing and enlarging. At first opportunity I bought a press camera, a *Speed Graphic,* which all newspaper and many commercial photographers were using.

A young Jewish friend and I established our own pictorial press service. That lasted a comparatively short time also, because I began specializing in photographing weddings. This kept me so busy that I practically lived on wedding cakes, ice cream and punch instead of good, wholesome food. In fact, I was so busy I once forgot a wedding I was supposed to shoot. I was terribly embarrassed when the bride called me, so I took the picture of her father leading her to the altar *afterwards* as well as some others, trying every angle I could think of to keep the empty pews from showing.

But the worst situation was the time I left the focal plane shutter closed, and none of the film was exposed. I spent a couple of sleepless nights before I got the courage to tell the bride that the record of the most important event of her life had for all time come to naught.

After the arrival of my parents, we bought a house on monthly installments, and I built a darkroom in the basement, where I did my own photo processing. My brother had married his Jewish girlfriend who had also come from Germany, so he no longer lived with us.

I befriended Sol Studna, a Jewish staff photographer from the *Kansas City Star,* our largest newspaper, and visited him at the newsroom whenever I could. Before long, the city editor gave me some photo assignments of special civic events.

At certain times of the day I went to the railroad station to await the arrival of the prestigious *Santa Fe Chief,* the most modern and the fastest train between New York and Los Angeles. Invariably, there were film stars on board who were heading for New York or returning to Hollywood after appearing in a Broadway production. Meeting them face to face was my most exciting assignment.

One of my friends suggested that on some evenings, preferably on weekends, I go to the various night clubs to take pictures of the patrons. Having had a few drinks, they would no doubt be in a jovial mood and would not mind having their picture taken with their buddies. If they would not want to give me their address, I could deliver the pictures to them at the night club a few nights later. Some might even pay me in advance, he thought.

When I went there the first time, I was surprised at the smoky and gloomy atmosphere and started to set up a stand with a big flood light because I hoped to save the cost of the rather expensive flashbulbs.

The people who were sitting at the bar, as well as some at the tables, many with their girlfriends, seemed startled. They started shuffling and moving around as they began to straighten up. Soon the proprietor came rushing up, shouting, "What's going on here? What do you think you are doing?"

I quietly — and innocently — said, "I only thought to take some pictures of your patrons while they are enjoying themselves here at your club!"

He screamed at me, "Turn off those lights immediately, before I lose all my customers — and get out!"

I continued to play dumb and ventured forth, "Wouldn't they like to have a remembrance of the good time they have here?"

He looked at me as though I were completely ignorant of present day social activities and felt he needed to "educate" me.

"Look," he spoke more quietly now, "these folks come here because they like the subdued atmosphere; they appreciate the freedom they find here, to relax and to amuse themselves without any restraint." Then, rather forcefully, he said, "Now grab your stuff and get out!"

Of course, I fully understood him, but it was several years before I found out that the Bible says people are condemned because light has come into the world and men loved darkness rather than light because their deeds are evil. (John 3:19)

Constructing paths between barracks during part of our basic training at the Med. Training Battalion at Camp Grant, Ill. (1941).

I Become a Soldier

IN FEBRUARY 1941, at the very beginning of the new draft law, I went into military service. At the induction center of Fort Leavenworth a photographer was urgently needed to take pictures for public relations and propaganda purposes. I was assigned to fill that spot, which made me extremely happy.

Since the induction center had recently come into existence and there was no photographic laboratory, I went with an Army truck and driver to bring all my darkroom equipment from home. For about a month I photographed the new inductees during their physical examinations, at mealtime in the mess hall and while trying on their new uniforms.

After a month, a new order was issued, that no soldier could be given a permanent assignment without first completing a three-month basic training course, not even a cook, a driver or a sentry. Nobody. I was given the choice of mechanized cavalry (tanks and heavy artillery) or medical aid training. The cavalry training would be at Fort Riley, Kansas; the medical aid training at Camp Grant near Rockford, Illinois.

Because I had always wanted to see another part of America, I chose the latter. Camp Grant had just recently been established, and upon arrival we were put to work pushing wheelbarrows and building roads between the newly erected barracks. Even while doing this, part of the time we were instructed in the basic methods of caring for wounded and sick comrades. Later we learned how to treat specific wounds caused by bullets and shrapnel, and how to place a wounded man on a stretcher or carry him alone over the shoulder like a sack. Our instructors were all commissioned officers, mostly first lieutenants and captains, doctors who had been drafted into military service.

This training brought us face to face with the vulnerability of human beings and the brevity of life. Being daily exposed to the frailty of our mortal bodies, many of us became rather morbid, though we generally tried not to think about it.

All our implements, the medical pouches, pressure package packs, instrument cases and even the ambulances carried the initials of the Medical Department of the United States Army: M.D.U.S.A. We would frequently say that these meant: "Many Die, You Shall Also."

Even at that time, I believe the Lord gave me a nudge to think seriously about what would happen to a person if he were killed in action. I didn't yet know the Scripture, "... *it is appointed unto men once to die but after this the judgment ...*"* nor did I know the antidote, "... *he that heareth my word and believeth ... hath everlasting life ... shall not come into judgment ... is passed from death unto life.*"**

As part of our training we went on forced marches carrying a heavy pack to prepare us for the rigors of future missions, usually leaving at five o'clock in the morning and returning in the late afternoon.

After three months of intensive training, our battalion was divided and assigned to various branches of the Armed Forces. Among them were the infantry, which none of us wanted, the engineers, anti-aircraft batteries, the signal corps and the air corps. Most desirable was the Army Air Corps, for we thought, and rightly so, that medical aid men would seldom go on bombing missions and never fly in fighter planes. We felt we would personally have little to do with actual combat.

When my unit was assigned to the Air Corps, I was sincerely congratulated and very much envied. Besides that good fortune, we were being sent to California, and soon we were on the train heading for that much praised part of our country, ordering whatever we liked in the dining car at Uncle Sam's expense.

I was thrilled when I saw the beautiful rolling hills and the semitropical vegetation, especially the tall palm trees. I watched the Pacific Ocean with amazement as we headed up the coast to Moffett Field, just south of San Francisco.

We were herded to a nearby aviation cadet training center which was in process of expansion to receive additional personnel. Meanwhile we were put up in big tents full of rows of beds with lockers between them. It was sunny and warm, and we felt as if we were at a summer vacation resort. I was soon assigned to the station hospital. We were issued clean white suits with caduceus on the lapels. I felt very privileged to wear the staff with two serpents coiled about and two wings at the top, the insignia of the U.S. Army Medical Corps.

Along with other orderlies, working among nurses and doctors, I made beds, took food to the sick and those wounded in various accidents

---

* Hebrews 9:27; ** John 5:24

— the war had not yet started — and carried and emptied bed pans. I did not particularly enjoy this kind of activity, so as often as I could I meandered to the nearby public relations office which had a large photographic section, just to see if there was any chance of being transferred to it.

One day I recognized one of their officers whom I had met in Kansas City when he was taking publicity pictures for an advertising firm. He was happy to see me again and asked me what my present duties were. In the course of conversation I told him I would very much like to work again as a photographer, whereupon he promised to see what he could do about it. Ten days later I was ordered to his department for new assignment to duty.

What great joy that was. I photographed the training of pilots, bombardiers and navigators and was taken to other training centers, sometimes even flown there, to do the same.

On the seventh of December, 1941, while eating in the mess hall, I heard some very excited buddies of mine say there had been a surprise attack on Pearl Harbor. We all hurried back to the radio in the barracks to hear the first fragmentary reports. We were stunned at the extent of the devastation. President Franklin D. Roosevelt, our President at that time, spoke of it as a Day that Will Live in Infamy and announced that we were now at war with Japan.

Our weekend leaves were all cancelled immediately, and our military service, which under the draft law was to have lasted just one year, was automatically extended to "the duration and six months." There was feverish activity everywhere. The pilot, navigator and bombardier training was greatly accelerated, and those who had completed it were immediately shipped to the various fighter squadrons. The entire military installation took on an atmosphere of somberness and deep concern.

I thought about those of my former training unit who had been assigned as medical aides to the infantry, artillery and other field units. I wondered if they would have to give their lives during the ensuing battles.

In contrast to their possibly so-tragic fate, I was in for a most pleasant surprise. I received orders to attend a nine-week photographic publicity course conducted by the famous *Life Magazine* in New York under the direction of the Army Signal Corps. *Life Magazine* was known as the very best picture magazine of its day, and its price was, believe it or not, only ten cents.

After the outbreak of hostilities, no civilian photographer was allowed on any military installation or permitted to photograph any military activities. Our photos, taken as military personnel, could, of course, be censored by military authorities.

We lived in a hotel in New York, and in the evenings we went to see Broadway productions, for which all members of the military received free tickets. Many good-hearted families invited us for meals to their homes. They wanted thereby to do their part for the war effort because they thought that we were lonesome, being away from home and from our families. What a life that was!

Film Greats Before My Camera

AFTER COMPLETION of this course, I received two more items of good news. The first was that I had been promoted to corporal; the second, orders had come not to return to Moffett Field but to travel directly to Santa Ana, California, as public relations and publicity photographer of a Radio Production Unit. This unit produced special programs in which the exploits and victories of our brave fighter pilots and bomber crews were dramatized and then broadcast nationwide.

These productions were called *Soldiers with Wings* and, besides actors, included an orchestra of about 30 first class musicians who had been drafted and so were now playing for Uncle Sam. Also now in uniform were composers, who wrote the special background music, script writers and even some aspiring young movie stars, and directors to produce the weekly presentations.

Probably the most fascinating for me to watch were the sound technicians who produced the street noises, car door slamming, dogs barking, plane engines starting and many more sounds to fit into the productions.

These sounds were pre-recorded on records; tape recorders did not yet exist, nor did television. It was 1943, and it was quite an art for the technicians in the sound booth to perfectly synchronize the sounds with the dramatizations. For me, it was all new and exciting.

The programs, held in an auditorium seating around 500, were attended by future pilots, bombardiers and navigators who were in training at a nearby flying school. They were produced not only for their entertainment, but also for their motivation, as well as for information and the inspiration of the American public and to recruit men and women for the Army Air Corps.

Since all this happened near the great Film Capital of Hollywood, many famous film stars were invited to most of the weekly productions to add special interest. They personally interviewed the returned, decorated pilots or bomber crews, and then took part in the actual dramatization of their feats as they were re-enacted or simulated according to the script writers' and director's scenario, and thoroughly rehearsed before going on the air.

I was to photograph these stars as they first greeted the heroes and also during their appearance before the microphones. Having been given the chance to actually see them, in person, these film greats whom I had idolized from my youth, was something I had never dreamed of. Talking to them and photographing them close up was beyond my fondest imagination.

I was completely in charge of them while they were before my camera, telling them where and how to stand or sit and what to do. My pictures were to show action and tell a story, rather than to look posed or stiff. So I had the double task of thinking up some natural or original activity as well as shooting it. To get a more unusual, unposed picture, I would sometimes take it while my subject was in the process of following my request.

My greatest desire at the time was to be photographed with them, and quite a few times I succeeded by handing my camera to a soldier friend nearby, after previously focusing it and setting the shutter. I then had him take the picture while I was standing or sitting next to one of the stars, engaged in conversation. Occasionally, I used the self-portrait method and triggered the shutter electrically with a small extension cable.

All my photos were hung up in the lobby of the Radio Production Unit. I quietly hoped to display them some day in my studio to impress my prospective customers. Because I did all my own developing and enlarging, I could make as many extra copies as I wanted. To this day I have photos of myself with Rita Hayworth, Hedy Lamar, Barbara Stanwyck, Gary Cooper and Dorothy Lamour.

My favorite one is with Marlene Dietrich. When I asked her from where she got her accent, she replied laughingly, "The same place you got yours!"

I could not have wished for a more interesting, challenging and satisfying occupation.

For a time I was under the administrative jurisdiction of the First Motion Picture Unit in Culver City, California, from which I received my promotion to Staff Sergeant. I still have the original "Special Orders" signed by Ronald M. Reagan, Captain, Air Corps, Adjutant, the commanding officer of that unit at the time.

One thing, however, disappointed me very much. Yes, it actually shocked me. Many of the so "beautiful" movie stars didn't look nearly as glamorous as I remembered them from the silver screen. Even the pancake make-up couldn't conceal the wrinkles and the blemishes of some of them.

One of them whom I had especially admired, Jean Arthur, asked me not to photograph her so close up. I moved back a ways as she requested, but then "enlarged her" in the darkroom.

There were several incidents the Lord used to make me think seriously about the frailty and brevity of life. One of the stars I photographed, a real glamour girl, was Carol Landis. I used one of the lighting set-ups I had learned at the *Life* Photography School, and the pictures turned out exceptionally well. I showed them with pride to all the fellows in the barracks.

A few days later while I was making my bed, one of my buddies walked by, and without saying a word laid a newspaper on it and walked on. My eyes fell on the headlines' big bold print: CAROL LANDIS COMMITS SUICIDE. I was so dumbfounded, I could hardly believe my eyes.

She was one of Hollywood's most glamorous stars, adored and admired by every man, at the pinnacle of her career, and without doubt one of the highest paid movie greats in the industry. The world lay at her feet, photographers followed her wherever she went. As far as possessions were concerned, there seemed to be nothing she desired that she could not have — an extravagant villa in Beverly Hills, who knows how many cars and how much domestic help.

She had everything her heart desired except, apparently, that inner peace, the peace which only God can give, the peace which "passeth all understanding" (Philippians 4:7), which nothing in this world can give and for which there is no substitute and without which she evidently could no longer live. So, one evening alone in her fabulous mansion, she turned on the gas.

By this time it was late summer, 1944, and as you can see, the Lord was preparing my heart to think seriously about my life and my eternal welfare.

Bob Wesley turned out to be that servant whom the Lord used to lead me along the way. When I at last accepted his invitation to photograph the gospel team, I had no idea how it would affect my future.

As I continued photographing the greats of the film industry, it was interesting to see how they fought so desperately against the natural process of aging and were determined to hide, or at least to delay its plainly visible symptoms. Such were my observations before I came to believe on the Lord Jesus. The following thoughts of my heart are written in retrospect.

These signs of old age, I believe, are very similar to the depraved condition of the human heart. A person may be able to cover them up for a while, but can never erase them nor in any other way put them to naught.

Such is man, just like Cain, whose sacrifice was not in accordance with the plan of God and thus was not accepted, in contrast to Abel's which pleased God. The result? It is written, "... his countenance fell ..." (Genesis 4:5). .

A more literal meaning would probably be that he was downcast, but the fact remains that because of Adam's transgression the entire human family became separated from God, dying spiritually, and at that moment began to die physically as well.

So now, sooner or later, the fallen countenance makes itself known. Manufacturers of cosmetics make millions by promising their customers that their salves, creams or tonics will lift those fallen countenances. They don't work, nor do massages, nor even plastic surgery, after a while.

No, the only sure solution comes from and through Him who "... knoweth our frame (and) remembereth that we are dust." (Psalm 103:14). He gives us the only perfect and eternal remedy: "But if the Spirit of him that raised up Jesus from the dead dwell in you, he that raised up Christ from the dead shall also quicken your mortal bodies by his Spirit that dwelleth in you." (Romans 8:11).

"... for the trumpet shall sound, and the dead shall be raised incorruptible and we shall be changed. For the corruptible must put on incorruption and this mortal must put on immortality." (1 Corinthians 15:52,53).

PART THREE

Life and Living

On a Sunday outing in our carriage in the spring of 1919 with Dad and Mother at right. I (4 years old) next to mother, then Gary (2 years old) by our governess and Anneliese (6 years old). Charlotte, my youngest sister, was not yet born.

Our entire family just before my brother and I left for America in 1934

During a short furlough from military service in 1945, my older sister had gone to Brazil to marry a boyhood sweetheart.

Mother and we four children at her 90th birthday reunion in 1979. Dad had died.

A Civilian Again

IN JUNE 1945 I was transferred to London, England, with other soldiers who were able to speak German, in order to translate captured German airplane construction plans sent there from our conquering forces in Germany.

It wasn't long until in London also, those who had truly trusted our Lord found each other and established a United Nations Gospel Witness Team. It was made up of military personnel from France, Holland, Britain, Canada and the U.S., who together were fighting for a total victory in Europe.

We met for Bible study during the week and went out to different churches on weekends to tell the Good News.

I had wished very much to see my homeland, Germany, again, and a few months after its surrender in May of that year, I was ordered to escort Dr. Alexander Lippisch and his assistant, "Dipl. Ingenieur" Norman Willich, back to the American Occupation Zone in southern Germany. They were the inventors of the first and fastest jet fighter plane of that time, the Messerschmitt 163 (Me 163) and had been brought to London for interrogation and to assist with the translation of the captured aircraft documents.

I was thrilled to travel with these two famous inventors, but far beyond that, excited to see the land of my birth again and my home town, Dortmund. I had left Germany only 11 years before, but what an unbelievable sight awaited me.

Under Hitler's reign it was to exist 1,000 years, but lasted only 12 years, four months and exactly eight days. Now it resembled a nearly endless rubble heap.

Of the many friends and acquaintances I hoped to find, I couldn't locate a single one. How sad it made me. It was during this time that I sat on the ruins of my former home and wept over our UN-real estate. I was in American uniform, returning as a member of the victorious armies, but I felt as one with these, my people, who had suffered so much and through those many agonizing years.

I went to Wiesbaden and there continued to serve as translator of captured German documents. Soon I completed my term of duty and was returned to the United States, though I would have loved to remain there somewhat longer.

Then came the great day of February the 9th, 1946, when I was discharged from the Army. I had served two days less than five years. Now my great apprehension — if I may call it that, was how to tell my family face to face about the Lord and about my new life in Him.

During the first few days the subject didn't come up because of the newness of being home again. My brother, a lieutenant in the U.S. Intelligence, had been in a German prison and had recently returned, so we were all glad to be together again as a family .

Then, a few days later while sitting at the table, Dad said all of a sudden (in German), "What is it, this foolish idea I hear about you having been baptized?"

Even though I had been baptized shortly after my salvation, I had never written them about it. But according to Jewish thinking, baptism is considered one's final step in completely turning from Judaism and Jewishness to embrace the "despised Christian religion."

As slowly and as gently as I could, I said, "Look, Dad, our Bible said that we are all sinners and that in order to obtain forgiveness and be accepted by God, a blood sacrifice would be needed. We used to have such in former times, when an innocent lamb was sacrificed to atone for our sin, but since then God sent us His only acceptable sacrifice, the Lord Jesus Christ who is called the Lamb of God, and I have accepted Him."

Dad had a difficult time controlling his anger; shaking his head, he burst out, "We are Jews, you hear, we are the Chosen of God, and what you have done by turning away from our God to some sort of a substitute, the religion of the Gentiles, shows great weakness of character, so you better think it over and come back and be a good Jew!"

I didn't reply and nothing more was said at the time.

I was not yet able to cite any specific Scripture. I thought to let my family get somewhat used to the fact I had an entirely new outlook on life and hoped for another opportunity to say more. While with the Gospel Team, some of the soldiers had told me about Dr. Walter L. Wilson, a former physician and author of various books on soul-winning. He lived in Kansas City, where we now lived, and was also the pastor of a good Bible-believing church. I wasted no time in looking him up.

He was most kind and gracious, and we talked quite a while about what I should do next. I didn't know he was also the founder and president of a small Bible school in our town.

After we prayed together, he encouraged me to attend his six-week summer Bible course without charge, in order to get established in the fundamentals of the faith. Then I could decide if I wanted to continue as a regular Bible school student.

The U.S. government was paying for any four-year or higher education program for those who had served in the Armed Forces during the war. Besides that, it was paying $90 per month for personal expenses.

I realized how needful it was for me to take at least the summer course, not only for the Christian fellowship, but to become able to show from the scriptures what I believed and why.

Shortly before this, dad had suggested I go into business with him and actually had business envelopes printed using his and my initials in coining a new logo for our new firm. His idea was to start out with a couple of seamstresses, who would sew pillows with big pockets on each side, one for an ice-pack, the other for a heating pad.

Now it was high time to tell my family I had decided to dedicate my entire life to my Lord and to prepare myself by going to Bible school. Because I had not brought this subject up before, my family had silently hoped my religious fervor might have worn off somewhat.

Hearing my sudden announcement, they were greatly shocked and dismayed and did not know how to cope with the idea their son was going in that direction.

Dad's face, full of rage and twitching with utter indignation and bitter resentment, the like I had never seen before, could hardly control himself. He tried to vent his fury by screaming, "Have you lost all your senses to have such an idiotic idea? Have you gone completely out of your mind?"

I left the room because I didn't want Dad to excite himself any more. The shock of my decision and the great disappointment to not have a father-son business seemed more than he could handle.

From that time on, Dad's face was very pale and we hardly spoke to one another. My mother and sister were not nearly as upset. At least, they didn't show it; yet there was a decided coolness between us at first, but it wore off as time went on. Not so with Dad.

One evening, however, as I came home from a prayer meeting, I went to stand by him at his desk, hoping that his anger had abated somewhat and he would talk to me. He was playing solitaire and smoking a big cigar. To my surprise, he told me of a closet he would like me to build for him. It would be easy enough, I thought, needing only one plywood side and a simple door in front, across the corner of a small room. It would be fun, too building it for Dad, especially now.

But when he showed me the detailed plans he had drawn for it, I had to keep myself from laughing. He had drawn heavy metal right-angle irons and crossbars; heavy bolts with nuts and washers, even lock-washers as though it would have to withstand the onslaught of ages.

I explained that such heavy metal ware was really not necessary and tried to show him how I could build it very sturdily without all those metal reinforcements.

He looked at me sternly and then said, "But this is the way I want it built." I tried to explain to him again how needless all this really was, and for a while neither of us was ready to give in.

Finally Dad said, "Wouldn't you like to do something for your old father the way he would like to have it done?"

In that very moment, and in a very clear, yet inaudible voice, which truly startled me, the Lord spoke to my heart to give in and build it exactly as he desired it, to show him I still loved him and honored him as my father, and as a testimony of the Lord's working in my heart.

I immediately switched, so unexpectedly I surprised myself. I turned to Dad and said, "All right, Father, I'll do it exactly the way you want me to. The first thing tomorrow morning I'll go to the hardware store and get the needed metal parts."

Dad looked at me for a moment in utter unbelief as though he could hardly believe my sudden and complete change of heart and then said very emphatically, "No, I've decided not to have you build it for me after all. You also don't have to talk to me any more about anything, and I even think it best if from now on we went our separate ways."

I could hardly believe my ears and in amazement said, "Why, Dad, I don't understand. You first asked me to build you this closet a certain way, and now that I'm ready to do it just like you wanted it, you tell me not to do it. What's the matter?"

His face became hard, with a hurtful expression, and he answered sternly, "No, I don't want you to do it at all, because I sense you have made your decision not because of me, but because of your religious viewpoint. And since you have evidently made it more because of your 'Lord,' as you call him, than for the sake of pleasing me, your father, you go right ahead and follow your sanctimonious ways and leave me completely out of it!"

From that time on, Dad spoke hardly a word to me. Because I, as his son, felt it my duty, as well as desiring with all my heart to have him understand Who it was on Whom I really believed and why, I went to the public library and in all quietness wrote him a long, detailed letter with many of the Old Testament Scripture references and sent it to him.

Whether or not he read this letter I do not know. But at least I had the satisfaction, the assurance and the peace in my heart, that I had done all I could, so he wouldn't go into eternity without knowing what the Bible had to say about salvation.

When he became very sick and was bedridden, I tried various times to go and talk and pray with him, but Mother was very determined that

I would not "overly upset" him and saw to it that I didn't go alone into his room.

Her statement to me repeatedly was, "I want Father to be able to die 'in peace.' "

He passed away on the 12th of June, 1952, shortly before I went to Japan. Eternity alone will reveal whether he read my letter and indeed obtained that "peace" of which Mother unknowingly spoke.

With a Japanese pastor and his family in Kansas City. My first contact with the Japanese in the summer of 1952 during my preparation in heading for the land of our Lord's choosing.

My "bed" in Maher-Shalal-Hash-Baz, while "on the road" for two years after graduating from Bible school in 1950. In 1952 I went to Japan.

Traveling in Alaska, I got acquainted with the source of my transportation and its tractless tracts.

9

To Bible School, Then on the Road

I WENT to the Kansas City Bible College (which later became Calvary Bible College), but continued to live at home until the last half of my fourth year when I moved into the dormitory of the school. (If we had been Orthodox Jews, my family would probably not have allowed me to continue living with them. But as I said, we were very liberal Reformed Jews.)

During these years I continued to take pictures, mostly of weddings and family reunions.

Bible school training consisted of the study of basic Bible truths along with church history, child evangelism, choir directing, fundamentals of phonetics for acquiring a foreign language and public speaking to better minister the Word from the pulpit. We also heard many foreign missionaries who were "home" on furlough. A good part of the afternoons were spent in hospital visitation, jails, open air meetings and on Sundays in Sunday schools, teaching and applying what we had learned.

One of the girl students, Augusta Thiessen, had my particular interest, but more about that later.

The class in which we learned how our Lord taught his disciples to "fish for men" presented the greatest challenge to me, especially since there was one of our students who was very adept with his hands, using his skill to attract the attention of people much like a fisherman attracts fish.

He changed a red handkerchief (illustrating sin) into a white one, showing how, "though our sins be as scarlet, they shall be as white as snow."* Again, he took three strings of different lengths, representing a little baby, a teenager and an adult, and manipulated them to become the same length, reminding us that "... there is no difference, for all have

---

* *Isaiah 1:18*

47

sinned and fallen short" of God's standard.**

My friend used these in children's meetings but found even the adults appreciated and enjoyed his clear, Bible-centered presentations. I became intrigued and soon learned how to do some of these object lessons myself. Before long, I had a suitcase full of objects with which I gave an entire Gospel illustration program.

Our Lord's call to His disciples to fish for men made a deep impression upon me. I continually found new ways to attract men, women and children to the things of the Lord and eternity. Some of the ideas I thought up may seem rather unorthodox or even somewhat extreme today, but I had dedicated them all to the Lord and to the honor of His name.

I became active in the then-popular Youth for Christ organization and took a part in their weekly Saturday night rallies and for a while even became their treasurer.

I spoke at high school Bible clubs, attended their Soul Winners' Club and became one of the counselors to help young people who wanted to trust the Lord.

I graduated in June, 1950, and left immediately, together with another student, in an old Chevy on a two-month evangelistic trip. One of our first stops was in a very small and poor coal mining locality in the hills of Kentucky, where a dedicated missionary labored with his family. He had no room for us in his small dwelling and took us to a tiny log cabin. It had two wooden bunks and a kerosene lamp and a make-shift table. The toilet, he said, was between some trees just down the hill a little ways, and in that direction also was a small stream at which we could wash.

With that, he left us for the night, pausing shortly at the door, turned around and said, "Oh, yes, and if there is anything you think you need, feel free to let me know and I'll show you how you can get along without it."

We traveled through much of the eastern United States, in response to invitations from churches, daily vacation Bible schools and youth camps, some of which had come as a result of my Youth for Christ contacts. At the end of the summer, my companion went back to finish his schooling, and I continued on alone.

I spoke not only in churches and youth camps, but also in orphanages, prisons, old age homes, mission conferences and public schools throughout America and Canada. At times there were even special get-togethers, arranged after people had heard my story.

I never lacked for a place to stay, and I had many good meals among a host of loving families.

Finally, I spoke also in Alaska, which at that time was still a territory, and to which I went by plane.

** *Romans 3:22,23*

The other distances I covered all in my old Chevrolet. I had the back of the seat next to me fixed so it could be unscrewed and laid down even with the back seat. With an air mattress on top, it made a comfortable bed, but I used it only when I couldn't make it to the next place in one day.

MY CAR AND I

Reading my Bible one day, I came across the verses in Isaiah 8:1 and 3. The Lord told the prophet to name his first-born son MAHER-SHALAL-HASH-BAZ, which loosely translated means: "Collapse and destruction draweth near." The name was a prophetic sign of the impending conquest of the land by the king of Assyria.

This, I thought, would be an unusual yet fitting name for my old car. Once the new and shining pride of its owner, it now showed the unmistakable signs of rust and corrosion, soon to be headed for some out-of-the-way junkyard.

So I had a big sign made, about two to three times the size of a license plate, with MAHER-SHALAL-HASH-BAZ painted thereon and fastened it to the front of my car. Whenever I stopped at a filling station or when asking for directions somewhere, people would invariably ask the meaning of that sign.

I would explain its biblical origin and then tell them that we all are very much like that old car of mine, hastening to our doom unless we have committed our lives to the Lord Jesus Christ. I compared my old car with the life of a person here on earth about whom it is written that his life "is even a vapor, that appeareth for a little time, and then vanishes away" (James 4:14).

I often quoted 1 Peter 1:24,25:

"For all flesh is as grass, and all the glory of man as the flower of grass. The grass withereth, and the flower thereof falleth away: But the word of the Lord endureth forever. And this is the word which by the gospel is preached unto you."

Another one of my unorthodox ways was in picking up hitchhikers, which I did frequently. After they got into my car, before I drove off, I would tell them it was not without risk, riding with me. Naturally they would look at me, sometimes fearfully, and always with a puzzled expression.

I would then point to the New Testament clamped to my dashboard, opened to First Thessalonians and asked them to read the portion I had underlined:

"For the Lord himself shall descend from heaven with a shout, with the voice of the archangel, and with the trump of God; and the dead in Christ shall rise first; Then we which are alive and remain shall be caught up together with them in the clouds, to meet the Lord in the air; and so

shall we ever be with the Lord" (verses 16 and 17).

When the hitchhiker would question its meaning, I would explain that I had trusted the Lord, and at His coming I would be caught up together with those believers who have already died and would be coming out of their graves.

Because this could happen at any time, even while we are on our way, he would find himself in a car without a driver and might end up having a head-on collision or in a ditch or against some tree.

The safest thing, I would explain, would be to trust the Lord "right now" and be not only fearless of the result of a driverless car, but be saved from all sin and for all eternity.

I remember at least one hitchhiker who made that decision right then. He wanted to be relaxed and unafraid while riding with me, and assured that at our Lord's coming he would be caught up, even as I.

10

An Encounter of Eternal Consequences

IN THE SUMMER of 1951, while attending a large missionary conference at Winona Lake, Indiana, I was surprised to meet many missionaries and former acquaintances. One special surprise was seeing Reverend Morken again, under whose ministry I had come to know the Lord about seven years before. He had been serving our Lord as missionary in Japan, and I was interested to hear all about his experiences there.

During our leisurely visit, he asked what I was doing and if I had any definite plans for the future. I told him of my graduation from Bible school and about the many opportunities I'd had to present the Word in many parts of America.

"Yes" he said, "but what are your goals?" Do you intend to keep on the road like that, going hither and yon for an undetermined length of time? Or has the Lord possibly laid a very specific ministry upon your heart?"

"No," I answered, "not that I am aware of. What did you have in mind?"

Slowly and thoughtfully he began to share with me the dire need of the people of the Orient who have no chance to hear of the true and living God, and are thus doomed to follow the heathenish practices of their ancestors before idols which neither hear, nor see, nor are able to save.

Then he asked a surprising question: "What do you think about going to them and telling them, maybe for the first time, about the love of God which is extended to them as it is to you and me?"

That sounded challenging indeed, but Japan was a faraway country. The customs and the entirely different lifestyle of the people (not to mention the enormously difficult language and the impossible way of writing it) were, after all, more than I would be able to handle. I was 36, not so young anymore, and I well remembered the difficulty I had to learn the English language 17 years earlier.

Reverend Morken suggested that I think about it, that I make it a special matter of prayer, and said he would talk more to me about it on the following day.

When I met him the next day, I had to shamefully confess that I didn't really care to pray about it, because — to say it honestly — I was afraid of any guidance which would lead me in that direction.

His answer was much more reprimanding than I had expected. "How do you hope to know the plan of the Lord for your life if you don't give Him the opportunity to reveal it to you?" was his straightforward question.

The mission conference lasted for five days, and I knew I would probably have to give an account to my dear brother again the next day about having prayed concerning this matter and how I believed the Lord was leading. So I decided to come before the Lord in all sincerity, knowing that he knew my heart and my innermost thoughts. Instead of mentioning Japan though, I told him I had been approached about becoming a missionary (which, of course, was true) and that I would be ready and willing to go to my homeland, Germany, where I knew all about the traditions, the conventional behavior and event he language of the people. I would thus be able to show what I could do for Him from the very outset.

That may have seemed like an easy way out in which I looked for a compromise, and in a certain way it was indeed such. When Brother Morken asked me the next day, I was completely honest and told him how I had prayed deep in my heart, namely that I was afraid my Lord would really send me to Japan if I would declare my readiness to go there.

I could immediately see the expression of deep disappointment in his face, and for a while my dear brother in Christ just looked at me without saying a word. I recalled the Word of the Lord in Isaiah 42:8, "I am the Lord; that is my name: and my glory will I not give to another, neither my praise to graven images."

It was as though the Lord was saying to me: So, by going to Germany where you know the customs, the traditions and the language, you want to show me what you could do for ME. If, however, you will follow my leading and go to Japan, where you do not know the thinking of the people, neither their customs nor their difficult language, I, THE LORD, will show you what I can do for you and you will have to give me the praise and the glory due to my holy name, for "MY GLORY WILL I NOT GIVE TO ANOTHER."

So I prayed that same evening, "Lord, I really can't call you by that name and not do what Your will is for me. And even though I have great doubt that I will be able to do in Japan what you desire of me (and I'm sure you know all about that, too), I'm ready to entrust my life and my future anew and completely into Your hands, being assured that You will guide me for Your glory."

The next morning I couldn't tell Reverend Morken fast enough of my decision, even before he had a chance to ask me. He was overjoyed and offered immediately to write a letter to the director of his mission. That, however, was a little faster than I had expected, just as I felt when, after my decision for the Lord, he had immediately asked me to appear on the platform with the team the following Sunday.

By this time, however, I had learned a fundamental principle which I have shared many times with other young people. Just as a vehicle, be it a car, bicycle or even a plane or a ship, cannot be guided unless it moves, so we cannot discern the guidance of our Lord unless we begin to move (even if haltingly at first) in the direction He has indicated. Never will we know His perfect will for us if we just sit and twiddle our thumbs. I was doubly assured of this when I remembered the Word of the Lord to his disciples to follow Him in order to become fishers of men. What would have happened if they had not obeyed?"

I, too, had followed Him in the true sense of the Word, that is, in heading out on the road with my "fishing tools," which our Lord according to His Word had taught me how to use and which He had abundantly blessed.

I recognized anew that in order to be completely happy and content, I had to continue following in the direction He indicated, abandoning my own plans and interests.

As soon as I could, therefore, I told Reverend Morken that I was on my way! What a joy to tell him to go ahead and write that letter.

He thus wrote to Dr. R.E. Thompson, the director of the Far Eastern Gospel Crusade (now called SEND, International), explaining how we had met, what I had been doing for the Lord since graduating from Bible school and how the Lord had been speaking to me. He unhesitatingly recommended me as a candidate for the Orient.

Only a few days passed before I received a direct answer from the Mission.. It was an invitation to come to Minneapolis to meet Dr. Thompson and to get personally acquainted with the brothers and sisters who worked there in the Mission office. How exciting!

During that time of great fellowship with them, I mentioned that I was already 36, that it had not been easy for me to learn English and that I was concerned whether, at my age, I would be able to learn the Japanese language. Most of their first-time missionaries were at least ten years younger than I. While I was ready to follow the Lord without reservation, I thought that in order to be absolutely sure of His guidance I would place a few hurdles in His way which He would have to overcome, possibly even in a supernatural way.

In my questionnaire I had to give the names of three of my Bible school teachers from whom a character report and a recommendation would be requested.

I chose three of those in whose classes I didn't make good marks and who therefore might have considered me lazy.

Through my Lord's wonderful undertaking, none of this stood in the way, and a few weeks later I was asked again to come to the Mission office. This time I received a set of questionnaires about my personal viewpoint or interpretation of certain Bible passages. Among these was Galatians 2:20:

"I am crucified with Christ; nevertheless I live; yet not I, but Christ liveth in me; and the life which I now live in the flesh I live by the faith of the son of God, who loved me and who gave himself for me."

Because I was still on the road with many scheduled meetings, I took these questionnaires with me but didn't stop to fill them out. Quite a few weeks passed. Mother always sent my mail ahead to the place where I would be, and one day there was a letter from the Mission asking how it stood with answering and returning those questionnaires. They also asked whether I truly had the intention of following the Lord or if I had decided not to do so any longer.

Those words spoke convincingly to my heart, and I asked permission of a family in Portland where I happened to be to spend the next few days there, so I could come before my Lord in prayer and meditation, asking for spiritual insight to answer those questions. I needed only my Bible and concordance, which I always carried with me.

The verse that was my great comfort and encouragement was Proverbs 16:3: "Commit thy works unto the Lord, and thy thoughts shall be established."

Upon that promise I began to write what I truly felt in my heart. The exact sentence construction I don't remember, but the essence was that I was assured that my Lord, through His blood sacrifice by His death on the cross had not only atoned for my sin, but had actually obtained, that is to say, He had purchased me. To substantiate that truth, I quoted 1 Corinthians 6:19b and 20. "… ye are not your own. For ye are bought with a price, therefore glorify God in your body and in your spirit, which are God's."

I explained that because of the price He paid for me I now belonged to Him, my great Purchaser, and I therefore did not have the right to do with this, His possession, the things that would please me. Rather, I would make it my mission to find out what His plans are for me, His new purchase, and then to always do exactly what He tells me to do, for His honor and for the glorification of His name.

By the grace of God, I'm seeking to still do that, even yet today.

11

I Become a Missionary

IT WAS SUCH A BLESSING to my soul to have been able to put the thought about my Lord as Purchaser into writing and to fully realize that these truths were indeed the convictions of my heart.

After I had returned the answers, the Mission sent me a specific date on which I was to meet the members of the Mission Board and be interviewed by them.

I was greatly impressed as these godly men, about seven or eight, stood up when I came into the room. Each one shook my hand with a big smile and a sincere welcome and then bade me to sit down.

Dr. Thompson introduced each man to me and then said: "Please, Brother Bill, tell us first very simply how you came to know the Lord."

I related to them how I was invited by a buddy to take pictures of a G.I. Gospel Team while I was a photographer in the U.S. Air Corps, where I heard the way of salvation for the first time and how after a great inner struggle I finally asked the Lord to come into my heart.

Then Mr. Richardson, a Christian businessman, asked, "How did your family react to your new-found faith?" So I told him about the great shock it was, especially to my father, but that I didn't suffer any outright persecution as would have been the case had we been orthodox Jews.

One of the Mission Board members, a pastor, leaned forward and with visible interest said, "Tell me, dear brother, how did you spend your time since you graduated from Bible school?"

It was so easy to reply to their questions, and I felt completely relaxed in their presence as I continued to relate my experiences throughout my extensive travels showing and telling the wonderful story of salvation.

They thanked me for having come, and after three of them had prayed for me, I was asked to wait outside for a few minutes. It wasn't long before the Mission chairman came out, shook my hand vigorously and congratulated me that without exception, the men had agreed to accept me as their new missionary candidate.

The great turning point of my life had arrived, December 15, 1951, five months and three days after I had said "Yes" to the Lord and to Rev. Morken.

Being now a new candidate, I next had to meet with the business manager and candidate secretary to find out what my new responsibilities would be. The paperwork and the other red tape was beyond my imagination. No questionnaires this time, but rules and regulations of this fundamental and interdenominational Mission organization, the Far Eastern Gospel Crusade.

Now that I was considered a member and therefore one of the Mission's representatives, I would need to be able to explain its origin, its function, its spiritual calling and, among others, the various spheres of its activities. So I had to study all that material given to me, but was invited to call, write or even drop by at any time for any needed help or advice.

I was also told to look to the Lord from now on for my immediate as well as future financial support. I received pledge cards which I could pass out to congregations at the places where I would speak and to other interested friends. These were to be signed by those who wanted to commit themselves to give a certain monthly amount toward my support, to the extent that the Lord enabled them for the next five years. This amount was to be sent to the Mission, which in turn would issue the donor a tax-deductible receipt and forward the amount to me now, and later, to Japan.

One of the Mission leaders advised me, however, not to visit churches and other places of ministry solely for the purpose of obtaining this support, but rather to minister the Word to the salvation of souls and the edification of those present.

With that I could also tell them of my calling to Japan and that I would go as soon as our Lord would make it financially possible.

I was free to explain that $150 in monthly pledges was required by the Mission before I could head out. Besides this monthly amount, I also needed money for my personal outfit and equipment, including a kerosene cooking stove, my overseas passage, including freight, and for my language study, the very first thing after my arrival.

With a definite goal in mind, my life took on a new meaning. I returned to many places I had been before to share how the Lord had wonderfully guided me and what my plans were for the future.

The Mission kept me informed about my pledged support, and all were greatly surprised at how quickly the needed support had come in. Before long, the Mission wrote that my pledged support exceeded the required amount. I had to write to some congregations to withdraw their pledge or to give it to other missionaries.

Thus, by the end of the following summer, I had not only my entire monthly support, but also the needed amount for my outfit, passage, freight and even for my language study. I thanked my Lord with all of my heart for all He had done for me so quickly and so unexpectedly.

Even though my family knew all about this, they were very much surprised to hear how quickly things had fallen into place. Mother especially was very concerned that I would go so far away and for such a long time.

The Mission had also required that I read and then write a comprehensive book report on a rather voluminous work titled: *The Chrysanthemum and the Sword,* which detailed the Japanese way of thinking and their behavior. Only upon completion would I receive permission to head for the Orient.

That was a great burden for me, because I had to sit, read, think and write. I would have much preferred to have kept on traveling and to speak at various places and have made further preparations for my departure.

As it was, I sat daily until late at night, trying to finish this task as fast as possible. I was to hear and learn and experience volumes more about the Japanese way of life in the months and years that were before me.

Showing my Gospel Illustrations to the combined Sunday School Assembly at a church in Tacoma, Washington in June 1951.

12

Farewell to Father

DAD DEVELOPED CANCER, and I ask myself sometimes whether it was his excessive cigar smoking or the agony over my having "abolished the faith of our fathers" that hastened his death at the age of 77.

He was bedridden for quite a few months before, and Mother had taken care of him practically day and night, until finally we were able to obtain a full-time nurse.

Although I was sad and heavy-hearted because of Mother's continual vigil in keeping me from talking to him, I knew I had at various occasions already been able to show him that Jesus Christ was the promised Messiah, the greater son of David.

One day, however, during the final days of my departure for Japan, Mother called me into his room, and we both stood by his bedside while he took his last breath.

As the eldest son I should have had the responsibility — and the honor — to make all arrangements and to preside at my father's funeral, according to the still-prevailing Jewish tradition, but Gary, my younger brother, with some of his Jewish friends met at our home. They greeted me very casually and made plans, ignoring me completely.

It was as though I had no right any longer to take part in family affairs, yes, practically as though I did not exist.

The many relatives and Jewish acquaintances who came to visit very coolly expressed their sympathy to me and then went on to stand in little groups chatting, while I was virtually ignored. What had I done to deserve this treatment? Wasn't I my father's son any longer? Didn't I bear his name? Could I not in some way pay homage to him even in his death, to him, who had raised me and who was God's instrument by enabling my brother and me to escape Hitler's wrath and thereby — though indirectly — permitting me to become exposed to the gospel of salvation through the son of the God of Israel, the One for whose cause I'm now being ignored?

Though it was sunny and warm outside, I felt myself within a gathering storm, threatened and exposed.

At the funeral I observed an old Jewish ritual, but I doubt the Rabbi thought much about the Biblical origin of its custom. At the beginning of the service, he came to my brother and me and pinned a small black ribbon on our lapels.

After the service was over, he came back to us and partially tore them.

I remember reading about Jacob, when he heard of the presumed death of his beloved son, Joseph. He rent his clothes and put sackcloth upon his loins (Genesis 37:14).

Ah, my beloved people. Tradition! Tradition! Tradition! So religious, yet so far from the Truth.

It was only the joy of the Lord and His inner peace that comforted my heart and sustained me.

13

Off to the Orient

IT WAS TIME to head for California and from there to the ship. Mother wanted to ride along to visit relatives in Los Angeles. During the birthday party there for "Tante Betty," one of Dad's sisters, to which also "Tante Jenny," the other sister, had come, I said good-bye to Mother and headed for San Francisco.

On October 13, 1952, along with Clarence Swanson from Chicago and Doris Hume from Iowa who were both also new missionaries, we boarded the *Indian Bear*, a freighter, and a very comfortable and yet economical way to travel.

"Swany" and Dorothy were as excited as I was, and we got along famously, telling each other how we came to know our Lord and how we knew that Japan was the place for us.

I remember heading for the very bow of the ship as we were passing under the Golden Gate Bridge, saying farewell to America. I somewhat self-consciously saluted my adopted land in soldier's fashion, and I couldn't hold back the tears of great joy as I was heading for the land of my Lord's choosing. Standing there all alone beside a heavy anchor chain, I said to him:

"Lord, now I know for certain that it is You who is leading me, because if I would have had anything to do with it, I would have headed in the exact opposite direction!"

Even now, while writing these lines and recalling that thrilling incident, my eyes fill with tears again.

"Trust in the Lord with all thine heart; and lean not on thine own understanding. In all thy ways acknowledge Him and He shall direct thy

path (Proverbs 3:5,6).

I was proving this to be true.

Since passage on a freighter is also much slower, it took us 23 days to reach Japan. We made a three-day stop in Guam, where the ship unloaded freight, affording us the opportunity to take a look around. It was hot and humid, though the tall palm trees were waving us an unexpected welcome.

The natives and their idyllic straw huts looked to us like those we had seen in picture books and which suddenly had become alive. We especially enjoyed the chocolate-colored children who seemed to have fun talking about these newly arrived bleached human specimens. We wouldn't have minded at all to have stayed there a little longer.

On the day of our expected arrival in Japan, we all got up before dawn to see which one of us would be the first to catch sight of the lights of Yokohama, our new home.

Our ship didn't pull up to the dock; rather we rode a small launch to the pier.

One of the first who greeted us was Ted Bollman, our Mission treasurer, who happily received the old-fashioned, hand-operated adding machine we had brought along, and then we rode on the left side through narrow, crowded and sidewalk-less streets to our Mission home, located on one of the small hills overlooking this great seaport.

Right inside the front door we were very heartily greeted by Mae Vincent, our new hostess. She wasted no time in telling us what became standard procedure. "Please take your shoes off and slip into these slippers." They had been set out in a neat row at the edge, half a step up on the highly polished floor that led to the offices, dining room and to some of the rooms occupied by our missionaries. By then, some of the domestic Japanese help had come up and bowed politely, among them Fumiko-san and Misako-san ("san" denotes either Mr., Mrs. or Miss), and from around the corner I could hear our field treasurer, Bob Foster, saying over and over again, "Hi, hi, hi." It was not a greeting, I soon learned, but he was talking on the telephone saying "Yes" repeatedly.

The home in general was constructed very much like a Japanese dwelling to acquaint us with Oriental living from the very start. We were then assigned to our respective rooms, and I was to share mine with Swany on the second floor, giving us a wonderful view of the city. On clear days we could see Mount Fuji in the distance, the famous mountain of Japan.

Before entering our room we had to take off our slippers because of the typical Japanese flooring, called Tatami, a very closely woven rice-straw carpet which is tightly stretched over pressed straw sections about two inches thick and with a standard measure of three by six feet. These sections are very snugly fitted into the room, making a smooth and unbroken flooring which feels like a thick carpet under foot.

Because of the finely woven rice-straw covering which snags easily, the Tatami may only be walked on barefooted or in stocking feet. Strange as it may seem, I felt completely at home there, from the very first moment.

Our first meal in the dining room with the other missionaries and some of the Japanese office and kitchen staff was typical Japanese style, including the ever-present bowl of rice, which is much more sticky than our American variety.

We immediately began to try eating with chopsticks, copying as best we could how others were holding them. One of them was to be held with the upper part of the thumb holding it in place, while the other one was pretty much like a scissoring motion pinched against it.

We easily became frustrated at first, using one chopstick in each hand and even tried to "spear" our food whenever possible, causing many laughs. It wasn't long, however, before we became quite adept.

In Japan the rice bowl is held close to the mouth while the chopsticks are used like a two-pronged fork, practically pushing the rice into the mouth. To pick up pieces of fish, slices of pickles or processed seaweed, one uses the chopsticks like small pincers. Soup, by the way, is tackled with neither chopsticks nor spoon. It is drunk as one would drink from a cup or a glass.

The afternoon of our arrival found us already venturing forth alone into the nearby community and shopping area for a first-hand observation of the Japanese at their daily activities.

THE JAPANESE CULTURE

It didn't take me long to become aware of a helpful similarity between what I saw and experienced in Japan and what I found in my Bible. Our Bible is basically an Oriental book, written in the Middle East, and thus full of Oriental customs.

The word orient signifies the part of the horizon where the sun first appears in the morning, thus, the East. In America we have an interesting usage of a word derived from it. We speak of orientation, and we also use the expression to orient oneself. This means literally, to easternize oneself or, in other words, to turn toward or to face the East.

The basic meaning comes from positioning a map in agreement with the points of the compass and to find one's position in relation to the East, thus "getting one's bearings."

A person, therefore, who has trusted the Lord Jesus Christ and is keeping his heart and his eyes on the East — where his Savior was born, lived, died, was resurrected, and to where He will some day return (when His feet shall stand upon the Mount of Olives, "which is before Jerusalem on the East" (Zechariah 14:4) — could be referred to as one who, in a spiritual sense, is well-oriented.

When I first watched my Japanese brethren read their Bibles, the characters of which are written vertically, I noticed how their heads and eyes always moved from the top to the bottom and back up as though they were nodding *Yes* to what they were reading. Here in the West, where the lines run horizontally, we have to read them from left to right and back again, which looks as though we are always saying *No.* In my meetings with Western young people I've often said that though of necessity we have to read our Bibles horizontally, we can with our hearts read them the Oriental way, namely up and down, so that in our minds we would be seeing a cross.

Figuring out many of the Oriental customs and expressions in the light of the Scriptures became one of my most challenging, but enriching and satisfying past times. One custom, however, stumped me for a while. It was the immediate Japanese reply when being congratulated upon graduation, marriage or even buying a new car. He would invariably respond with, "O'KAGE-SAMA-DE" (it is thanks to your honorable shadow).

What would one's *shadow* have to do with it? When I came across the Biblical account in Acts 5:12-16, I found some light on the subject. I read there about the many signs and wonders wrought by the hands of the apostles, insomuch that the people brought out the sick and laid them in the streets that at least *the shadow of Peter* passing by might *overshadow* some of them. It was the power of God manifested through Peter, even through his *shadow,* whereby the sick were healed. One could well add, through the labors of love of those who carried the sick into the streets.

Another instance was when Jonah was angry that God did not destroy Nineveh. He sat outside the city, and the Lord caused a gourd to grow up to provide a *shadow* over his head. Jonah was exceedingly glad for its *shadow.*

In both accounts, the *shadow* speaks of kindness, benevolence, favor, helpfulness, interest and other similar characteristics. It is these for which a Japanese wants to express his gratitude. He feels that by merely knowing you, or by you knowing him, he is being looked after, *overshadowed.*

The greatest joy for me in understanding this was that I could use it in telling the Japanese that the God of all creation wants to reveal Himself to them even through parts of their daily expressions which have a Biblical origin.

Another Oriental custom which reminded me of Biblical times was the Japanese custom of bowing rather than shaking hands. The lower one bows, and the more often, the more respect one shows those to whom one is bowing.

We read that Abraham bowed before the angel that appeared before his tent; Jacob bowed seven times low to the ground when he came near his brother Esau; the brothers of Joseph bowed themselves before him In Egypt with their faces to the ground.

At first it seemed rather awkward for us foreigners to get used to this custom, but after many years it became so much a part of us that we were not conscious of it and even bowed before our relatives and friends when home on furlough. Once, here in America, I picked up a suit from the cleaners and kept bowing to the counter girl as I walked backwards through the door.

After I was married, we moved to a small provincial town. There was an old, very poor woman, extremely bent over, who frequently trudged by our house. She would carry a heavy bundle of twigs on her back, twigs she had gathered in the nearby forest to use for her firewood. We decided to give her some of the old lumber pieces from our moving crates. At first she refused to take them, but when we insisted, she finally accepted them, though hesitantly, which we ascribed to her (typical) Japanese humility. Two days later she returned with a dozen eggs as an expression of her thankfulness.

We had learned before that there is a social law, unwritten, yet by most Japanese diligently adhered to, that for every gift one receives one must reciprocate with something of the same or greater value. Not to do so would be an offense not only to the one who had given, but also to the conscience of the beneficiary.

We were shocked when we realized the predicament we had put this poor woman in, for we recognized that she had hardly enough to meet her daily sustenance; but we had to accept her gift in order not to offend her.

Shortly thereafter, we seemed to have learned our lesson though it really hurt, because when we saw a very needy man hobble by, my dear wife said something which would have sounded strange to an un-oriented person — strange and contrary to common sense: "Honey, please don't give him anything. Don't you see how poor he is? — He wouldn't be able to reciprocate." (There *is* a way to help such a person, by making sure he doesn't know the source of the help.)

After I told the story of our Lord's wonderful and free salvation to a group of high school students who had come to me to study English, I was not too surprised when one of them asked the question on the heart of all the others: "What does one give to such a great God in return for all you said He has done for us?"

Had I not remembered these experiences, I might have answered by quoting Ephesians 2:8 and 9 or even John 3:16 to show that it is a GIFT. But I could no longer do that. By this time I had become *oriented* and understood that if something was indeed entirely free, the giver evidently obtained it for nothing or at very little cost, so it probably wouldn't be worth much.

To have my pupils think that way about our Lord's priceless sacrifice on the cross for them would have been in exact contradiction with the Truth I had come to Japan to teach and preach.

I explained to them the best I could the indescribable price it cost God to send His Son to become sin for us. I asked them what they thought the acceptable price in such a case should be. They all agreed that there was probably no return gift in all the world that would be valuable enough. Thereupon I showed them (from Romans 12:1 and 2) that God Himself had set the only acceptable and reasonable reciprocal gift which alone would be able to satisfy His loving heart; to give one's self whole-heartedly to Him in one's entirety, that is, without reservation.

In the Japanese room that I at first occupied with my missionary brother, there was not even one piece of furniture, only a built-in type of closet. This closet had light-weight doors that slid in wooden grooves and could be easily lifted out. The doors were covered with bamboo paper having typical Oriental design. Behind these doors were our bedrolls, *futon,* which were filled with cotton, as were also the covers under which we slept wonderfully warm. In the morning we would roll up the futon and the covers and stick everything behind those closet doors. The futon, however, was less resilient than the mattresses we had been used to.

Prior to this, I had always had a problem understanding the story of the man sick with the palsy, who, upon Christ's command "took up his bed" and went his way to his house. Now I understood. It was another of the many times I sincerely thanked my Lord for sending me to the Far East to get "oriented!"

14

I Learn to Speak Japanese

THE STRANGE LANGUAGE SIGNS looked to us *impossible* to learn; yet we were all eager to begin our study of them as soon as possible. There were thirteen of us new missionaries who had all arrived about the same time. Within a few days we were divided into three groups of three or four, into separate classrooms in our Mission Home, each with its own Japanese lady teacher. In that way each of us could be given more personal attention and the opportunity to use right away what we had leaned.

We learned first that the Japanese have three ways of writing, and those funny signs form the backbone. They are called KANJI — KAN (pronounced Khan) was the name of the Chinese province from which they originated, and JI (jee) means *letter* or *character;* thus KANJI means a letter from the KAN-province.

At the time these originated, about 1700 years ago, the Japanese had only a spoken language. They adopted these Chinese ideographs (characters) and superimposed them over their already existing Japanese words. They continued to also use the Chinese pronunciation when two or more characters were joined together. Thus there are at least two (and sometimes as many as four or five) different ways in which these ideographs may be read: the present Japanese way and the way the Chinese read them when they first were adopted.

These KANJIs consist of many strokes of variant lengths, which we had to learn, *as well as the correct order of writing them.* The most complicated ones had 20 to 25 different strokes, some of which have been recently simplified (!) into 12 to 18.

A sixth-grade child in Japan knows 2000 of these KANJIs. The local newspapers use 3000, stocking up to 2000 more of the less frequently used ones. We missionaries had to be able to read, write, pronounce and know the meaning of 1350 KANJIs before we could "graduate."

Along with the KANJIs there are two other ways of writing: HIRAGANA and KATAKANA.

HIRAGANA is written in script or running style and has 48 basic signs or letters to show particles, declension and in some cases the correct pronunciation of a KANJI character.

KATAKANA also consists of 48 letters which look more angular and are used for foreign personal names, foreign places and items not native to Japan, for example, *Jones, Chicago* or *Brussels sprouts*. Using these "letters," they write the phonetic pronunciation of the original, coming as close as they can to the sounds of the word.

We were not permitted to use any English in class, although the grammar and study books were in English. In our first class period, the teacher came in, bowed politely and wrote her name on the blackboard in Roman letters. We would call her by that name with the word *Sensei* following it, this way: *Ninomiya-sensei,* or just *sensei* (teacher), which literally means *born before,* thus more experienced and therefore wiser.

Holding up a book, she said, "HON." So, we figured, a book in Japanese was a HON, pronounced *HONG,* as in *Hong Kong.* We were encouraged not to revert to English by saying to ourselves, "A book is a HON," but rather to look at it as an object we were seeing for the first time and which was called a HON. When she picked it up again, pointed to it with her other hand and said, "KORE WA HON DES!" we surmised correctly that she was saying, "This is a book." That was the very first sentence we learned to say in Japanese in November 1952.

The grammar became more and more complex. We were told that nothing less than two hours of personal study would do for every hour spent in the class room. There were times we felt it was absolutely impossible to conquer Japanese; and one or two of a previous group had a psychological breakdown because they weren't able to keep up with the rest. We were often reminded not to neglect our daily private devotions and to look to the Lord continually for strength and grace and in utter dependence.

Beginning the very first Sunday we went to a nearby small Japanese church, hearing for the first time Japanese singing, praying and preaching. Of course, for quite some time we understood very little. After a few weeks, however, we were told, for our encouragement, to speak to the congregation using a couple of simple sentences, which we had well rehearsed. For me, that was a thrilling experience, and I was the first one of our group to go forward.

One of our Japanese-American lady missionaries, born and raised in America of Japanese parents and who spoke both languages fluently, was to introduce me. She had me walk to the front ahead of her. Nearing the platform, I stepped aside to allow her to walk to the pulpit before me. I thought it to be the polite, Christian thing to do, but she motioned me ahead. I wasn't too willing to do that, and for a while we just stood there, each one trying to have the other one go first.

Finally, she firmly insisted and promised to tell me the reason for it later. I went on ahead of her, and after she had introduced me, I happily spoke for the first time in Japanese to a group of people sitting before me in a Japanese church, "WATAKUSHI WA IESU-SAMA O AI SHIMASU," (I love the honorable Jesus) and "WATAKUSHI WA NIPPON GA DAISUKI DES," (I like Japan very much).

The explanation for preceding her onto the platform, I learned later was one of the ancient customs of that land: many others I was still to learn. In Japan, the man is the absolute "ruler of his castle": his home and his family. This is a position he must diligently hold and defend at any cost — not only before his relatives but before the entire community, including his place of employment and his business associates. Otherwise, he becomes their laughing stock and considered henpecked, a weakling and a coward. This is so deeply imbedded in the Japanese that it reaches into every aspect of their lives. To this day it is still noticeable in the local churches. The congregation would have thought it strange indeed if I allowed a woman to precede me onto the platform.

In the overcrowded trains, busses and street cars, one continually sees all the available seats occupied predominantly by men. Women, often with heavy packages in one hand, stand in front of the men, holding on to the straps above them with the other hand. After I was married, my wife always refused to sit down, and the moment a space became available quickly told me to sit down. She refused, under those circumstances, to take the seat herself, lest both of us become the object of their disdain. Lately, however, men do get up when they see a pregnant woman or one who is carrying a small baby.

On the subject of babies, a family who has a newborn girl is generally quite disappointed and disheartened. The reason is that after going through the expense of raising a daughter to marriageable age, she leaves the home, and in most instances moves into the home of her in-laws, to become an unpaid maid to her mother-in-law while her husband is at his job. She is often taken advantage of, having to do the most menial tasks. In case of a boy, on the other hand, there is great rejoicing and a big celebration, for when he gets married, he will bring a free helper into his parents' home.

It was interesting to hear from older missionaries about their experiences in their various associations with the Japanese. For example, **four** is associated with death because in Japanese both words are pronounced the same (SHI). So, four of anything, such as pieces of fruit or cake or flowers or anything else, are never placed on a table. Many hotels have no "fourth" floor for no one would want to live there. The floors are numbered: 1, 2, 3, 5, etc.

We had national Japanese pastors and church workers speak to us about the difficulties which they had to overcome before they felt free to truly trust the Lord for salvation. One big problem is the one facing the oldest son. He is expected (required) to do the honors at the god-shelf daily, presenting rice and other offerings. Especially constraining is the necessity to bow when performing these rituals.

These guest speakers answered a multitude of questions concerning their culture and tradition. We were amazed to learn that much of the Japanese outlook on life, and their seemingly strange thinking processes could be better understood after we had studied their language.

The Japanese language consists of a nearly uncountable number of "honorifics." It would be easy to hurt a person's feelings, embarrass him or even insult him, without intending to. On the other hand, by wrong usage one might appear proud or arrogant.

Everything that is one's own, even oneself, one's wife or one's children, has to be expressed in a grammatical form that conveys humility, lowliness and submission; everything about the other person has to be highly esteemed, exalted and honored. But since all this is done most indirectly and unobtrusively, it is — when one has mastered the grammatical form — most pleasing and natural.

For example, KUDASAI, the simple word *please,* does literally mean "down" or "below"; so that one is actually saying, "Let me — that is below you — receive it at your hand; do this for me who is in a lowly position." (The Scriptures, full of Oriental customs such as bowing, reflect this concept.) When people show their respect, they put themselves in a lowly "position" by referring to themselves or the members of their families as "servants," as in the account of Judah before Joseph (Genesis 44:18-34).

Again, AGEMASU, *to give* to someone, is literally "lift up," to "hoist" or to "elevate."

Another example is the word for *wife*. Since personal pronouns such as "my" and "your" are seldom used, it is **the word itself** that conveys possession and who the possessor is. If it is *my* wife, she is KANAI, "the ordinary thing in the living quarters." If she is yours, she is OKU-SAMA, "the exalted lady in the inner chamber."

After I was married, I had an embarrassing situation happen to me as I met an acquaintance on my way to the bus one morning. He asked me about my family, and in telling him that my wife wasn't feeling too well, I inadvertently used the word OKU-SAMA. He looked at me, puzzled, and then said, "Very strange. When I left her a little while ago, she was feeling quite well." He was probably wondering how I happened to know so much about the condition of his wife. A very delicate situation indeed, which, fortunately, I was able to quickly correct. The Japanese generally understand the problem we foreigners have with their difficult language and readily make allowances for it.

THE KANJI

I learned after I came to Japan how their complicated signs had come into being. This became an immense blessing and an abundant joy to my heart. Eventually it became one of the most helpful fools in proclaiming the Word of God to the Japanese.

I discovered that these signs had originally been **pictographs,** simple sketches of things which people saw around them, especially in nature. For instance, a mountain ⼭ , the shape of which can still be seen in today's Japanese character for mountain, 山 YAMA; or river 川 , which the symbol used today still has a resemblance to a current 川 KAWA.

The Bible tells us that God, through that **which He has made,** has revealed unto us the invisible things that may be known about Him.

"For the wrath of God is revealed from Heaven against all ungodliness of men, who hold the truth in unrighteousness; ***Because that which may best KNOWN of God is manifest in them; for God hath SHOWED it to them.*** *For the invisible things of Him, from the creation of the world* ***are clearly seen,*** *BEING UNDERSTOOD BY THE THINGS THAT ARE MADE, even His eternal power and Godhead; so that they are without excuse.**

or again in Psalm 19:1-4:

*The heavens DECLARE the glory of God; and the firmament SHOWS his handiwork. Day unto day UTTERS speech, and night unto night SHOWS knowledge. There is no speech nor language where their voice [in evidence] is not heard. Their [guide]line is gone out through all the earth and their words to the end of the world.**

The Apostle Paul writes that "faith comes by hearing, and hearing by the word of God." Upon the question, "Have they not heard?" comes the startling reply, "Yes, truly. THEIR SOUND went into all the earth, and THEIR WORD unto the ends of the world."*

That last phrase, "THEIR SOUND went into all the earth and THEIR WORDS unto the ends of the world," are the same as in Psalm 19:4. **Their sound** and **their words** refer to the heavens which **declare,** to the firmament which **shows,** to the day that **utters** and to the night that **shows.**

Indeed, GOD HAS REVEALED HIMSELF TO THE ENTIRE WORLD, "through the things that are made." AND THE PRESENT DAY JAPANESE CHARACTERS, which are derived from what men saw as

---

* Romans 1:18-2
* Romans 10:9,10

they looked at nature around them, SHOW FORTH EVEN YET TODAY, **His eternal power and Godhead.**

Our Lord had seen to it that my family name would be BAUM, meaning **tree** in English. This turned out to be one of those unforeseen blessings in Japan. Later, when I taught German at the Meisei University (Tokyo), I introduced myself to my students by writing the Japanese character for TREE on the blackboard. (Perhaps the early Chinese at first drew themselves a tree as they saw it 𣎳, but as time went on it was simplified to look like this 朱 , and eventually like this 朮. Today it is written basically the same way: 木 , pronounced KI.

In my class, I called their attention to the center, the basic part of which is the cross 十 . I explained that because of the cross and because of the One Who died on it for me, the 十 has a very special place in my heart. Interestingly enough, a cross in Japan is pronounced JU (Jew).

The word "cross" as such is not in the Japanese language. The character is rather the symbol for their number **10.** So when a Japanese thinks about a cross, he pictures **10** in his mind. A street "cross"-ing is thus to him literally a "ten"-ing. This may seem rather strange until we remember we use letters from our alphabet in the same way to speak of a "U" turn or an "S" curve. To the Japanese our Lord died on a "number 10 construction."

I pointed out to them that his body and outstretched arms as He was being crucified formed a perfect "number 10," thereby reminding us that He was the only one Who kept all the 10 commandments, which the law of God had demanded, and that He did this in our place.

There is a KANJI, my favorite illustration because it uses my name: BAUM (tree) 木 . The Japanese have an abbreviated or contracted symbol for **person** which is イ and which forms a new symbol when it stands immediately in front of the tree 木 . This new symbol, 休 , means REST and appears in the Japanese Bible in Matthew 11:28: "Come unto me all ye that labour and are heavy laden, and I will give you 休 **REST."**

I kept my students in suspense by writing 木 in the middle of the blackboard and イ (PERSON) in the lower left hand corner. Then I would explain that the One who hung on the 木 (TREE) with His outstretched arms invited whosoever will to come to Him. This イ (person) heard it but was not interested, and neither were many other イイイ (PERSONS). But finally, one decided he wanted the forgiveness of sin, and went to the 休 (TREE) and thus obtained 休 REST for his soul.

You should have seen my students' expression of amazement as they suddenly realized from their own Japanese calligraphy, that when a 亻 (person) comes to the 木 (tree) on which Christ died for him, He will of a surety find 休 (REST).

It was also in Japan I became further **oriented** by gaining an unexpected understanding of the Trinity from reading my Japanese Bible. Being a Jew whose background denied this great Truth, this was of particular importance. I had heard many illustrations given to simulate the Trinity, such as a rope made up of three strands; or an egg which consists of a shell, yoke and egg white; or even of water which becomes steam when heated, and ice when frozen, thus it is a liquid, a vapour and a solid. But none of these satisfied me, especially since I was now to proclaim the only true, eternal Godhead to idol-worshipping Japanese.

My first Bible classes began with Genesis 1:1-3, telling my students about the Eternal God and His Creation. In connection with that, I turned to John 1:1: "In the beginning was the **WORD** and the **WORD** was with God and the **WORD** was God." Seeing the Japanese language symbol which stood for **"WORD** 言**,"** I was startled because I had seen the very same symbol in Gen. 1:3, but there it stood for **said,** where I read: "And God **said,** 言 Let there be light." I realized that instead of "God said," it could just as well have been, as it is in Japanese, "And God WORDED"; God created the world by means of His **spoken Word.**

With other words, the symbol for the word **SAID** in the Genesis account, used for God speaking different aspects of this world into existence, was the same symbol as the one used for **WORD** in John's Gospel. Now I could explain to my students the truth contained in John 1:2 that "The same (that is, the WORD) was in the beginning with God," that "all things were made by Him" (John 1:3) and that He (the Word) "was made flesh and dwelt among us."

I showed them that: "(God) hath in these last days SPOKEN to us by His Son ... The Lord Jesus Christ — BY WHOM ALSO HE MADE THE WORLDS." (Hebr. 1:1,2)

So the WORD of God does really two things: It speaks and it creates, as we read in Psalm 33:9, "For He spoke, and IT WAS DONE, HE COMMANDED and IT STOOD FAST." Thus, in a way, we have a double revelation of God: an INSIDE BOOK, the Bible; and an OUTSIDE BOOK, His creation. In Revelation, He who is called KING OF KINGS and LORD OF LORDS is also called the WORD OF GOD. (19:13,16).

The four horizontal lines of this Japanese character which stands for both **WORD** and **SAY** (or **SPEAK**), though they are not a character in themselves, could well symbolize the vocal cords (for there are actually two pairs which project into the cavity of the larynx), while the bottom portion is the Japanese symbol for mouth ☐ . Both of these, the vocal cords as well as the mouth, are needful to produce a word, but they both would be of little value were it not for one more important part, the BREATH to vibrate these cords and without which there could be no sound.

In the Scriptures, this BREATH (Hebrew, **RUACH)** is called the SPIRIT of God. "Spirit" basically means AIR or a**spir**ation (breathing). We speak of "spirit drinks," referring to those which have an ethyl alcoholic base which causes evaporation, "becoming air." The word **expire** (die) basically means that the validity or the BREATH of life is gone.

This Breath, or **SPIRIT** of God, is mentioned in the second verse of Genesis, chapter one, even BEFORE God began to SPEAK the creation into being; so we actually should not refer to this member of the Trinity as the **third** person of the Godhead, but as **one of the three** that constitute the TRI-UNITY.

I showed my students, that through their language, possibly more than through any other, these eternal truths have been revealed to them. That the Holy Spirit is as much God as is the Father and is the Son, for He in fact is the ONE who empowered the WORD of GOD to become audible even as without the breath none of us would be able to utter a word and that without Him, this world could not have come into existence, as may be clearly seen from Psalm 33:6, "By the Word of the Lord were the Heavens made; and all the host of them, **BY THE BREATH OF HIS MOUTH.**"

15

The First Step Is Hardest

THROUGHOUT OUR TRAINING, we had gone out on weekends into the surrounding communities to visit our active senior missionaries, some of whom worked with Japanese who either had come to know the Lord under their ministry or who were already believers. Seeing and learning first hand about living and ministering among the people of Japan was a most valuable and needful exposure. It helped us to think through how we would fit in, and to consider what particular aspect of ministry into which our Lord would lead us in the days ahead.

We went with these missionaries from house to house, distributing invitations to their Bible classes. We sat in while they taught, listening to the many questions and the answers; and we went along to their street meetings. During these weekend visits we were given much opportunity to try our wings, using what we have learned.

I had my first real chance at this while visiting our missionary, Shelton Allen, in Utsunomiya. After church and after we had eaten our lunch of rice, broiled fish with soybean sauce, pickles and seaweed and the usual unsugared Japanese tea, he said to me: "Let's go now to our street meeting and I'll get you started!" I really didn't think I was ready for what I was pretty sure he had in mind. We drove to a nearby playground with one of the Japanese co-workers and set up a P.A. system and started to sing. It wasn't long before some curious housewives, a few students from the nearby university and some children gathered around. Then Shelton walked up to the microphone and said (in Japanese, of course): "I brought a special friend with me today. He has only been in Japan a few months and is still studying the language every day, so that he can tell a most important story. Remember, he is still very new at this, but would you like to hear him speak?" They all applauded and laughed and clapped their hands and shouted, "Hi! Hi! o'negai itashimasu!" (loosely, yes, yes, we would ask that favor), and with that Shelton motioned me to the mike.

I had everyone's attention and first told them that I liked Japan and the Japanese people. Then I began in the best way I knew how, to tell them what the Lord Jesus had done for all of us, but soon after I thought I was getting across because all seemed to agree, nodding "Hi, hi," Shelton suddenly interrupted me and slowly pushed me aside and what he then told them made them all burst into laughter.

I didn't know what had happened until a little later when Shelton told me. I had used a seemingly insignificant but wrong grammatical construction. Instead of saying, "Jesus gave His life to save me from my sin," I had said, "I gave my life to save Jesus Christ from His sin."

While it was a very wrong statement, I believe our Lord used even that for His glory. By having to correct my statement, the emphasis was made on Who the One was Who gave His life, and for whom it was that He gave it.

The missionaries we visited on weekends were in a variety of activities of ministries. Some were evangelists, others were pastors of new congregations, others specialized in primarily reaching students. Some were in charge of Christian bookstores and sidewalk book tables, some were radio preachers and some taught in newly formed Bible schools. They were also active, as occasions warranted, in other phases of ministry.

I was particularly interested in talking to people I met "by the way," looking for a very natural opening to tell them of the Lord.

As I was buying some very cheap red grainy paste that doubled for jam at that time, I met a very friendly, nicely dressed middle-aged man. He gave me a friendly smile, and I thought it would be easy to talk to him. I told him where I was from and the purpose for having come to Japan.

He listened attentively and asked, "Tell me, what did you find different over here from what you are used to in America?" so we carried on a most interesting conversation. His friendly manner and openness encouraged me, and when I told Shelton about it he said right away, "Oh, he must be the man whose wife was killed in a tragic accident just three days ago."

I shook my head and told him, "That can't very well be; this man was cheerful and happy as a lark, and he in no way showed any signs of grief or sorrow."

"Exactly," Shelton said, "typical Japanese, not wanting to burden others with his personal grief and thereby making them also feel sad and mourn with him, for he realizes that each one of them has problems of his own and he feels it wouldn't be right to burden him with his personal grief."

Another typical Japanese way of thinking is seen when there is a question of borrowing money from someone or lending it. A Japanese would rather borrow than lend. The reason in his thinking is that if he were to lend money to a friend and the borrower would be unable to return it at the appointed time, he would probably be so embarrassed that he would try to avoid the lender, and thus, our good man would lose a friend.

In June of 1953, when I was still in the beginning stages of freely conversing with people, I wrote the following account in a prayer letter home.

The local trains still are the sphere of my current most practical service for the Savior. I've been passing out tracts and have engaged English-speaking nationals in conversation, which gives me a wonderful opportunity to talk to them about eternal values.

A short while ago, I saw a Japanese high school girl sitting in front of me, engrossed in reading an American comic book. I practically fell over backwards when her reply to my question if she understood what she was reading came forth in faultless English. These teenagers are really students. Having never left Japan, many also know German, French or Spanish.

I asked her about her hopes beyond the grave, and a look of bewilderment and uneasiness came over her face. So anxious was she to find the answer that she willingly gave me her address so that I could write to her. The other day I received her reply:

"Dear Mr. Baum,

I thank you very, very much for your kind letter and a valuable book. I read it and three leaflets. I think they gave me a chance to think seriously about life. I used to be very blue when I consider, for I find that I don't know the purpose of my life. (I can't believe what my high school teachers said about.) I know how sinful I am. Oh, I hate myself and don't know what to do with me, and in such case I want to die and think I need death, because I feel it gives me a solution for everything. But, Mr. Baum, it's good to forget, it's good that we can live on this earth without thinking. Oh, I'm sure heaven doesn't want me to enter (but is there a heaven really?) Mr. Baum, please help me as I can believe. For me believing is everything now."

I guess it expresses better than I possibly can the despondency of the disappointed and confused younger generation. I pray that He may grant me a ministry among them.

P.S. The writer of the above quoted letter called me the other day from the Yokohama station. I met her there and was able to show her the plan of salvation from God's word and then put her in touch with a Japanese Christian girl of her own age. Please remember her in your prayers.

At times I was invited by other missionaries, even those from other missions, to talk about "Biblical Judaism," a Judaism that points to **Yeshua Cha Mashiach** based on the Old Testament prophecies, and also to show some of my object lessons.

In Kumamoto, one of the southernmost cities in Japan, I inadvertently got into the wrong street car. Not until we arrived at the end of the line did I realize my mistake. I told the conductor, hoping he would let me ride back with him without paying again. He was most kind and evidently quite impressed with the efforts I made trying to speak his language and granted my request. By that time, a number of passengers had entered, waiting for departure, and had listened to my plea to the conductor. They were whispering to each other and seemed amused at this foreigner who went in the wrong direction.

Because they were all looking at me, I thought I should say something to them, but didn't know exactly what or how. Then I remembered a verse (Proverbs 14:12) and quoted it to them, in Japanese, of course: "There is a way that seemeth right unto a man, but the end thereof are the ways of death." And directly thereafter, John 14:6, "I am the Way, the Truth and the Life; no man cometh unto the Father but by me."

Then I explained that I thought I had gotten on the right street car, but not being able to read the sign, I made a big mistake and ended up going in the wrong direction. At first I spoke very hesitantly because I didn't know what their reaction would be. But when I realized they were all intently listening, I became bolder and explained in the best way I knew how. I told them what and Who was the right way to Heaven and exactly what one would have to do to get there. When I finished, nobody said anything, but when I got off, a young man followed me and asked if he could get some more information about this "Jesus man." I spent two hours with him the next day, and then gave him the address of a missionary who lived in that town, for I could think of nothing more to tell him, at least not in Japanese.

We were still in intensive language study and had been told that for every hour in the classroom we were to spend no less than two hours in private study. Nearly all of the new missionaries in our group were ten or more years younger than I (I was then already 37), and when I realized how much ahead of me they were, I was desperately trying to keep up with them and nearly "went to pieces" and felt like packing up and going home. There was one who actually did so in a previous group.

Our mission leaders were very much aware of this and warned us not to compare ourselves with others, but rather to keep our eyes stayed on the Lord.

I remember how I tried to vent my frustration even at the expense of the Japanese one day when I went with Shelton into an electronic shop in Utsunomiya. The salesman called one of his men, introducing him with the words, "Nishimura-san here speaks very good English and would be very happy to help you."

With that the clerk greeted us with: "Goodo moningu sah, can I herup yuh?"

What I did then was not exactly the thing to do, but I'm relating it here for the record. I spoke to him in a jumble of English and German, saying something such as: "I would versuchen this aparat mit zwei wires to helfen the Kolben at the robinkel to function independently."

He smiled sheepishly while, no doubt, his brain worked overtime and he probably went home to tear up the diploma he received at his English conversation course. As we walked out, I heard him say to his boss — and these were his exact words: "Zen, zen, wakaranakatta!" (Absolutely incomprehensible!)

Shelton frequently reminded me of what I said the moment we were on the street again: "I really hate myself when I do things like that!"

PARTINGS

After the nine months, although we could by no means freely converse as we would have liked to have done, our basic and most intensive language study came to a close. We were being sent forth into the various places of service for our Lord. Yes, it was this for which we had come to Japan; yet it proved to be a very emotional and sorrowful experience.

The 13 of us who had arrived and had studied together had become a very closely knit family. We had many hours of precious fellowship, prayed and even cried together and tried to encourage one another the many times we were frustrated when it seemed so hopeless to comprehend the seemingly impossible language.

Parting also meant no more visiting in one another's rooms, not eating together any more, not exchanging the exciting discoveries we made in solving some difficult grammar construction nor sharing our frustration trying to make ourselves understood in some Japanese department store.

We also had many laughs together. While as a group of new missionaries, we were taken to a Japanese hotel for an overnight stay. My good friend and roommate, Clarence Swanson (Swany) wanted to show his Japanese speaking ability, picked up the house phone to call the desk, and instead of saying: Moshi, Moshi, o'cha o kudasai! (Excuse me, [or Hello, hello — an attention-getter], please send up some tea), he said: Mushi, Mushi, o'cha o kudasai! (Mushi is the Japanese word for insect or vermin.)

Wanting to ask for some toothpicks, Conrad Miller, one of our senior missionaries, told us that when he first came to Japan he asked for "Wood for my teeth."

I thought about the many partings I had gone through in my life. There was the one as a teenager when I sorrowfully left my parents, my many friends and the land of my birth. Having been reunited with my parents many years later in America, I had to say good-bye again when I became a soldier. Then there came the good-bye from all my buddies with whom I shared the barracks for many months. The parting from the precious members of the G.I. Gospel Team under which I had come to know my Lord came next. After that I went through the very painful and most deeply felt spiritual alienation from my family after I became a Christian, and I keenly sensed the farewells I had to say to my classmates with whom I had spent four blessed years in Bible school.

Now another most difficult parting confronted me, though it was only after nine months. I had become one with this group of new missionaries like being stranded together with them on a distant island, a long ways from home and faced with a seemingly unconquerable language and among many strange customs. That parting, however, could not be compared with this, one of my most difficult partings, namely that from our entire mission family, when it became time to "retire" and return to America.

It was a parting from a part of my life, one to which I had given myself to unreservedly and with all that was within me. Thereupon came uncountable partings as I began to travel all over Europe, to Africa, South America and China, among others. They were, so to say, "little partings." But only as to the length of stay in each place. I often had to tear myself away emotionally as well as physically from some of the most loving and dedicated people I have ever known. Even yet in my dreams I see them accompanying me to my car as I slide behind my steering wheel, roll down my window so I could wave to them as I drove away, even yet while seeing them through my rear view mirror still waving until I was out of sight.

A parting of a completely different, and also of a much more far-reaching and emotional impact, was that from our daughter, Mary Esther, in 1975 when we took her to the Tokyo airport to return to America to enter nurses' training, and later married to eventually return to Japan as a missionary. Our boy Tim came home with us to America when we "retired" in 1980, but soon parted from us to go to Bible college in Pennsylvania where he also married and then settled there.

These partings taught me a wonderful spiritual lesson. My Lord doesn't want me to tie myself to any temporary associations on this earth, regardless of how compelling or entwining they might be, so that I would not be restrained by any earthly ties when He, the great Bridegroom and Lover of my soul comes to call me into His eternal presence, never to have to part again.

16

Finally: To Get Really Started

OUR MISSION LEADERSHIP had talked with us periodically about how and where we thought the Lord was leading concerning our ministry following the basic language study at the Mission Home. By the time we actually finished, each of us had already found his or her place of ministry. Most of us went to work with a missionary in one of the places we had visited on weekends.

It was understood that we were to continue language study on a private basis by hiring a Japanese teacher at the place where we would be actively engaged in proclaiming the Good News to the Japanese.

There were four successively difficult and complex language books that we had to complete and take tests on before we would no longer be under the guidance and jurisdiction of our Language Training Committee, to which we also had to send periodical reports about our progress. For the official tests we were to go to Tokyo to a well-known, well-reputed language school headed by the authors and publishers of our textbooks. It would be nearly three more years before I would finally conquer all those hurdles.

Two or three of the new missionaries had befriended young Japanese students during their free time and had even visited them repeatedly in their homes. After a while, the families became so attached to them that they offered to take them in to live so they could begin their ministry in those surrounding neighborhoods. Though these families were not necessarily believers, they were nevertheless not opposed to the Christian teaching.

What an example to be a believer living among them! The missionaries who did this soon spoke Japanese more fluently than any of the rest of us because they were exposed to it all day. They had to use it continually to make themselves understood. We others would converse in English when we were with our senior missionaries.

When finally the time for moving arrived, I hired a three-wheeler "truck," a Japanese motorized tricycle with handlebars. We loaded my suitcases and crates into the back and headed for UTSUNOMIYA, the capital city of the TOCHIGI Prefecture, about 140 km north of our Mission Home in Yokohama.

The driver sat in the open, and I perched precariously on a skimpy fold-up seat next to him. We drove that way for nearly five hours over dusty, bumpy roads. Several times I nearly fell off when, at the last moment, my driver tried to avoid a chuckhole.

Shelton Allen, my missionary brother whose co-laborer I was soon to be, was somewhere "about his Father's business" when we arrived. His extremely small, typical-Japanese house was in the very poor section of the town and *literally* on the other side of the railroad tracks.

We unloaded all my baggage, and I paid the driver, who left me sitting dejected, on one of the crates. Nobody to meet me, strange new surroundings, not yet able to handle the language adequately.

Before long, a whole gang of poorly dressed children came running up, looking at me as at a strange foreign creature that had invaded their neighborhood. They all pointed their fingers at me, laughing and shouting, "HANA GA TAKAI DES NE!" over and over again. (What a high—tall— nose he has. Just look!)

I tried to win their friendship by playing along with them, telling them that my nose was indeed "TAKAI" (high or tall), complimenting them on their cute little noses. I said I wished mine were as theirs. They only laughed louder at my funny way of expressing myself.

When later I told my brother Shelton about the incident, he laughed also but for a somewhat different reason. He explained that the children, although laughing, were elated to see a man with such a "high" nose and were indirectly paying me a compliment.

To the Japanese, such a nose speaks of prominence, stateliness and literally of something "outstanding." It seems that every Japanese silently wishes for a "tall" nose instead of the short, flat one with which he was born.

In their fashion magazines nose clamps are advertised to be worn while relaxing at home and at bedtime to make their noses "taller" even while they sleep.

On special festivals for children when parents take special pride in showing off their offspring, dressed in colorful kimonos, their hair decked out in glittering array, the bridge of their noses are painted with a white streak to accentuate them.

Our house was typical Japanese, one room, with *Tatami* (tightly covered, pressed-straw sections) making up the floor, except for the three-by-six foot kitchen area, which was wood. In the kitchen, over the small sink, was the water pump which was our only water supply. Also in the tiny kitchen was our typical Japanese bathtub, called an *ofuro.*

In Japan it is the custom to wash one's self in front of the *ofuro,* scooping the very hot water out with a clean dipper and mixing it with cold water in a basin. After washing and rinsing this way, one climbs in and SOAKS. Japanese relax that way, sometimes for a half-hour or more, until the skin is as red as a lobster and the sweat runs from the forehead. The one-time filling is used by the entire family. The water remains clean because the bathers wash and rinse themselves outside the *ofuro.* The father is the first to use it, then the sons according to age, then the mother and, last of all, the daughters.

For me, it was too hot to soak in, so I just washed, rinsed and dried, without climbing in. But not my brother Shelton. He got in just like the Japanese and soaked. Coming out, with his body literally steaming he would put on his clothes without drying himself. He did the same when taking a shower when he visited missionary friends in whose home there were such.

Shelton and I slept, Japanese fashion, on *futon,* just as we had done in our Mission Home.

For cooking, we had a three-burner kerosene stove I had brought from America. An elderly neighborhood lady, AOYAGI-SAN,* prepared our noon meals, mostly fish, and always rice. She was a quiet and dear lady, the mother of two children, and she sincerely trusted and served our Lord. She also did all our shopping, cleaned the house, did our laundry and often gave us helpful insights into typical Japanese thinking.

The food she served was throughout Japanese, which we ate while kneeling (that is, with our feet folded under, actually sitting on our feet) on a flat cotton pillow on the *tatami* in front of a low table. For me, that was always a most uncomfortable position. Aoyagi-san knelt alongside us, as the Japanese custom was, replenished our rice bowls out of a big pot by her side and refilled our tea cups when necessary.

We gave her $12 each month, which she didn't want to accept because the usual amount for such work was only $8 . We insisted, and she finally, though reluctantly, accepted it. Also, we asked her to please eat together with us, especially because she was our sister in Christ, but it wasn't easy for her to break away from the Oriental custom. To her, a servant must be in submission in all aspects, that is, subservient to his or her master; so she could not eat with us at the same table.

We finally convinced her that we had come as servants of our Lord, and that our service and dedication to Him did not in any way surpass hers. Hearing that, she at last consented to eat with us, as long as we would allow her to sit and eat at a lower table alongside ours.

---

* *SAN after a name may mean either Mr., Mrs. or Miss.*

The breakfast and evening meals we conglomerated ourselves. We usually ate directly out of the pot or the frying pan to avoid washing dishes. Frequently we received food packages from home, mostly canned goods.

Shelton was a pretty good cook; at least he knew how to heat the contents of those cans. When he looked at the paper labels, he would always say, "Let us first read the 'destructions.'."

I didn't yet know what a brain he was and how well organized. He played the guitar and composed his own music. He also played a saw with a violin bow, vibrating it while clamping the handle between his knees. By bending the end of the blade with his right hand, he produced the desired notes.

He also had a private pilot's license and during the war had been part of a Radio Control Station on one of the war ships. He was a real genius when it came to mathematics and electronics. In 1952 he had built his own simple computer and in-between time had taught himself "Esperanto," an auxiliary language for international use, and corresponded with members belonging to Esperanto speaking clubs which existed in other European countries. When he wrote to those in Russia about the Lord, he used a fictitious name.

Besides all this, he had a command of the Japanese language such as very few of the entire missionary community in Japan, many of which had been there years longer than he, and I had made the colossal mistake of thinking what he could do, that I could do also.

I became very disheartened and was jealous when I heard him preach and converse so freely with others. Though I had now a private language teacher, my progress was much slower than I had hoped. I had to admit that a person my age (I was 38 then and Shelton 28) would have a comparatively greater difficulty in learning a new language, especially such a difficult one as Japanese, than a person who was ten years younger.

Shelton was very sympathetic and encouraged me however he could. One day he said to me, "Bill, you keep right at it, and in a year form now you'll also be able to speak fluently."

I marked that date down and struggled along without making much progress. A week or so before the anniversary date of Shelton's encouraging remark I acted unusually cheerful, although I was really quite discouraged. Shelton came up with, "Hey, Bill, what's the reason for your happy disposition these days?"

"Don't you know?" I said to him, three more days and it will be the 22nd of September. I can hardly wait!"

"Wait for what?" he wanted to know.

"Don't you remember, it will be the anniversary of the day you told me that I'd be able to speak as fluently as you; what a day that will be."

I found out that he was also quite eccentric in its truest sense (from the Greek: "out of, or outside the center"), which is generally the case with brainy people. After brushing his teeth, he wouldn't rinse them but swallow the toothpaste and go on about his business. He had a very common and down-to-earth appearance and indeed a most humble disposition. It absolutely amazed me. No one would have suspected what all was in his brilliant, intelligent head.

It was then the custom in Japan, and still is in many parts of the Orient, to ask for a reduction in price, especially when buying clothing or household goods. I soon found out that his and my heritage were miles apart. Not only did he never bargain, but when I would ask what he had paid for an item he had just purchased, he would say, "I have no idea, I just gave them what they asked for." He also never brought back a receipt.

Memorizing KANJI was our major language study activity; it consumed most of our time in our first months and even years in Japan. We used 2-1/2-inch-square cards with the KANJI characters printed on the front with the meaning and pronunciation on the back. We started with the first card, memorizing the character and the sequence and number of strokes required; then turning it over, memorized the meaning and the pronunciation. After committing about ten of these to memory, we went back, looking at the back side first — trying to remember what the matching character looked like and drawing it with a finger on the palm of the hand. Then it was the character we looked at first, trying to remember its meaning, looking on the back to see whether we had it correct. Back and forth, back and forth, until we really knew them. Then we would start on the next ten; finishing with that set, we'd revert to the first set to double-check our memory.

I always started with five cards each time, slowly increasing the number. We had a system in which we daily reviewed the former day's set, then every second day, and so on. Some of us could memorize 20 to 30 that way, or maybe even 40. But not Shelton. He had set his goal for 100 per day. He got up at five o'clock in the morning, had his devotions and then walked for two or three hours through the nearby fields, taking a stack of KANJI-cards with him. After his walk, he came in for breakfast, then headed out again. What a guy!

One day it began to rain while he was out, and I expected him back any moment. It wasn't until mid-afternoon that he showed up, with his clothes sopping wet.

"I had to come home," he said. "Look at my cards. They are so soaked I couldn't flip 'em any more."

By that time I had learned not to compare Shelton's accomplishments with mine, but neither did I stay outside when it rained! The village streets, however, and the roads between the fields remained my daily constant companions. I knew every path and every turn of the road even better than the Japanese characters I studied while walking. I could have walked them with my eyes closed, which I saw myself doing in my sleep.

Every once in a while I would run into Shelton doing the same as I. We would usually just exchange a few words and walk on. I often asked myself what the Japanese thought when they saw us walking everywhere with those small cards in hand.

Most of the time I wrote my characters in the air with my finger. At times, when I didn't understand a pronunciation or the exact usage of a particular character, I would stop a farmer or laborer who happened to come by. But most of all I liked to ask the young school children on their way to or from the nearby grade school. They were so natural, down-to-earth and sincere, I couldn't help but love them instantly.

Shelton and I talked about how wonderful it would be to adopt one of them. The moment I began talking to them and showing them my cards, the others who were farther back would come running up wanting to see also. The children could read the cards as fast as I could turn them. I could hardly believe it! They were only 10 or 12 years old and I was 38. They were making a game out of it while I was sweating it out! Only once in a while, when it was a character they hadn't learned yet, they would ask one another. It was one of my greatest joys and a real tonic during my otherwise rather monotonous memorizing routine.

Once, while riding the train and memorizing my cards, I did something that my missionary brothers made sure I wouldn't forget. The moment I turned a card to see the English meaning of a character, the Japanese man sitting next to me volunteered the information, either trying to help me or to impress me with his knowledge of English. I turned around so I could concentrate on the meaning by myself, but there was another man standing alongside me in the aisle who took over. I was rather annoyed, but didn't want to spoil their fun. Suddenly I thought of a ruse, although I knew it wasn't exactly the Christian thing to do. My next card showed the character for the first season of the year. The man said, "Spring."

I said, "No, it isn't."

He tried to get a closer look, and emphatically said, "Yes. It's SPRING."

I shook my head again and said, "No, it's FRÜHLING."

When he continued to insist it was *spring,* I pulled out my Japanese-German dictionary, turned to that particular character and showed it to him: *frühling.*

Seeing it, his face turned red with embarrassment and unbelief. He bowed deeply, apologized and retreated. That's when *I* felt bad; it was my turn to apologize to my Lord for this unchristian behavior.

KANJI: RIGHTEOUSNESS

In Japanese there is a character for "LAMB" 羊 (Hitsuji). One can still recognize the two small horns and its short tail.

I became aware of a very startling spiritual truth when I saw another character written immediately underneath it.

That was the character for the self-centered egotistical "I" 我 (Wareh), also often called the perpendicular pronoun of the "I specialist."

The prodigal son in Luke 15 referred to himself as such when he came to himself (realized his sinful condition) and decided to return to his father.

When the selfish "I" stands directly under the "Lamb," so close, as a matter of fact, that its small tail is omitted, the two become an entirely new character 義, pronounced simply GI. But what an enormous message it conveys, for it means "RIGHTEOUSNESS."

I've drawn it hundreds of times in Japan, to show that when a person puts himself under the head — or lordship of the LAMB OF GOD, Who takes away the sin of the world (John 1:29), God no longer sees his self-centered sinful condition, but looks at him through the cleansing and redeeming power of His dear Son, and bestows upon him His "RIGHTEOUSNESS."

Standard procedure every time the teacher enters the class room in Japan.

"Today is the first day in the new classroom, Sept. 6th 1954." is written in English and in Japanese on the blackboard. I was the invited guest with a "Special Story" for the children in this grade school near our home in Utsunomiya.

17

My Earliest Evangelistic Efforts

TOGETHER WITH LEARNING those KANJI characters, I began to memorize Bible verses in Japanese. Otherwise how would I be able to freely proclaim His Word? I tried to find an unusual and yet a thoroughly natural way to bring the Gospel to the attention of the people. I started to go into small stores and shops or even to vegetable stands alongside the road and "innocently" say, in Japanese, "Pardon me. I'm engaged in studying Japanese. Could you please help me a moment?"

The answer, nearly always, was, "Yes, of course. What can I do for you?" (The Japanese are always impressed and feel honored when a foreigner goes through the trouble of learning their difficult language.)

I would hand them my Bible opened to a salvation verse such as John 3:16. Pointing to it, I would say, "I'm trying to learn this verse. Please tell me if I'm pronouncing it correctly." With that, I'd quote it to them.

Very often, they would ask me what the verse meant. I would try to explain it to them. Or sometimes I would say why I had come to Japan, and why I wanted to learn their language. That always led to further conversation. Before leaving I would give them an attractive tract as an appreciation for their kindness, together with an invitation to come to our Bible class.

Some of us missionaries used Victrola records with Gospel messages. I had brought a *Webcor* tape recorder from America and copied some of those messages onto tape. I went with this new invention into the homes of the neighborhood to demonstrate it. I let the neighbors first hear the message, then I recorded their voices and played back the tape, much to their amazement. (It was eight years after the end of the war, and the Japanese tape recorder industry was not yet that far advanced. The SONY company was in process of being established and looking for investors, but my regenerated Jewish nose did not catch the scent.)

It was winter, the best time to find the entire family at home because of the cold. Their houses were not heated, so they spent most of their time sitting around the KOTATSU, a square, low table set over a hole of the same size in the *tatami* floor. Here the family members would sit, hanging their legs into the hole. A small pot of glowing charcoal kept their legs warm. A thick, cotton-filled blanket covered the table, extending enough to cover their laps. By leaning forward they could even cover their arms and shoulders. They all wore heavily padded, loose-fitting Japanese jackets to keep their backs warm.

People continually invited me to sit with them, drinking the ever-present, bitter green tea and answering their numerous questions. I missed a family atmosphere, so these invitations were immensely gratifying. More importantly, it gave me a natural opportunity to talk to them about those things which matter most in life, and I could freely read to them from the Bible stories Jesus told.

Their question whether this Jesus was a man or a woman was not new to me. It came up continually because the deity they worship is a woman, the sun goddess Amaterasu Omikami. According to their thinking, the present Japanese emperor is her direct descendant. While they worship her, they adhere to the teachings of Zen Buddhism which originated in India.

Sometimes there was a humorous incident, at least it seems humorous as I look back. Both Shelton and I had bicycles. We couldn't even think of owning a car, so we rode to our Sunday morning services, as did most of the Japanese, and we parked our bikes next to theirs. To them, owning a fancy bicycle is the equivalent of our owning an expensive automobile.

One time when we returned home, Shelton asked me if I had noticed the lady dentist who had come that morning for the first time. I told him I hadn't paid that much attention to it. He said, "I think she must be pretty rich; you should have seen the bicycle she was riding."

Shelton is now retired, as I am, but nearly every time we write or see each other, I remind him of his proclamation of amazement, "Did you see the BICYCLE she was riding!"

We had a dog, completely black, and so named *Kuro,* Blacky. Just for the fun of it, I always called him *Shiro,* Whitey. To the Japanese of our neighborhood, such American humor was incomprehensible. They tried their best to make this "stupid foreigner" understand the difference between those two colors. They explained I had mixed up those two words; they showed me something white, and said *Shiro,* and then something black, saying *Kuro.* I nodded in agreement. But I persisted in calling our dog *Shiro,* so they gave up, shaking their heads in utter unbelief.

Because all young Japanese would take advantage of every opportunity to learn English, it wasn't long before one after another came to us with the request, "Please teach us English." We finally made an agreement with them that after each English period we would have a Bible lesson. Most of them were willing to do that, but we soon realized that some of them excused themselves and left after the English lesson. We changed the order and taught the Bible first, which worked quite well.

We also noticed that our students were predominantly young girls, while our single women missionaries told us of the strange phenomenon (!) that most of their students were young men.

JAPANESE EVANGELISM

During my visits in the homes of Japanese families, I realized every moment that I was among a people whom our Lord loved and for whom He had died. I knew He had placed me there to "show forth the praises of Him who had called (me) out of darkness into His marvelous light" (1 Peter 2:9). I continually looked for different ways to introduce the Japanese to the Good News of Salvation, even though my language ability was still greatly lacking.

One day we were invited for dinner at the home of one of our missionary friends. I watched the wife as she prepared an instant pudding-dessert; that gave me an idea.

Before we left I asked her if she would let me have an extra box of that pudding power, for I would want to use it for a special purpose. The next day I took a bowl of water, an egg beater, a number of small wooden spoons which one receives when buying Japanese ice cream cups and a manually operated record player, along with my Gospel records.

I sat down with all this at a wide spot in the road not far from our home. Before long, some curious housewives came by. I motioned to them to come closer to see what I was doing. With that, I poured the powder into the bowl of water and began beating it with the egg beater. More women stopped to see what was going on. By handing them all a spoon and pointing at my bowl, I gave them to understand that I was offering them what I was about to prepare.

Pointing at my watch, I indicated to them to wait a few minutes until my pudding stiffened. While they were waiting, I played my record for them. When the pudding had sufficiently thickened, I gave each of them a tract and passed the bowl around.

Evidently they had never tasted any dessert of that kind, for they showed their approval by smiling and nodding their heads, saying, *Totemo oishii des ne!* (It's really delicious, isn't it?, A couple of them even came up and patted me on the shoulder.

After that I was the "pudding evangelist" to my missionary colleagues.

I had gone to the Philippines to propose to and get engaged to my favorite missionary nurse.

We were married in our Mission home in Japan, and some of our national workers were our special guests.

18

It Is Not Good That Man Should Be Alone ...

SOME OF THE JAPANESE GIRLS in our Bible classes had made definite decisions for the Lord, and we were much encouraged to see them grow in the knowledge of the Truth. Among them were a couple who caught Shelton's and my particular interest, and we quietly (and sometimes not so quietly) entertained the thought that they would make very devoted life partners, as Japanese women are especially endearing.

Our Mission policy, however, prevented us from continuing our thinking on this matter. The policy was that none of their missionaries could marry a Japanese National. This was mainly because the American occupation forces were still in Japan, and U.S. military men were seen everywhere in the company of "certain kinds" of Japanese girls, often in questionable places. The populace frowned upon these relationships, and if an American missionary were to be seen going about with a Japanese girl, it would certainly be misunderstood. Who would know that in our case she was the wife? That would have greatly hindered our ministry and testimony for the Lord. (This policy was changed some years later, and today there are some missionaries who serve in Japan with their Japanese wives.)

Shelton and I talked and prayed about some of our Mission's single lady missionaries, but there were no direct leadings.

During this time, I kept thinking about a girl I had met some years before in Bible College, Augusta Thiessen, whom I have already mentioned. Gussie, as she was affectionately called, and I had attended church and other Christian activities together. I had met her older brother and her parents, who were farmers in a small community about 200 miles west of Kansas City. She had become a registered nurse, and the Lord had

93

led her to the Philippines shortly after I left for Japan. She was in charge of a nursery of babies who had been separated from their leprous mothers lest they also become infected.

We had written each other occasionally, but only about the work of the Lord in our respective areas. Yet, now I could not get her out of my mind. I realized that she was the only qualified person in her needy and very specialized field; she was with a different mission, one newly founded, and she was in Manila, miles away from Japan. Besides, this dear girl was 28, while I was 40.

This was all happening about three years after I had come to Japan, and Shelton and I headed for our yearly mission conference at our Mission Home in Yokohama. The only thing I could think about throughout the entire conference was Gussie, and I meditated on the ways of the Lord, looking to Him for guidance.

The verse that comforted me greatly was Proverbs 3:5 and 6: *"Trust in the Lord with all your heart and lean not to your own understanding. In all your ways acknowledge Him and He will direct your paths."* I knew He had already performed a mighty miracle in saving me and calling me into His service, and I trusted Him to perform another one. Humanly speaking, the situation seemed utterly impossible because, to be perfectly honest, when we had been together on previous occasions it had been entirely on a basis of Christian fellowship. Having already learned that unless one *moves* one cannot be *guided,* I slipped out of one of the meetings and went back into our room. There I rolled up one of the futons and, using it as a desk, began to put my thoughts on paper.

It wasn't easy to write this letter across so many miles and years since Gussie and I had last seen each other and, on top of it all, to write for the first time what was in my heart. We had never before even approached the subject of marriage.

One of the most difficult and most painful things for me was to bare my soul or emotion in expressing my love for this girl. Going out on a limb. To have it broken off by being told, "I'm sorry, but I'm not interested," would have hurt me to the core. It was quite a chance I took.

I didn't have her address with me at the conference, so I took the letter home to mail it. That gave me time to re-think what I had done. Shelton tried to encourage me to go through with it. He even offered to drop the letter for me into the red pillar mail box slot just around the corner from our house.

Back in Utsunomiya, I was not so sure that I wanted him to do that. Then one evening as we were going out to a small eating place for a typical Japanese meal of fried fish, sliced salty cucumbers, pickled cabbage and the ever-present bowl of rice and the bitter green tea, my dear brother said to me, "Why don't you just take that letter along; let's just see how our Lord may lead us." As we passed the red mailbox, I tried to ignore it and kept on talking to Shelton, hoping he would keep on walking. He stopped, however, and said, "Would you hand me the letter if I promise not to do anything with it unless you tell me."

I finally did so very reluctantly. Then he came up with, "Bill, didn't you actually write that letter with the explicit intention to change your present status? Remember, he continued, "what you yourself once told me, that one could only discern the Lord's will if one gave Him the chance to reveal it! Why don't you give Him that chance?"

He then approached the mailbox, saying, "Well, what is your answer?" With that he stuck my letter part way into the slot, holding it tightly between only his thumb and index finger.

"You can still change your mind, even yet," he said, "while I'm holding your destiny between two of my fingers." He was having fun with me now. "If I should relax the muscle just a fraction, it will be gone."

I decided to completely trust my Lord and put my destiny entirely into His hands. "Let it go," I said.

As it so often happens with us frail humans, even when we have committed a matter to the Lord the very best we know how, we tend to entertain doubts whether we have really done the right thing. I was no exception. I became keenly aware that the adversary was mightily at work, causing me to spend a few days wondering and wavering.

About ten days later, while studying with my language teacher, I heard the mailman at the front entrance and excused myself to see whether the anxiously awaited reply had arrived. It was the only piece of mail that day, and for a moment I considered opening it right away. But then I wondered how an adverse answer might affect me and, in turn, be noticeable to my teacher. I decided to leave it unopened until after she left. I could hardly wait.

Then, with the unopened letter before me, I knelt down, "Lord," I prayed, "in this letter lies my destiny, the future of my life, Lord, please encompass me with thy love, give me the strength to face whatever the answer might be."

The reply was unexpectedly, yet understandably vague and indefinite. Gussie asked why I hadn't said anything about this matter before. She added that it would not be easy for her to make such a momentous decision without both of us praying about it and talking it over with one another.

The next day I went to our mission director with this letter in hand to ask his advice. His answer greatly surprised me. "I suggest," he said, "you take the earliest plane to Manila and talk to that dear girl and pray with her, just as she suggested, and together seek the Lord's will in that matter. I'll even be glad to take you to the airport.

I went directly to the Philippine Embassy in Tokyo to apply for a visa, which was issued to me the same hour. After booking a flight to Manila at the travel bureau, I sent a telegram to Gussie giving the date and time of my arrival. Our mission director took me to the airport as he had promised. I couldn't help but feel that he, in fact, the entire mission leadership as a whole, was convinced that it was decidedly advantageous and a more effective testimony to the community, for missionaries to serve together as husband and wife than to carry the responsibility as a single person.

Close to midnight, five days after having received Gussie's letter, I arrived in Manila — June 1, 1955. Gussie and one of her co-workers met me, and we went directly to the Mission Home of the International Christian Leprosy Mission.

Gussie had three local girls to help her care for the 15 infants in the nursery at that time. They had to prepare the correct formula for each of the babies as well as the more solid food when needed. Besides giving daily care, she took them to the doctor for regular checkups and when they became ill.

She was on night duty when I arrived, and she busily continued her work in the nursery kitchen while telling me about the different ministries of her Mission. Shortly after midnight she made a lettuce sandwich for me, and I told her the whole story — how our Lord had directed me, even that of laying her so very definitely upon my heart, and then we prayed together.

After her work was done, she sat down and we continued talking for another couple of hours, getting to understand one another's hearts. Then we prayed again, and then she said, "Yes, Bill, I too believe that our Lord would be pleased to have us serve Him together."

How unspeakably happy I was! It was after 3 a.m. when I finally got to bed, but I couldn't get to sleep for a long time.

The next day while eating breakfast with Gussie, a friend of the Mission came by. Gussie introduced me to him. What she said I will never forget. "Mr. DeGuzman, I'm going to Japan to marry Bill!"

My own Mission Board, the Far Eastern Gospel Crusade, had missionaries in the Philippines also, many of whom had gone to language school with Gussie, and they knew her well. She was no stranger to my mission "family."

Something else wondrously arranged by our Lord was that my own Mission had its Annual International Conference while I was in Manila. The main leaders from the Home Office, as well as many of their staff, were present. Since Gussie would soon be a member of the Mission, it was most convenient for her to be interviewed and accepted by our Board. Besides this, decisions were made concerning her coming to Japan as soon as a suitable replacement could be found. She would first of all begin the study of the Japanese language.

I remained in the Philippines for about a month, taking ample opportunity to visit many of the missionaries in outlying districts and making use of my object lessons which I had brought along.

It was mid-summer when I returned to Japan, the hottest, most humid season of the year. During this time, most missionaries spent a few weeks at a higher, cooler location. One of the favorites was KARUIZAWA, a well-known summer retreat and tourist resort nestled high in the cool mountains. It was frequented by well-to-do businessmen who lived either in their private summer homes or in one of the big hotels. They often ate in the many fancy restaurants in the area.

We missionaries and our acquaintances from other missions browsed in the interesting souvenir shops, went for walks in the nearby woods or took advantage of the healthful mineral baths.

Most of us attended the Inter-Mission Bible Conference which convened there every summer. Invited speakers were from America, Australia or England, including special musical presentations. It was a time of great spiritual refreshing, as were the home Bible study groups. The Tokyo Language School conducted a summer language course there, but I continued my language study with a young Japanese student who wanted to earn some extra money.

One of the surprises was seeing the present Emperor of Japan (then Prince), Hirohito, when he was still in his early 20s. He and his equally young lady friend, the present Empress Michiko, played tennis together and walked freely along the popular mid-town promenade with the rest of us vacationers.

On October 13, 1955, my "bride" finally arrived in Tokyo, and I greeted her with an orchid for her dress. Shelton and some other missionaries went with me to the airport to meet her and take her to our Mission Home. I stayed in Yokohama a few days longer to introduce her to everyone before returning to Utsunomiya. Thereafter, I was able to go back to Yokohama to be with her only on weekends.

Our wedding date was set for December 15. The ceremony and the reception took place in our Mission Home, and our local mission director married us. Shelton Allen was best man; his future wife, a childhood friend of Gussie's, who had also been with her in nurses' training, was the maid of honor.

Most of the guests, about 150 people, were local Japanese Christians, missionaries from other Mission organizations and our own "Mission family." We had to rent that many pair of slippers, as is the custom for such celebrations. Shoes may not be worn inside because of the *tatami*. For our out-of-town guests we rented *futons* with heavy cotton padded covers and laid them wherever we could find a spot, even in the meeting hall and in the dining room.

For our honeymoon we went to ATAMI, a small, idyllic fishing village known for its healthful mineral springs. After a week there, we moved to a small house very near our Mission Home in Yokohama.

One night as we were about to retire, the front doorbell rang. When I went to open it, there stood a fearsome-looking man with an open knife in his hand, trying to force himself past me and into the house. I was terribly scared and instinctively withstood him. He lifted his knife, and in trying to defend myself, I received a cut on my hand. Then the man suddenly backed up, turned around and ran out. I don't know why, except that our Lord had miraculously intervened.

My hand bled profusely, and when Gussie saw it she became hysterical and screamed at the top of her voice. We had no telephone and didn't dare leave the house, so we called to our neighbor from the window and asked him to call the police. Half an hour later five policemen came running into the house, waving their wooden clubs and shouting, "Where is he? Where is he?" We could hardly keep from laughing.

They took me to a doctor who sewed up the wound, and though it wasn't very big, I still have it "at hand" as a long-lasting memento.

It was not easy to assure my dear wife that an incident like that was very unusual, occurring very rarely in Japan. She had just come from the Philippines where burglaries and assaults happened very frequently, so she was difficult to convince. She particularly worried about what would happen if someone like that should come to our door some evening while I was out at a meeting. She asked me for some way to let her know in advance that I was the one nearing the house. We decided that I would begin singing while still a few yards away. My song from that time on was *Onward, Christian Soldiers.*

Being afraid that my old motorcycle might get stolen if I left it outside at night, I pushed it into our bedroom, which bordered on a low terrace in the back, only a small step up from the ground. Not many homes have a full-sized motorcycle as part of the bedroom furnishings.

My honey was soon able to shop by herself, although in the beginning there were a few surprises. Once, when we had fish for supper, she salted it according to the ways of the West. My facial expression told her that salting is done in a Japanese store, sometimes in over-abundance.

I, too, didn't always fare too well. One day Gussie asked me to drop by the butcher to get some beef heart. My dictionary being my trusty companion, I looked up the word for *heart* and saw it was KOKORO. So I asked the butcher for the KOKORO of an USHI, cow. The butcher couldn't keep from laughing and shared my request with his helper, who was equally amused.

There are two different words and symbols for *heart* in Japan. One of them is SHINZO, the organ that keeps the blood circulating. The other, KOKORO, means *the mind, the seat of one's emotion,* as for instance when we say a person is kind-hearted. I had asked for a half-pound of a cow's *emotion!*

19

Nagahara —
From My Prayer Letter May 3, 1957

WE HAVE BEGUN a tent campaign, and I'm driving our Mission jeep through the narrow streets of our neighborhood. *Reiko-san* (our new helper since Gussie and I were married and live in Yokohama, and whom I was privileged to lead to the Lord) sits beside me in the jeep and makes the announcements over the P.A. system. She now also teaches during the children's hour in the tent each afternoon.

Shelton preaches each evening. He was married not too long after I was. Amazingly, his wife, one of our missionaries, is one of Gussie's best friends. They not only came from the same home town (Buhler, Kansas), but were roommates during nurses' training and graduated at the same time. She plays the pump organ during the meetings, and she and Shelton sing together.

Each morning I go to the Mission Home to conduct the devotions for our Japanese staff and the missionaries who are living there at present. Besides this, I've been asked to be the chairman of our forthcoming missionary conference, so I'm being kept mighty busy.

On top of all this, we'll be moving this month into the home of one of our missionaries who will be going home on furlough. It is in Nagahara, a part of Tokyo (which now has a population of 11-1/2 million).

My language study will hopefully come to an end when I have finished this last half of Book #4 and will have taken my final examination within another month. By then I will have spent two and a half years at that task.

In the meantime, our Lord has *presented* us with a daughter, Mary Esther, who at *present* doesn't seem to be too interested as to whether I'll finish my *present* lesson. She doesn't leave me alone and tries continually to pull herself up on my pant leg, so that I have a rough time concentrating. She also doesn't want to be restrained by being put into her playpen. It isn't as though we as missionaries and Christian parents wouldn't know how to solve such a problem for, after all, what are playpens for? They offer a wonderful place to study undisturbed without having to restrain one's daughter, who now stands on the outside holding on to its bars and looking in on Daddy without being able to get to his pant leg, at least not for a while.

In Nagahara, we took over the Japanese maid, *Kubota-san,* who had served the previous missionary, and Mary Esther was soon big enough to go along with her to the nearby market where she became the great attraction of the many Japanese housewives. They were intrigued by her blue eyes, wanted to touch her blond hair and feel her light skin and then, of course, they asked who her father was and whether he would teach English. Wherever they went, it never took very long before they were being asked that same question, and Kubota-san knew how to reply, so we soon had four to five weekly English classes, giving us the wonderful opportunity to present the Word of God. Mary Esther has become our best advertisement.

End of Prayer Letter

"YES" COULD MEAN "NO"

While living in Nagahara, I became newly aware of a typical Japanese behavior. These dear people have a very difficult time saying NO when they feel it could in some way offend or be considered unkind. A mother, for instance, would tell her child when he or she goes to school to always say YES to the teacher, regardless of whether it knew what was involved.

We once had a Japanese couple join us at our table in a crowded restaurant. When we found out they were planning to visit Germany, I became most interested. Gussie suggested we invite them to our home for a meal. It would give us an opportunity to tell them some of the German customs, answer some of their questions and witness to them of the Lord. They promised to come.

My wife prepared as best she could a typical German meal for that day. We were in great anticipation of having that couple with us, when about a half hour before their expected arrival the telephone rang. It was the husband who thanked us for the kind invitation. He explained that he had been at our house, but since he couldn't find a parking place he went back home.

"Maybe some other day!" were his last words before he hung up.

Even though the house we lived in then bordered on a big vacant lot, but rather than decline our invitation which would have been a breach of etiquette, they took the only other way out even though they knew it was a weak excuse. Perhaps they chose such a one purposely to make sure we knew they had no intention of coming in the first place.

I should have sensed a similar situation after we moved to Nagahara. We didn't have a telephone at first, and I asked our neighbor lady whether we might use hers occasionally. She cordially gave us permission.

Since the Japanese were more favorably inclined toward the Germans, who were their allies during the war, than toward the Americans, who defeated them, I told her I was from Germany. She was quite elated, telling me her son was majoring in German at college. Thinking it would be an excellent contact, I offered to meet him and answer any questions he might have. The mother expressed her sincere thanks, saying she would tell her son and he would no doubt be anxious to get in touch with me.

When I used the phone 10 days later, I asked whether she told her son. She said she did so right away and that he was planning to meet me. A month later I met her in town and asked her again.

She replied, "Oh, yes. My boy has been very busy with his studies, but he will be over any day now."

When two weeks later he still hadn't shown up, I should have sensed that neither he nor his mother was interested. But again I went over, this time to make a definite date: the following Sunday afternoon, for coffee and cake. She said Sunday would be fine, and we decided on four o'clock.

Gussie made a cake, I cleaned up my desk, and at four o'clock began to look out the window. Four o'clock came and went and so did 4:30. When by a quarter to five he had not yet come, I went over to the house to see if he had possibly forgotten.

His mother met me at the door, and her answer surpassed any human reasoning. "Oh, no," she said. "My son has not forgotten. But when he saw how nice and warm and sunny it was, he decided he would rather go for a walk."

Without saying a word, just shaking my head, I turned around and walked out. I never got to meet him.

Through one of my students, I learned another oriental-thinking process which may be more correct than ours.

I came about in a natural way when Takekawa-san told me he couldn't come to our next Bible class meeting because he would have to go to Tokyo that day. When he showed up at class, I was surprised and asked, "Did you not go to Tokyo?"

He answered, "Yes."

My next question was how he had come back so soon. He looked startled and asked, "Back from where?"

"Back from Tokyo, of course."

"I didn't go to Tokyo."

Now I was truly confused. I told him I had just asked him whether he had gone to Tokyo, but he quickly corrected me, saying that my question was, "Did you NOT go to Tokyo?"

"Had you left our the word NOT," he continued, "and said, 'Did you go to Tokyo?' I would have answered with 'NO.' But by asking me whether I had NOT gone to Tokyo, I took it as your assumption *that I had not gone to Tokyo.* Therefore my answer was 'YES,' because *you were right in thinking that I did not go.*"

This way of thinking has become so ingrained in us that it still creeps up, every once in a while. The other day I came home and asked, "Didn't anyone call for me?"

When my wife answered, "Yes," I asked, "Who?"

"No one," she answered. Her "Yes" meant my assumption that "no one did call" was correct.

During our time in Nagahara a new colloquial Japanese Bible was being published. Written in the everyday conversational language, it was much easier to understand than the former stiff literary style. Since I, like most, had already memorized many verses the old-fashioned way, the re-learning of them was very frustrating. I frequently mixed one with the other, but we soon realized that the youth especially could understand the new translation much better.

Across from us was a "Union" church whose young people soon came over to learn English, along with two of the Sunday school teachers and the pastor's wife. After I taught that forgiveness of sins and eternal life could only be obtained by a personal acceptance of the Lord Jesus Christ — and emphasized that He is the One who died for us, was buried and rose again on the third day — only the young people kept on coming. They brought with them so many new ones that we hardly had enough room to take care of them all.

20

Our First Furlough

OUR LORD WAS BLESSING so abundantly that we didn't really want to think about our approaching furlough, but it was time to start taking care of the many details. We didn't know what we should take with us because we had no idea where we would be living. We prayed daily for our Lord's leading. Neither Gussie nor I had been back to the States since we had first come to the field, and now we also had a one-and-a-half-year-old daughter with us. Another missionary family would be taking over our work in Nagahara, and we had to introduce them to our students and acquaint them with the particulars of our ministry.

We were greatly surprised to find that so many of our Japanese friends came all the way from Tokyo to the pier in Yokohama to see us off. We had a most difficult time saying good-bye and separating ourselves from them.

Our passage home was on the Japanese passenger liner, *Hikawa Maru,* and there was another missionary family traveling with us. The accommodations and the attention given us on the ship was excellent and so was the food. We could choose between Oriental and Western dishes, or we could have both. For Gussie and me there were many foods we hadn't eaten for a long time. While we enjoyed cakes, pies and cream tarts during afternoon coffee time, Mary Esther and the other missionary children headed for the typical Japanese treats: candied soybeans, rice cakes and other Japanese tidbits.

On March 1, 1958, we arrived in San Francisco. A Christian family I knew met us at the pier and helped us obtain a 1954 Hudson Hornet. It was an enormous auto but, sad to say, it is not being built anymore.

We visited many friends in the West and Southwest United States and our families in Kansas and Missouri.

Our mission required of its returned missionaries a very thorough physical examination at a special clinic in Chicago, so we headed there. How happy we were that, except for some minor dental work, we were in top condition.

Then we had to make a major decision. We had been offered a completely furnished house in Kansas City where we could have lived throughout the entire year. That would have been the easiest and simplest thing to do. However, we had written to many of our prayer partners and supporters, and they all wanted to see us and hear about our ministry in Japan. So we decided to spend the entire year on the road.

We traveled nearly 2,000 miles visiting friends in Wisconsin, Ohio, West Virginia, Oklahoma and Arkansas, and in some of the Canadian provinces.

We spoke in churches, Bible schools and at youth camps. In the camps, Gussie served as camp nurse and I encouraged young people to not only trust our Lord as Savior, but to give themselves completely to serve Him.

At times I used the following poem to challenge them:

Christ has no hands but our hands to do His work today;
He has no feet but our feet to lead men in His way.

He has no lips but our lips to tell them how He died;
He has no help but our help to lead men to His side.

We are the only Gospel the careless world will read;
We are the sinner's Bible; we are the scoffer's creed.

We are our Lord's last message written in deed and word;
What if the type is crooked; what if the print is blurred:

What if our hands are busy with other works than His?
What if our feet are treading where sin's allurement is?

What if our lips are speaking of things His lips would spurn?
How could we hope to serve Him and hasten His return?

In Canada we visited Niagara Falls, putting on special rubber coats and head gear to walk behind the cascading, plummeting torrents of the Falls. Seeking a natural opportunity to tell our guide about the Lord, I told Him that my Father designed this great phenomenon. He was very much surprised and wanted to know how long ago that was. I told him, "About 6,000 years ago." Then I told him what else my heavenly Father had accomplished.

A very special blessing was our visit among the folk at the church in

Santa Ana, California, that had taken me under their wings when I first came to know our Lord. What a thrill it was seeing again my many friends and having them receive Gussie into their hearts.

It wasn't easy to be continually moving in and out of the many homes we visited and taking care of Mary Esther while on the road. We were eagerly looking forward to the day when we would be back in our adopted homeland.

When we finally made it to San Francisco, our point of departure, we went to the Japanese Consulate for the verification of our Re-Entrance Permit, which had been issued before we had left Japan. To our dismay, we were told that the law had been changed and we would have to get our verification from the consulate in Chicago, the area office for our hometown.

I feared having to postpone our departure and flying back to Chicago, when a member of the Consulate suggested calling our Mission and having them ask the Chicago Consulate to authorize the San Francisco office to process our papers. Done! and on March 3, 1959, we were again on our way to the Orient.

This time it was a freighter, the *Sagami Maru,* but it had limited passenger facilities also. As soon as I was on board among the Japanese crew members, I felt back home once more.

Shortly after leaving San Francisco, I inquired about religious services on board. Being informed that they had none, I gave my qualifications and told of my willingness to conduct these if they so desired. They invited me to speak the next Sunday morning and posted a notice on the bulletin board. A number of passengers attended, as well as some of the crew and the captain.

Though it was the first time in over a year I had preached in Japanese, it went unexpectedly well. I distributed some Japanese tracts, and by the time we arrived in Yokohama, it was as though I had never left Japan.

Every once in a while, after having come home from overseas and told of our Lord's blessings there, some kindhearted soul came to me after the service and offered to buy me a new suit. That always puzzled me because the one I wore, with the nice wide lapels and which I had bought right after graduation from Bible school in 1950, was still perfectly good, I thought. I finally realized that it was considered "old-fashioned" according to present-day styles in America, and this dear saint wanted to have me look "up to date." It finally became my most valuable garment because whenever I saw the need for a new suit, I would wear this "old-fashioned" one. Thereafter I referred to it always as my "suit-getting suit."

Sitting around the "Kotatsu" with a neighboring family has given me the much-longed-for home atmosphere while still living the life of a loen bachelor with Shelton Allen in the winter of 1953. A Kotatsu is a table covered with a thick blanket. A small charcoal fire in the hole in the floor underneath keeps the lower extremities warm. (Note the Shinto God shelf at the left and the Buddhist home shrine at the right.)

21

Back at the Task

AT FIRST we again lived in our Mission Home, hoping to move into one of the smaller towns as soon as possible. I started out alone by train and then walked through the narrow streets and byways of various small communities. Japan was and still is enormously crowded since it is lacking in livable flat land. Empty houses are almost non-existent.

I went not only to real estate agents, but to newspapers, post offices, city halls and even to the mayor of one city. All to no avail.

On the way back to Yokohama, I befriended a Japanese student who was studying German and who asked me to help him with it. He brought along some of his buddies, and so we started a German-Japanese Bible study at the Mission Home.

In the meantime also, I was invited by some of our missionaries to come to their communities and show my object lessons to their people in their Bible classes and in Sunday school, but especially in the children's meetings. I was most happy to be used of the Lord so soon after our return.

One weekend I went to a town in which our Mission was particularly interested because there was already a small group of believers. The Mission hoped for me to work among the younger generation there since it was a university town. English and German were being taught, which would give me an unusually great opportunity to reach many students for the Lord by offering to help them with their studies. However, I wasn't successful in finding a place to live, so one of the Mission leaders came along to support my efforts by helping me look.

Arriving in that particular town, as soon as we left the station we stopped by the side of the street and prayed. Then we headed toward one of the main streets, the ASA-HI-CHO (the *Morning Sun Block*). My missionary brother couldn't keep from laughing about my going into one store after another instead of to the real estate agency. It was funny indeed to see the confused expression of the sales clerk when "this foreigner" said he would like to rent a house. My brother tried repeatedly to stop me from using this unorthodox method.

I walked into a motorcycle shop with the same request. The owner told me to have a seat while he went to make a couple of phone calls. He came back saying he had a small house nearby in which his mother-in-law was living, but that she would be happy to move in with them.

The owner walked with us a half-block up the busy thoroughfare, turned into a small side street, and after two more blocks came into a very narrow dead-end alley with open drainage ditches on both sides.

There, in the middle of the block, stood "our house," small and clean-looking, the only one-story structure on the alley. It was clean inside also, but from the windows on one side we could see only the adjacent two-story buildings; on the other side we could even see some parts of the sky!

The house was typically Japanese, with *tatami* flooring and a Japanese-type toilet. (That meant one would have to crouch over a hole in the floor. Covered with a wooden lid, it had a big cement container underneath — about the size of a large drainage pipe set on end. It would be emptied once very month or so, by means of either a scoop on a long handle or by a more "modern method," vacuuming with a good-sized flexible hose. In either case, the contents were discharged into a large drum mounted on a truck. This process was called *Kumitori*, which the dictionary translates as *the dipping up of the night soil.* We were also told that the house might be somewhat small by American ideas, but that there was the possibility of adding a room.

It was the only offer we had and decided to at least look at it. I had silently dreamed, though not prayed, for a large house with a big room for meetings and a typical Japanese garden. We had seen such on calendar pictures and had hoped for one with a nice lawn, or else one bordering on an open field where Mary Esther could play and run.

The name of the town was KOFU, the capital city of YAMANASHI prefecture. It was located in a fruitful land basin famous for its delicious grapes and peaches, but form where we would be living we wouldn't be able to enjoy the beautiful mountain ranges surrounding us.

The neighbors looked us over with typical curiosity, animatedly talking to each other about these strange newcomers who might soon come to live among them. We responded to their wondering looks with a friendly smile. These people — not the fields, gardens or open spaces — were indeed the ones who needed to hear about our Lord, and we couldn't possibly be any closer to them. As we looked around and thought about it, we felt it was the right place to which our Lord had directed us. The rent wasn't too high, and with the promise of an additional room, we accepted the offer and went back to Yokohama to get ready for the move.

Before we had gone on furlough, we had put all of our belongings into the Mission store room — all our furniture, our pots, pans and dishes, as well as Mary Esther's bed and toys. Now, we took everything to the railroad yard, and other missionaries helped us load it into a freight car. (At that time, self-loading and unloading was the cheapest and safest way to transfer one's household goods.) At the other end, we hauled it all to our new home with a rented truck.

It seemed that the whole neighborhood had come out as we began to unload. To have them see all of our many belongings, especially our big new refrigerator we had brought back from America — the like of which was not yet known in Japan — was very embarrassing.

After only a few days, Mary Esther had a great many playmates. They daily came either into the house or to the entrance calling *asoboh* (let's play), thereby inviting her to come outside.

She soon spoke Japanese so fluently we couldn't tell which voice was hers when they were at play in front of our house. There were even times when we would ask her to interpret for us when somebody came to the door with some official business.

Our Lord also gave us a very faithful household helper named FURUKAWA-san. One morning after our daily family devotions, she asked the Lord Jesus to come into her heart. At the entrance of the room she occupied in a very run-down tenement house was a propane bottle, above which hung a typical Shinto paper emblem dedicated to the fire god to invoke his protection. She told us that, right after she had trusted the Lord Jesus as Savior, she took this emblem into the back yard to burn it. One of the neighbor ladies, recognizing her intention, came running up to warn her of the terrible consequences. Furukawa-san told her, "Let's see who is more mighty, this fire god or my Lord." With that, she put the fire to it.

At the funeral of her mother she stood in line with her seven brothers and sisters for each to light an incense stick for the tranquility of their mother's departed soul. When it was Furukawa-san's turn, she couldn't bring herself to do it, so she quickly turned and walked out of the place.

There was one thing with which she had great difficulty: to follow her Lord in baptism. We had seen the same with other new believers. They realize, and rightly so, that it is the last and final step in giving themselves completely to the Lord Jesus; that it is a public testimony and confession of their absolute trust in their resurrected Lord; and that it means a complete and conscious separation from the things of the world.

When we left Japan to come home for good in June of 1980, Furukawa-san had still not consented to be baptized.

* * * * *

I had "graduated" from my former motorcycle, having bought a more powerful one on which I had a sidecar built. Now I could take my wife along, and Mary Esther, too, by having her sit on Gussie's lap. At times, a third person perched on the back seat when, for instance, one of the workers from the home office in America came to visit.

Often when I had some business downtown and Gussie was busy, I would take Mary Esther with me. She dearly loved those rides with her Daddy. One day coming back from such a trip and parking my vehicle, I realized that Mary Esther was nowhere to be seen. I was wondering where and when she might have fallen out and was shaking all over as I went into the kitchen to tell Gussie. She looked at me and nearly screamed, "Honey, what has happened, you're white as a sheet!"

As I tried to tell her, Mary Esther came running in with a cheery, "Hi, Daddy! Did you miss me?"

"Where have you been?" I blurted out.

"It was fun," she smiled, "hiding underneath, way up in front!"

I didn't know whether to scold her or to hug her.

When the three of us visited our local zoo, we were amazed by how nice and warm it was in the building where the elephant was spending his winter. We were having a difficult time keeping our home even somewhat comfortable with our portable kerosene heaters. I told Gussie I was about ready to seek employment as animal keeper at the zoo.

* * * * *

Mary Esther and I (she was four or five then) distributed tracts in front of the nearby high school, inviting the students to come to our English-and-Bible classes in our home. Very soon we had a group of 12 to 15 who attended regularly twice a week.

We started by singing hymns, first in English and then in Japanese. Gussie served some fruit and Japanese soybeans — or rice cookies. Mary Esther was always the center of attraction, because she was blond and blue-eyed.

One day, I told the story of Moses and the serpent, and explained that the Lord Jesus Christ used that historical event as an example in speaking to Nicodemus, a Jewish ruler, telling him that just as Moses had lifted up that serpent in the wilderness, so must He Himself also be lifted up, that whoever would believe in Him should not perish but have everlasting life.

Afterwards Takekawa-san, one of my most poorly dressed students, stayed behind to talk to me. He told me he had resolved to "Believe on Lord next time." Although our conversation was in Japanese, he chose to say that phrase in English, possibly to emphasize its importance.

For a moment, I was puzzled as to why he wanted to put off such an enormous commitment for an entire week. I was about to tell him he could do it right then when he added that the time to do it would have to wait until we would meet again the following week, "for they all have already gone home!"

I tried to figure out what I had said to cause him to make that statement. Then I remembered that toward the end of class I had referred to the words spoken by our Lord, *"Whosoever therefore shall confess me be-*

fore men, him will I confess also before my Father which is in Heaven" (Matthew 10:32). Evidently Takekawa-san had not yet definitely decided to trust the Lord until after the other students had already left, and in order to be absolutely certain that his salvation would be assured, he felt it to be needful to "confess Christ" before all his classmates — a most admirable and unquestionably also a most scriptural conviction.

The following week, when I was again with these students and we had sung a few songs, Takekawa-san suddenly raised his hand. When I nodded to him, he stood up.

He said that at our last meeting he had understood about Moses lifting up the snake in the desert. Even though it happened a long time ago, it was done to show us that Christ has to be lifted up on the cross to die for all of our sins. He knew this included his own as well. Then he said: "I want all of you to know that I have thankfully accepted that Christ has done this for me." With a big smile on his face, he breathed deeply as though greatly relieved. "Now I am assured that Jesus has received me."

None of the other students said a word. Only our Lord knows what transpired in each of their hearts.

I soon realized that my new brother in Christ was not the typical Japanese who had made a decision for the Lord. Before he left that day, I asked him whether he would like to come along to the baptism scheduled for the following Sunday in a nearby river.

He immediately accepted and asked what he would have to bring along.

"Only your Bible," I told him.

"But won't I get all wet?"

It took just a moment for my thoughts to catch up with his. I told him to bring along an extra pair of pants and a shirt. It really amazed me to see so great a difference between the reluctance of our household helper, Furukawa-san, and the readiness of Takekawa-san to follow the Lord in baptism.

I soon found out that he lived in the poorest of family circumstances. His father, a highly respected physician, had left his mother when she became incurably ill. (This is often done in Japanese society.) Takekawa-san moved her into a very old house and moved in with her to take care of her at every available hour when he wasn't at school. He also prepared their very meager meals. Through his testimony and his dedication his mother also came to trust our Lord for salvation.

Even though he was still finishing high school, he immediately became active, teaching the children's Sunday school class of our small congregation, which at that time was meeting in an old garage.

His three brothers were all physicians, and his father wanted him to become one also. I don't remember how the subject of Bible school came up, but it wasn't long before Takekawa-san decided to attend one in Tokyo where two of our own missionaries were on staff.

His father was very upset to hear about it and threatened not to give him any inheritance. He let his father know that nevertheless he was determined to follow the Lord by preparing himself to serve Him. He indicated that his heavenly treasures were by far more desirable than any earthly ones. His father gave in and withdrew the threat.

After Takekawa-san graduated from high school, the wife of one of his brothers took over the responsibilities of caring for his mother by moving her into her own home. Takekawa-san headed out for the Bible school in Tokyo. Most of our church folk and those who had been with him in our Bible class during the time he had come to know the Lord went to the station to see him off and to pray with him once more.

22

Architect and Missionary

OUR MISSION BOUGHT a low-lying rice paddy not too far from our home in Kofu and gave me the responsibility of building a simple structure there to be used as a meeting place. I started by looking for fill-in to raise the ground and establish a firm foundation. I looked for building sites in the town where excavations were in progress and offered our "free dumping lot." Many people gratefully accepted this offer. It was an encouragement to me to see the big trucks piled high with dirt pulling up to our field, dumping their loads.

Then I needed a retaining wall. The local prison was most cooperative in supplying not only huge rocks from a nearby stone quarry, but some of its inmates as well, including guards, to build up that embankment.

To have the responsibility for it all was a great challenge which cast me continually upon my Lord for wisdom and ingenuity. I felt completely free to use the ideas and methods which He put into my mind and heart.

I even found a mound of huge stone pieces left over from the construction of a Shinto temple. After obtaining permission, I rented a truck and hauled them to our site. What a diversified "foundation" our church would be built upon!

From the military we heard about the discontinuance of many of the Army camps because the greater part of the occupation forces would be returning to the United States. They offered to give certain of the family living quarters (including the fixtures) to mission and welfare organizations that would tear them down and haul them away.

Some of our missionaries undertook that project for us, bringing large beams and girders. There were complete windows, doors, even pipes, faucets and bathroom fixtures. These were all unloaded onto the now-completed church foundation. The missionaries helped erect the side beams and supported them in place, leaving me to finish the construction.

Takekawa-san came to help me each day after school and during his vacation. We always prayed together before we began. When Gussie came with our afternoon refreshments, she brought little Timmy along, our recent addition to the family.

After about a year, we had the floor, walls and ceiling completed and covered with plywood. The lights and switches were in place; and, in Rube Goldberg fashion, we had even constructed two Japanese-style toilets.

Takekawa-san continually looked to me as his spiritual father and advisor. It made me realize anew, and keenly, the relationship which the apostle Paul must have had with *his* "son, Timothy.."

After Takekawa-san had been in Bible school for about three years, he came unexpectedly to our house one day, bringing with him a young girl he had met there. He introduced her to me and then asked me to talk to her to see if she would be suited to be his wife. I was amazed at how much he looked to me, his spiritual father, for this important decision, probably the second most important one in his life.

I had a precious time talking with her. We read the Scriptures together and prayed. When I told Takekawa-san I had absolutely no objections, they left happily.

At about that time the local YMCA director invited me to teach one of his English classes.

"I can only do so," I told him, "if I'm permitted to also tell some biblical truths in Japanese since most students do not understand English too well."

"No," he said emphatically, "we already have a class where the Bible is used, but you are permitted to talk about the Bible in your class; however, only in English."

My class consisted mainly of young sales and office girls from the largest department store in Kofu. At the end of one of my first class periods, one of the girls, ONO-san, came to me saying she had attended the regular Bible class there. She said my teaching was entirely different; she didn't understand it at all, so would I explain it to her in Japanese?

I told her I was not allowed to do it on the YMCA premises, but I would be most happy to explain it in detail if she would come to our home. She came two days later. I told her in the simplest way possible what God says about our sinful condition and what He has done to remedy it. She had never heard that there was a "really living God," and she was very much afraid of such a God, but she promised to come back the next day.

She didn't show up, however, and when I went to the mail box to get our mail, I found a note she had written: "I have come just as I had promised, but what you have told me is too scary for me."

When I saw her the next time at the YMCA, I invited her again and promised I would not talk about a fearful God, but about a very loving one.

She came and listened most attentively. Understanding God's love *for her,* she joyously trusted Him for her salvation.

Coming back two days later, she bubbled all over. "Sensei (teacher)," she said, "the other day after I asked the Son of the Almighty God to save me at your house, I stopped at a small garden on my way home and told the rocks and all the beautiful flowers that the God who has made them has made me beautiful, too, on the inside."

One day she told us that her parents had some time before picked out a husband for her, as the custom was in Japan. She would, therefore, soon have to marry him. She told us he was a Buddhist and didn't want to hear anything about the Lord. I showed her from the scriptures that her loving God didn't desire her to be joined to an unbeliever. After she understood that and had told her parents they found another husband for her, but she refused to marry him as well.

She knew that Takekawa-san had gone to Bible school. Realizing that she couldn't do anything better to prepare herself completely for the service of her Lord, she decided to do the same. Her father, however, was absolutely set against it. So she waited until the Lord would in some way open the door for her. She became our regular house guest, took an active part in our small congregation and announced our evangelistic meetings over our car's PA system as Reiko-san had formerly done.

Ono-san's father, a doctor in a small suburb, died about a year later. She looked on as many of the distinguished citizens of the community came to his pagan funeral, conducted by priests of the nearby Buddhist temple.

Tradition demanded that everybody bow deeply before a picture of the deceased and burn incense for the repose of his departed soul. When our Japanese pastor also came to the funeral with others of our congregation, she was greatly encouraged and with them she slowly passed by the picture without bowing. They all then bowed before the members of her bereaved family to express their sympathy.

Ono-san herself broke the traditional period of mourning by continuing to attend our regular Bible class. This class had come into being when she invited as many as she could of those who worked with her at the department store. With tears in her eyes, she repeatedly encouraged them to be bold in telling their family and friends about the only One Who was victorious over death and the grave. She urged them to believe Him before it would be eternally too late.

Then she told them that now there was no longer anything or anyone that stood in the way of her going to Bible school. She left soon thereafter.

Both she and Takekawa-san came back during their summer vacation and taught Sunday school classes. When Takekawa-san was asked to give a short testimony, he would usually preach for half an hour.

It wasn't long before the Lord led Ono-san to that one special student in the Bible school (or led him to her). After graduation they were married. Before long they became the spiritual leaders of one of our congregations.

In November we heard that a strong *Taifun,* pronounced TY-FOO, was nearing Kofu. (The characters of this word, roughly translated, mean *towering air.)* About a year previously, a *taifun* had struck during the day-time. Our back wall, made of clay mingled with or supported by bamboo wickerwork, had become so soaked from the pounding rain that it collapsed. We had tried to keep it from falling inward instead of outward, and we partially succeeded. None of us were hurt. The wind had lifted the roof off our neighbor's house and slammed it down into an empty lot next to ours. It was a scary sight.

As soon as the rain and the wind had ceased, the nearby living families converged on the house and constructed a new roof in less than two days. Amazing!

This time, we saw our neighbors board up their windows, especially their glass doors which made up the outside of most of the Japanese houses. We were busily doing the same. When the lights went out at six o'clock, we took our sleeping mats, pillows and covers, and made our "beds" in the center walkway of our house. That would be the farthest away from any glass windows or doors, and thus the safest place.

We also wore all of our clothes and had our important papers, such as our passports, close at hand just in case we felt that the house might not stand the onslaught. Then we committed ourselves completely into the protecting hands of our Lord. When the Taifun struck a few hours later, it rained in torrents and the entire house shook so violently that we thought it would collapse at any moment.

Though the Japanese use very few nails in their building construction and the beams are set within each other by an intricate system of notches so that they will "give" when moved, we believe that it was our Lord who really held the house together, and we thanked and praised Him for His protection.

When Mary Esther was six and a half years old, we took her to the boarding school for missionary children in Tokyo. It was properly named the Christian Academy in Japan, but we all referred to it as C.A.J.

Either Gussie or I would go every weekend to pick her up and then take her back again late Sunday afternoon. It took about four hours from door to door, including the train ride with transferring.

All this always brought some real hardship, not only for our little girl but for us parents as well. Since it hardly ever happened without tears, it was most painful to have to say good-bye for another week.

After an extended vacation, such as Easter or Christmas, the parting was the more agonizing, and we prayed earnestly to know our Lord's direction about how to solve that problem.

CHRISTMAS IN JAPAN

Christmas time in Japan offered us a natural opportunity to tell how it came into being. All downtown stores played popular American Christmas music like *Jingle Bells, White Christmas* and even *Rudolph, the Red-Nosed Reindeer.* The large exclusive department stores displayed gaudily decorated Christmas trees and a portly Santa Claus who partially succeeded in bowing politely to the buying public.

We tried to offset this worldly atmosphere by having a home-made manger scene. The back and side of the stable was made of small, tightly interwoven branches, as was the tiny crib. The roof was made of tree bark. We had brought the plastic figures from America. A tiny bulb from an electric train suspended by two nearly invisible wires served as guiding star. We even had a tiny flickering red light bulb underneath some branches to imitate a fire around which some of the shepherds stood and a very small spotlight directed on the Christ child in the crib.

All of our students and visitors stood and looked at every detail, while we told them the Bible story of His birth.

After listening intently, one student said, "How amazing that His birth should coincide so perfectly with just the time that we celebrate Christmas."

We received many invitations to speak at Japanese schools, even in sanitaria and orphanages, to tell how we celebrate Christmas in our home country. Often it was more for a cultural exchange than for any historical or Biblical insight into the real meaning of Christmas. Yet we couldn't have wished for a more wonderful opportunity to convey the message of God's love for all mankind.

In one place, however, the leader of the group that invited us stood up after I finished and said, "We here in Japan, of course, don't believe all that which we have just hard, since that is a Western idea. For us here in the Orient, our god is HOTOKESAMA (the honorable Buddha)."

But at another school, the director asked us to give each student a pamphlet, and afterward said to the entire student body: "Read it diligently and do not dispose of it but give it to a friend since it contains a very important message."

A few days later, a teacher who was present invited me to speak to his anthropology class, and I joyfully accepted. I came away wondering whether he was more interested in having his students hear about the destiny of man and his relationship to God or in having the students be able to tell their parents that a foreign professor had been invited to lecture on a very interesting subject.

For variation, I occasionally went to the U.S. Occupation Forces (military) bases. I introduced myself to the chaplains and told them of my ministry.

They had various programs, some geared especially to the families

117

of the troops. When I showed them some of my object lessons with their spiritual applications, I received more invitations than I was able to accept.

At Christmas time special programs were planned, one of which was a Family Christmas Celebration. I was featured to "tell the Christmas story by means of easy-to-understand visual illustrations." That was more than a challenge, because I had never yet applied my object lessons to the events surrounding the birth of Christ. Our Lord blessed mightily, and I had absolute liberty to tell about the birthday of the King in English, a welcome change from having to speak in Japanese.

Each military family was to bring a gift for the missionary as a token of their appreciation. These were put into a huge, crate-like box at the beginning of the "performance." I received canned goods of all kinds: vegetables, soups, jams, fruit, nuts, cookies and even a whole ham, all of which the military could buy at the local Post Exchange stores. For us, who lived on the Japanese economy, these were impossible to obtain. I could hardly get everything into my station wagon. We celebrated Christmas for weeks to come.

Because of my connection with the chaplains, I was also permitted to visit Army hospitals where the most severely wounded men of the Viet Nam War were sent for emergency treatment before being shipped back to the United States. I prayed with them, wrote letters home for some, distributed tracts, showed object lessons and even made a phone call home from the bedside of one of them. Because of severe burns over most of his body and face, he was almost completely bandaged. He couldn't manage more than a whisper. Having gotten his family out of bed (it was two o'clock in the morning at his home in America), I told them, trying to comfort them, that I was sitting by the bed of their severely wounded boy. They wanted to talk with him, but when I held the receiver to his ear and he heard the voices of his loved ones, all he could do was cry uncontrollably.

23

Globe-Hopping

IN JUNE OF 1963, our second furlough was due. As before, we felt that it was too soon after establishing a fruitful ministry. This time, a much greater adjustment awaited us because our mission was interested in expanding its ministry into Europe. Since I was the only German-speaking member of our mission, it was decided after many discussions and much prayer that following our furlough we would head for Germany rather than to return to Japan. We were to be temporarily assigned to the *Bible Christian Union*. We would work in conjunction with them because it was an organization already established in Germany.

What should we do with the numerous household items we had accumulated during nine years in Japan, everything from washing machine to egg beater? Shipping them all to America, where we would be for a year, and then to Germany would be most impractical and expensive. We were able to sell a few of these cheaply; the rest we gave away.

We spent a comparatively short time with my mother and Gussie's parents and then drove to Brooklyn, New York, where the headquarters of our new mission board was located. There we met other missionaries-in-training. Together we became acquainted with the specific work we were to undertake in Europe.

We also took part in local evangelistic efforts. One day it was my turn to man the small stand in front of a nearby university, one that had a large Jewish student body. We were giving away New Testaments with the fulfilled Old Testament Scriptures printed in dark type. A big sign announced that any student could have one of these just by asking.

Students walked by, reading the sign but showing no interest. I was searching for a way that would prompt them to initiate the contact rather than I myself, so I turned the sign upside down, standing there looking bored and uninterested, as though unaware of my sign's position.

Soon a student stopped, saying, "Stupid! Haven't you noticed that your sign is upside down?"

Aha! A contact! It worked so well I kept on doing it. The scene went like this, with slight variations, depending on the student. I would compliment him for being so observant, and he'd say something like, "Any fool would be able to notice that."

Depending on how the conversation would continue, I'd ask whether he had noticed that God in His Bible has said He would do the same with the way of the wicked: *"... the way of the wicked he turns upside down ..."* (Psalm 146:9). Very often that would develop into a profitable conversation.

On January 29, 1965, our ship sailed for Bremerhaven, the same port I had left some 30 years before, during the time of Hitler. We were stationed in Frankfurt with a small congregation where we were to serve while the local missionary went to America on furlough. Now I could for the first time proclaim the Word of God in my mother tongue. What a thrill that was!

Mary Esther went immediately to a German grade school, not knowing one word of German. Our boy, Tim, went to kindergarten. In only a few weeks they both spoke German better than my dear wife, who was struggling to learn it.

Now we had to obtain the furnishings for our home to replace those we had left in Japan. We bought a washing machine (and even an egg beater!), but built our own bed from purchased lumber. We made bookshelves from some crates. Then we noticed announcements in the newspaper that the city would pick up discarded furniture and household items if they were placed on the sidewalk near the street by a certain hour. Driving around, I found some yet very good mattresses, as well as a desk and even what would now be considered an antique wardrobe.

My ministry soon included speaking at youth conferences and summer camps, passing out invitations to our church services among the strollers along the Main (pronounced *Mine*) River, and helping in evangelistic efforts. My greatest adventure was a trip to Israel with one of our mission's youth leaders and a group of the Young People.

After they returned to Germany, I stayed a few days longer in Israel to visit some Jewish friends who had left Germany as I did at the time of Hitler. Primarily I wanted to tell them of the Messiah, even though I knew what their reaction would be.

Mother had kept in touch with a family from Wittlich, her birthplace, and had given me an address, not knowing my purpose for wanting to visit. When I rang the doorbell there in Haifa, I immediately knew it was my old playmate, but she didn't recognize me. When I told her who I was, she scrutinized me in unbelief, as 35 years had passed since we had last seen each other. Then she wrung her hands over her head in amazement, calling others of her friends and family who happened to be there. It was a "wonder" for her to see me, who had also been fortunate enough to escape Hitler.

There was hand-shaking and embracing as I was being introduced, and so many questions came at me I hardly knew where to begin. In the meantime, my old friend had gone to the telephone to plan a big welcoming celebration.

I knew I would have to give my testimony before all the drinking and dancing started. I also realized the unspeakable hurt I would bring upon their hearts when I told them. In a way, I wished I would not have to be "that cruel." But I started by saying, "I have something very important to share with you."

They tried to persuade me to wait until later, but I insisted that it could not wait. So they all sat down, and I began with Abel's sacrifice in comparison to Cain's, and jumped over to what the children of Israel had to do in Egypt to prevent the death of their first-born son.

It is not the custom in *reformed Jewish* homes to talk about religious issues. My dropping in so unexpectedly and my insistence on not waiting to tell them something of great importance made them suspicious of what I wanted to say.

While I was still speaking, the husband stood up and, trying to control his quivering voice in spite of his bitter resentment, said, "Of all things, THAT is something I would not have expected from a person like you. I know exactly what you are trying to tell us. We were so thrilled when you came in and told us who you were and that you had escaped the Nazi persecution.

"We would have liked to hear how you got out of Germany, whether your parents are still living and about your brothers and sisters, where they are and what they are doing. To have you try to tell us this shocking episode is the very worst thing you could have done to us." In a very rough tone he continued, "I must ask you to leave here as fast as you can. And don't you dare to ever cross our threshold again! THERE IS THE DOOR!"

I saw the agony in the faces of those present. As a Jew I felt in my own heart the great pain I had inflicted upon them. I left crestfallen in spirit, yet deeply satisfied and thankful to the Lord for giving me the courage to testify of Him before my own.

Back in Europe, one of the unusual events was the time a member of our congregation came very excitedly to me, saying that a woman in the nearby park had claimed she was Jesus Christ. I could hardly keep from laughing, but not even my explanation that our Lord was not a woman would satisfy him. He was convinced that she was indeed Jesus Christ and wanted me to see for myself.

I went along with him, praying for wisdom to disprove her ridiculous claim. But to me also the woman insisted that she was Christ. My brother stood wondering what I would do about it. I thought for a moment and then asked her to show me the palms of her hands, which she did. Looking at them, I said, "My Lord has nailprints in His" (Zechariah 13:6). She turned around and walked away. My brother was satisfied and sincerely thanked me.

In the spring of 1967, our Japan Mission decided not to pursue its plan for extending its ministry into Germany. They gave us the choice of remaining in Germany with the other mission or to return to Japan with the Far Eastern Gospel Crusade.

Our hearts were still in the Orient; and even though it meant packing and disposing of goods and starting all over again, on June 1, 1967, we left for Tokyo once again after nearly two and a half years.

24

Back to Japan

OUR FLIGHT TO JAPAN went this time the Eastern route, from Germany by way of Iran and India, where we stopped over to visit missionary friends in Teheran and in Hyderabad. Our small son, Timmy, continually asked, "Daddy, what country are we in now?"

As we were nearing Bombay, seeing the lights of this intriguing city, I turned to Mary Esther and said, "Think of it, sweetheart, BOMBAY, the famous, mysterious city of India, with its temples and strange heathen customs and where the cows are considered holy and walk freely among all the traffic. Where the fakirs and dervishes try to find peace and tranquility doing their penance. We'll soon be among them, seeing sights that most people won't ever get to see."

Our dear little girl, whom we had dragged with us all over the world, truly was not impressed. Looking up at me, she barely audibly muttered, "So what?"

* * * * *

Back in Japan, we began looking for a place to live, finding furniture and other necessities, for we had again disposed of our goods before leaving Germany. We felt more and more like Abraham, as *"strangers and pilgrims on the earth."* In reality we, as Abraham, were looking *"for a city which has foundation, whose builder and maker is God."* Born in Germany, emigrated to America where I came to know the Lord, 13 years in Japan, three times back to America on furlough, two and a half years in Germany, and now back in Japan!

My dear friend Shelton, with wife and four children, was living in another part of Utsunomiya. He invited us to come there to work with him again, and we found a house very close to his.

I began to teach English in two high schools and in one private school, where I was given absolute liberty to tell of the Lord. Besides that, I was invited to teach English to the office staff of an industrial firm, and to those of the Daiwa Fishing Reel Company, and even to the workers of the Aiwa Electric Company which had one of its main television manufacturing plants in Utsunomiya. In all these places I used the English-Japanese New Testament exclusively, supplied to me by Gideon International. I couldn't have been happier with all the open doors our Lord had given me to proclaim His Eternal Word. Except for one thing.

Mary Esther, 11, and Tim, 5, went to the boarding school for missionary children in Tokyo (CAJ). They both cried incessantly when it was time to take them back to school. We had a real battle on our hands every Sunday afternoon and even more so at the end of every vacation.

We were aware that because of our much traveling and readjusting, our children felt very insecure. We prayed much and talked to our mission leadership about it. Finally we came to the conviction that the well-being of our children would be by far, yes by very far, more valuable than all our missionary service.

I remember writing home in our prayer letter: "For what shall it profit a missionary, if he shall gain the whole world and lose his own children?" We had heard from another mission that some of their children had become so estranged from their parents that they eventually got into trouble with the law. The sorrow and heartache it caused their parents became so severe they could no longer fulfill their missionary calling.

We decided to move into Tokyo, as close to the school as possible so our children could come home every day. For me, it meant giving up all of my contacts. Even after we had packed everything and were about to move out, I had another phone call. A girls' high school invited me to come and teach English there also.

Leaving Utsunomiya was most difficult. I sadly walked along those streets where I had so often driven my car. I tried to comfort my heart with saying that our Lord never takes anything away without giving something far better. How much better I was soon to find out, and to a greater degree than I could have imagined. It actually began some time before we left.

25

I Become a University Professor
(Thanks to an "air conditioner")

BEFORE LEAVING UTSUNOMIYA, we had become friendly with the wealthy owner of a large manufacturing establishment and his German-born wife. We had many times been invited to their home for dinner. Before they moved into their newly completed villa, they had given us their antiquated "air conditioner." It consisted of an oversized car radiator through which an electric pump circulated cold well-water, which flowed back into the well or into the gutter. Behind the radiator was a big fan to blow the cold (?) air into the room. I had built it into our Japanese house in Utsunomiya, but the air was very clammy, and the result was most unsatisfactory. We had taken it along to Tokyo and were about to discard it when I mentioned it to a Christian brother.

When he showed great interest in it, I gave it to him. Afterward, I realized that, without intending to, I had obligated him (according to Japanese tradition) to reciprocate. Knowing that my greatest desire was to reach students for our Lord, he soon fulfilled this obligation, not by giving me something but by inviting me to meet the president of MEISEI University, with a view of teaching German there.

I was completely bowled over. I couldn't have dreamed of this in my wildest imagination.

I met the president, who seemed impressed with my ability to converse with him in Japanese. But when he asked me whether I could consider teaching German to four classes, three days a week, I had to swallow mighty hard. I knew the school was founded on the teachings of Confucius, and I felt the president should know what I believed and why I had come to Japan. He listened to me attentively, but seemed to have no objection.

I considered it impossible to teach German to university students, especially in Japanese. It was a wonder to be asked to teach so many, and I wanted to be absolutely sure it was *the Lord* who had opened this avenue of service for His glory.

So I went one step further and told the president that I would take the position only if I had the absolute freedom to tell my students about the way of salvation as the Bible teaches it. I thought this would surely be denied, and I would be legitimately out of this tight spot. He thought for a moment and said that his institution was based on Oriental ideals, but he would not deny my request as long as I would do it "moderately," and none of the students objected or complained to the school authorities.

I conferred with our Mission leaders. They realized this was an unusual case and agreed that our Lord must indeed have opened this door of service. They wholeheartedly supported me and prayed for God's great wisdom in reaching these students with the Good News of Salvation: that I would be *"... in the midst of wolves ... as wise as serpents and harmless as doves"* (Matthew 10:16).

If I had not been sure this was my Lord's leading, I would not have ventured into this new situation. I had not attended any school of higher learning, had no teacher training, especially none in the German language. Although German was my mother tongue, it did by no means qualify me to teach it. I had not spoken it for a while and felt that my usage of the language wasn't what it should be. On the evening before my first lesson, I earnestly prayed that our Lord might return before the next morning. I was scared, wondering if I would be able to meet their expectations. The following day I felt great comfort in His word that "His grace is sufficient for me" and that *"His strength is made perfect in weakness."*

There were only young men in my first class. They knew they would have a "foreigner" as their teacher. (Some classes were men only; some women only; some mixed.) Before I entered the classroom I could hear their lively discussion, but the moment I walked in it was absolutely quiet. All stood up, as is the custom in Japanese schools. At the command of one, everyone bowed and I did the same.

When I introduced myself in Japanese, I heard their sighs of relief. They had no doubt thought the entire lesson would be conducted in German. When I wrote the Japanese character for my name (Baum=tree), I sensed their surprise that I would write in KANJI. Only later did I give its spiritual meaning.

I spoke to them not as a teacher, but as a friend. I thanked them for the privilege of being permitted to teach them German. I added that in myself I didn't have the wisdom to do it adequately, but that I knew Someone who would be able to help us all. The students had never heard a teacher speak to them like this, and they relaxed completely. I told them that there is One Who knows all languages and Who would enable them to learn German and added that I wanted to talk to Him about it.

I closed my eyes, bowed my head and talked to the Lord in Japanese, thanking Him for the joy of meeting all these students, and asking Him for "grace and wisdom upon them as well as upon me as I teach them." While I was praying I could hear some of them whispering, and some self-consciously snickering. But now they all knew I believed in the Lord Jesus Christ.

After class one student came and thanked me for having the courage to pray. He said he too believed in the Lord, as well as his parents, but that he thus far hadn't had the strength to let his faith be known.

I thanked the Lord for this token of encouragement and went on in the same way in the other classes. In one, a student came to me saying that his grandmother had talked to him about the God Who had sent His Son to earth. He wanted to know if He is the same One I believed in.

During another class, I said how nice it would be if we wouldn't have to study another language, but if everyone would speak the same. When they agreed, I told them that "many years ago" there was indeed such a language, but a great problem arose which changed the situation. Naturally they wanted to know when and where this was, and what the great problem was. I told them what happened at the Tower of Babel, putting emphasis on the presence of sin in the human heart and its result. In nearly every class my Lord provided me with natural circumstances to tell about Him. It fitted perfectly into existing situations. I wasn't prepared for what I saw one day when Miss Aramaki came to the blackboard to correct a mistake in a German sentence.

While she was writing, I noticed this patch sewed to the shoulder of her jacket. (It is very popular in Japan to have foreign phrases printed on various items of clothing.) After she had returned to her seat, I wrote that sentence on the blackboard, just as it appeared on her patch: "HELL! DON'T FOLLOW ME! I'M LOST, too!" and challenged my students to read it.

They stumbled through it; remember, this was a German class. No one seemed to know what those words meant, least of all Miss Aramaki, who until then had never given any thought to what was written on that round piece of cloth.

At first she was a little embarrassed. I put her at ease by telling her that by wearing that patch she was conveying a most important fact of life and asked the class if they would like me to explain its meaning. Of course! Anything, not to have to study.

I told those who had an English-Japanese dictionary to look up "HELL." It's pronounced *Jigoku*, (literally: *Territory of Prison*). The dictionary defined it as the "Bottomless Pit" or "The Infernal Regions," and I explained that both denote the same place and that the Bible is the only Book that authoritatively speaks about HEAVEN as well as about a place called HELL, which is another word for "The Infernal Regions." Then I told the story about the "Certain Rich Man" who lived a sumptuous life here on earth but neglected to make the necessary preparation before he died for the comfort of his eternal soul. While "HELL" itself, where he found himself after he died, cannot speak, the rich man spoke on Hell's behalf the very words written on Miss Aramaki's patch. He cried in desperation to a person he saw in HEAVEN, "Send someone to my home on earth to warn my five brothers so they DON'T FOLLOW ME to this place of torment!" For the rich man it was forever too late to trust the ONE Who came to seek and SAVE that which was LOST. Therefore he wanted to warn those of his family who still had a chance to make this all-important decision.

Of course, I told all this in Japanese, adding that God recorded this 2000-year-old account so we would not make the same mistake as the rich man. I thanked Miss Aramaki for making it possible for me to share this story with the students. (The literal meaning of the two characters that make up her name are Ara = rough, rude, harsh and violent; and Maki = to roll or to be rolled up, like a scroll.) I told her I would gladly pay for the patch if she would remove it and give it to me the next day.

I have that patch before me on my desk to remind me to pray for her. I also gave her a small book which told in detail what the Lord Jesus had done for her and what a great difference it would make in her present life and in eternity if she would follow *Him*. May God grant her to be completely RE-rolled and re-wound into a scroll for everyone to read, a scroll of loveliness, of grace, joy and peace.

Each student wrote his or her name and address on a small card. I read these off at the beginning of each class period to see who was absent. Having up to 120 students in some of the classes, I did not know the name of everyone. At times, when I read a name, the reply sounded rather vague. I suspected someone else had answered in this person's place — as seemed to be the custom. In order to be sure, I read the same name again. Usually there was no answer except suppressed laughter. They realized I was aware of the deception.

Something similar happened when I doubted whether the person who answered was really the one whose name I had called. I walked down the aisles to count the students. As I turned to count the next section, I saw out of the corner of my eye one of them in the back row move quickly over into the section I was about to count. Although I caught him, he acted unconcerned and indifferent. So I went back to my desk and thanked them for helping me prove the Bible to be correct.

They, of course, wondered what I meant. I opened the Bible and read, *"The heart is deceitful* (in Japanese = *cunning, tricky* or *crafty) above all things, and desperately wicked: who can know it?"* I told them the answer to that question: *"I the Lord search the heart, I try the reins, even given every man according to his ways, and according to the fruit of his doings"* (Jeremiah 17:9, 10). After that I would freely tell the remedy for such condition and frequently pass out tracts with testimonies of Japanese believers.

Once I had more students than I had cards. I looked all over to see if I had dropped any. When I was sure I hadn't, nor left any in my pockets or brief case, I counted the students again. I was really puzzled. Finally one of the girls raised her hand, "Professor!" she said timidly, "I'm the guilty one, I invited two of my girlfriends to come along, because I wanted them to hear what you always tell us about the God who is alive, will you forgive me?" I assured her that I would and that she had really done nothing wrong.

The students were generally glad when I digressed from my lesson and told them a Bible story. I had to be careful not to do this too often and connect it as much as possible with my regular German instructions. I was pretty certain some of them were strongly opposed to the proclamation of the Gospel.

For variation, I asked if they would like to learn a German song. Of course, they were in favor of this, and it fitted in perfectly with my subject which, after all, was German.

I wrote the first word on the blackboard, pronounced it and asked them to do so after me. Having corrected their pronunciation, I went on to the next word, and so on. It was a portion of a Christian hymn, and I wanted to make sure they felt the emphasis was on the German words rather than on the message of the song. Eventually I had it all on the board and sang it for them:

"Yesterday, today forever, Jesus is the same, (in German = "God's Lamb is unchanged"); All may change, but Jesus never, Glory to His Name."

The students liked the melody and the rhythm, and there was a lot of repetition. I taught and sang it in all my classes. Those with many girl students sang it especially well.

What I had feared did happen one day, but our Lord transformed it into one of the greatest blessings I could have imagined. A student stood up and spoke out boldly in front of the entire class. "Professor, you continually talk only about the one Western religion. Should you not by all rights also tell us about our own Eastern religions such as Buddhism, Shintoism and Confucianism?"

My first thought was that this would be the end of my missionary activity, at least in that class. I replied that there is truly only one God, the God the Bible speaks about. I said that from now on I wouldn't talk about Him anymore during our class period. I invited those students who were interested to hear more about what the Bible had to say to meet me after class. Five or six came, and together we went to ask the school authorities for a room in which we might conduct a Bible study. Amazingly, it was granted us immediately.

After that, we met there three times a week, sang, prayed and studied the Word. I made this known in all my other classes, and students invited their friends. Soon we had 12 to 15 who attended regularly. Before long, they all had asked the Lord to come into their hearts. Not only that, they decided to meet three times a week, a half hour before school to pray for their unsaved classmates.

In all of my other classes, I continued to use every opportunity to speak of the Lord. One day, one of the girls raised her hand, asking to be excused early to visit her mother in the hospital. Immediately after I excused her, and without any further thought, I said, "I think we ought to pray for her." I folded my hands, bowed my head and began to pray.

My students were not too surprised, because they had heard me tell about the Lord. The following day, the girl thanked me sincerely for my prayer and said how happy her mother was when she told her. After the mother was released from the hospital, the family invited me to their home for a meal, giving me a typical Japanese picture of a bamboo plant. A week later the girl came along to our church.

The remuneration I received for teaching, according to the law for missionaries, could not go to me directly, but to my workfund at the mission. From this I could draw any expenses in connection with my ministry, such as printing prayer letters, postage, gasoline and upkeep of my car. After some time, these funds enabled the mission to purchase a small used house trailer for use in my ministry. We parked it alongside our house and used it as a classroom for our home Bible studies and for taking students into the countryside to sing, give their testimonies and pass out tracts.

26

Not Quite a Choir Director

ONE DAY I received a phone call from SHOBI MUSIC ACADEMY in downtown Tokyo, asking if I would consider teaching German pronunciation to their girls aspiring to sing opera and operetta. A German lady missionary who had been teaching them was going on furlough and had recommended me. I accepted immediately, realizing it would be a lot easier than teaching grammar, and a lot more fun. I kept my position at MEISEI UNIVERSITY, Mondays, Wednesdays and Fridays, going to SHOBI on Tuesdays.

The words which I first taught were to the tune of a very well-known German folk song. [They had much difficulty pronouncing the German *ü* (there is no Japanese nor English equivalent), and the gutteral German *ch,* as in *Johann Sebastian Bach*]. After the 50 or so girls had repeated the words several times, they were ready to sing them. One girl went to the piano and played the tune while the others hummed along looking at the song sheet.

Being their teacher, I was expected to lead them in singing what I had just taught. I had never in my life directed a song. There was no way out. I lifted my hands, not so much to direct as to beseech my Lord to help me. Suddenly I was "directing" a choir of 50 Japanese girls. With perfect pitch and with brilliant, crystal-clear voices they were singing my so-well-known tune. I felt like being "home again." Tears of happiness filled my eyes.

My great desire was to have them sing to the glory and honor of our Lord and to get to know Him personally. When December came, I taught them Christmas songs and later on other Christian hymns I had copied from German hymn books. So they would know what they were singing,

I translated the text into Japanese and asked them what they thought might have inspired the author (or composer) to write these hymns. Most felt it must have been the influence of Western culture, just as they adhered to Eastern thinking.

After I had given each of them a tract so they could read what had actually influenced the writers and had told them that the contents were also very important for their own lives, I invited them to our home for Sunday afternoon which they considered a great privilege. My dear wife was the perfect hostess, providing "Western" pie or cookies, yet always also Japanese refreshments, including the typical green tee. We sang Japanese Christian hymns, which was something new for them. Their happy and beautiful singing left no doubt that they enjoyed it. Since it was our home, we freely presented God's Word in their language and answered their questions.

I had decided not to take any more offers to teach English, but there came one I just couldn't refuse. It was at the Kaetsu Junior High School, an all-girls' school in another part of Tokyo. I went there twice weekly by commuter train.

The trains which took me to that school in the mornings came every three minutes and were so enormously overcrowded that stations employed special "pushers" who forced passengers into the already jam-packed cars so that the doors could be closed. People then are squeezed in so tightly they can hardly move. Some have lost their glasses, heels from their shoes and even their false teeth. At times, people are shoved against the passengers seated along the sides so that often window panes are broken out. Once I wanted to scratch my leg, but couldn't bend down, so I used my other leg to do it. When I tried to put it down again, some other foot was in the place.

It may seem unbelievable to Western minds that the railroad authorities had computerized how many extra cars would be needed in the winter when the commuters would be wearing heavy underwear and padded overcoats.

For all of my classes at Kaetsu I used only the Gideon half-English, half-Japanese New Testaments. All my lessons were Scriptural accounts, such as the story of Christ's birth or of the prodigal son. I had the students read first the Japanese side so they would be familiar with the text, and then I taught the English side word for word.

One of my most treasured photos shows them wearing their identical uniforms, sitting with their hands folded and eyes closed while I was praying, as we did in every class every morning. We also sang, "Jesus loves me, this I know, for the Bible tells me so ..."

On the blackboard, I wrote Bible verses for the girls to memorize, erasing one word at a time. They considered this great fun.

We had picture cards, which they pointed to while telling the Bible story. I strongly suspected that the school authorities knew I used the

Bible and Bible story picture cards as a means of teaching English to their students. They didn't object, seemingly glad that they had a native (?) English teacher on their faculty. In one of the last classes, I asked the girls who truly wanted to ask the Saviour into their hearts to unashamedly stand up. After just a moment of hesitation, 16 of them did so. I truly expect to see them one day in glory.

By now it was June 1980 and I was 65 years old and at the age at which to be retired. Mary Esther, our daughter, had finished her nurses' training in the States and had married one of her former classmates whose parents also were missionaries in Japan. She and Mark, her husband, were preparing to return to Japan to minister to the hearing-impaired Japanese. Tim had just graduated from CAJ and was returning with us to the States.

27

Finally "Retired?" — Or What?

AFTER OUR RETURN to America, my greatest longing was to go back to the land of my birth, a Jew whose people the former anti-Semitic leaders had sought to annihilate. I yearned to tell them that there was no animosity in my heart, but rather a great love because of the wonderful reconciliation I had found for my own soul. I wanted to share with them this important Truth of Salvation.

While ministering in Germany for two and one-half years with the *Bible Christian Union,* I had made many contacts. Also, I had gone back there a year before our retirement to help the first German missionary of our Japan Mission with his support needs, so I had numerous connections and places of service I could now revisit.

Earnestly desiring to see Dortmund, my home town, again, I started out in 1981. I hardly recognized the now completely rebuilt lively and beautiful city, flourishing on the location of the "town that had died," named so by the city fathers, because of the severe bombings which had all but leveled it during World War II.

I yearned to locate some of my former non-Jewish friends and classmates again, but was only partially successful through the phone book, and yet in for a shock. At the first three numbers I called, the person I asked for had died or had never been heard from since the war. In one instance, the man had fought in the battle for Stalingrad.

One person was now the owner of a flourishing electronic business. He put me in touch with another one of my old school pals, now the director of the city's most prestigious hotel. It happened to be the hotel in which my Bar Mitzvah (Jewish coming of age) celebration had taken place when I was 13. The original building had been leveled, and now there was a new one with the same name, *Zum Römischen Kaiser* (to the Roman Emperor) stood in its place. My buddy arranged for my free stay there in one of its fancy rooms. He also contacted another of our former classmates, who now worked for a local newspaper.

So it was that when we three met one evening, a reporter and a photographer showed up, too. The next day our picture was in the paper with my story: I, the son of a Jewish family who once owned a well-known bedroom furniture store, had gone to America during the Hitler regime and had now come back for a visit.

During the next few days I received many phone calls from former employees and from the sister of one of them who had lost his left arm during the war. She gave me her brother's address in East Germany, north of Magdeburg, and I visited him later.

One other call was from a classmate of my sister Anneliese. This classmate invited me to meet others of their class (non-Jews) at an afternoon *Kaffee* to tell about my sister's present life and about the rest of my family. I took my tape recorder along and recorded all their greetings to my sister and sent it to her afterwards. (She had escaped to Brazil and married her childhood Jewish sweetheart where they still lived.)

I told them that I, a Jew, had trusted Him of whom Moses and our prophets had spoken. But when I explained the main reason for my return to Germany, the atmosphere became noticeably cool and the conversation stilted. I left shortly thereafter. I realized anew that *"... the preaching of the cross is to them that perish foolishness ..."* Nevertheless, I had the great satisfaction of showing that even an old Jew was happy to return to the land that had once persecuted him, to witness of the grace of God in his life.

A Mennonite brother had given me the name of a local pastor. He suggested sending out invitations for a special meeting in his church where I could tell "My Whole Story." There were some who remembered my parents and our store. So I told how and why we had left and settled in America, but especially how I had come to know the Lord and about our subsequent ministry in Japan.

After the meeting a lady came up to thank me for my lively account and introduced me to her mother who had just come to visit from Sangerhausen, East Germany. Until that time I had never met anyone from the other side of "The Wall." When I found that she loved the Lord and even had Bible classes in her home, I became desirous for an opportunity to minister "over there" as well.

I wasted no time telling her so. She not only invited me, but offered to help me with the necessary immigration paperwork to get there. She gave me her address, and from that time on I kept in constant touch with her and with her daughter in Dortmund.

Then came more open doors. One of these actually had its beginning nearly ten years prior to that. In the late 1970s, a repatriated Mennonite

Christian brother, David Klassen from Russia, came to Japan to tell of the severe persecution which his people there had suffered and of his own exile in Siberia because of his faithful witness for our Lord. Since he spoke only German and Russian, I was asked to help with the interpretation from German into English as he shared his experiences for the English-speaking missionary community. At that time he also invited me to speak at his own congregation if I should ever come to Germany.

Now there, I was enjoying especially the younger generation that had recently come from Russia. They received me with wide open arms because I also had come from a persecuted people, and thus I felt very close to them. But even more so, because though a Jew, I believed as they did on the greater Son of David. They arranged meetings for me in a wide circuit of German Mennonite churches made up entirely of those who had recently left Russia.

er möchten
ᵣ den Besuch

suᵢ
lern
maᵢ
ᵢ sel
ᵢ zu
des
nen
: Fe-
An-
wer-
Rei-
eler-
5.30
Bau-

ernhof" (mittwochs 14 bis
15.30 Uhr) und „Afrika-Safari"
(freitags 10 bis 11.30 Uhr).
Diese offenen Führungen rich-
ten sich an Einzelpersonen
und Kleingruppen (2 DM pro
Person, Kinder frei).

Über dieses Angebot hinaus
bietet der Zoo auch allgemeine
und spezielle Führungen mit
einem Blick hinter die Kulis-
sen an. Anmeldungen:
5028580. Auch Zoo-Ralleys
können gebucht werden.

ᵢt gegen Dr. Hammad:

Grünen
ᵢtikerehe
ᵌht grün

eheᵢ
nem
ptet
aktiᵢ
. Riᵢ
rᵢker
liedᵢ
" (O-
ᵍen
bge-
mad
e.

land zu ermöglichen. War er
da noch mit seiner deutschen
Frau verheiratet? Die Berliner
TAZ streute solche Gerüchte.
Richard Kelber tut es auch.

Erst einmal verschickte er
mit großem Verteiler ein Ma-
nuskript für einen Radiobei-
trag (Offener Kanal, 1. Okto-
ber) mit eindeutigen Anspie-
lungen. Und gestern legte er
noch einmal eine sechsseitige
Wurfsendung nach - mit Foto-
kopien von Urkunden, die, so
sie denn echt sind - die Eheschließung dort einen Hei-
ratsvertrag bestätigen. Daß sie
staatlichen und nicht nur un-
verbindlich kirchlichen Cha-
rakter hatte, liegt danach auch
nahe. Die Kopien hätte er, so
Kelber zur WR, in seinem
„Briefkasten gefunden".

Die Dokumente seien auch
den Landtags-Grünen seit Mo-
naten bekannt. Die aber hät-
ten nur mit einer Ehren-
erklärung verabschiedet. Und
Kelber will auch noch wissen,
daß die Eheschließung mit der
in Dortmund lebenden Palä-
stinenserin am 2. April 1996
erfolgt sei, dieses Datum im
Eheauflösungsvertrag aber auf
„September 1996" verlegt wor-
den sei. „Hat es da Überschnei-
dungen gegeben?" fragt spitz-
findig Kelber.

Ihm geht es, wie er sagt,
nicht „um die politische und
gegebenenfalls strafrechtliche
Verantwortung des Herrn
Hammad, sondern um die politische Verantwortung der
Grünen und den Schutz der
Frau". Hammad, der in Cas-
trop-Rauxel eine Kieferortho-
pädische Praxis hat, sagte gestern, er habe zwei Rechtsgut-
achten vorliegen. „Weder juri-
stisch noch moralisch muß ich
mir was vorwerfen."

ᵢber-
von
zum
- aus
ᵃaten
ᵢ-Ge-
ᵗtrof-
ᵍlich
„wie
Ger-

(46)
ᵢserin
ᵢ hät-
liche
ᵌhlie-
ᵢ der
ᵗsch-

Gestern vor der Petrikirche: Wilhelm Baum sucht Glaubensbrüder.   (WR-Bild: Schmitz)

82jähriger ist ein Weltreisender des jüdischen Glaubens:

Einst mußte er fliehen - die Liebe zu Dortmund blieb

(har-) Er ist in Dortmund ge-
boren, in Dortmund zur
Schule gegangen. Als 19jäh-
riger, im Jahre 1934, mußte
er wegen seines jüdischen
Glaubens flüchten - als Nazi-
Schergen mit der „Ausrot-
tung des jüdischen Volkes"
begannen. Und dennoch hat
der heute 82jährige Wilhelm
Baum seine Heimatstadt tief
ins Herz geschlossen: „Ich
träume davon."

Alle 10 Jahre, da besucht er
Dortmund, immer nur für
zwei, drei Tage. Und immer
auf den Spuren seiner Ju-
gendzeit. Er schaut sich das
Bettengeschäft Hutt an, das
einmal seinem Vater gehörte.
Da verlebte er seine Kinder-
zeit. Mit dem heutigen Inha-
ber habe er einen freund-
schaftlichen Kontakt. Er geht
zur Krüger-Passage am We-
stenhellweg, mit der ihn Ju-
genderinnerungen verbin-
den. Oder zur ehemaligen
Oberrealschule an der Brüg-

mannstraße, die er besuchte.
„Da stehen noch die alten
Bäume, an die ich mich ange-
lehnt habe."

Haß auf das, was mit seiner
Familie, was mit ihm gesche-
hen ist - keine Spur. „Dortmund ist immer noch meine
erste Liebe", sagt der alte
Mann mit grauem Vollbart,
der wie ein 60jähriger
wirkt: blitzende Augen, tem-
peramentvoll im Gespräch.
Denn Wilhelm Baum ist ein
überall geht es um den
jüdischen Glaubens,
seit rund 50 Jahren.

28 Jahre lang
in Japan als
Missionar unterwegs

Das hat ihn im Anschluß
an den Krieg, den er als Foto-
graf bei der amerikanische
Luftwaffe erlebte, nach Japan
gebracht. 28 Jahre blieb er

dort, kehrte schließlich mit
einer Frau und zwei Kindern
nach Amerika zurück. Er lebt
in Cansas-City. Von da reist
er ohne Unterlaß mit seiner
Bibel durch die Welt: Ruß-
land, China, Kenia, Brasilien,
Pakistan, und in diesen Ta-
gen missionierte er vor der
Petrikirche in Dortmund. Am
Mittwoch macht er sich zu einer Deutschlandtour auf.
Einladungen lägen vor von
Andernach, Ludwigsburg,
Schorndorf und Stuttgart.
Und überall geht es um den
jüdischen Glauben.

Die Kosten seiner Reisen
um den Erdball bestreitet der
82jährige ganz allein: von einer „kleinen Rente" und den
Spenden, die ihm die Gläubi-
gen zustecken. Sein sehnlich-
ster Wunsch vor seiner Abrei-
se aus Dortmund: Er würde
gerne alte Bekannte, Mit-
schüler treffen. Wer ihn wie-
dererkennt, könnte ihm eine
Freude machen mit einem
Anruf unter ☎ 525979.

In 1997, my home town paper published my picture and article about my ministry. I'm holding the Japanese character for BAUM (German: "tree") The caption read: "Once he had to flee, - the love for Dortmund remained."

28

Tromboning Through Europe

IN 1982, I went again to Germany, this time making arrangements for a big trombone team trip in 1983.

Our son, Tim, had come back from Japan with us and was attending a Bible school in Pennsylvania, where he majored in Bible and music, specializing in playing the trombone. His music teacher was a talented man who had organized an elite trombone team to which Tim belonged. The teacher asked me about taking him and the team on a tour of Germany. Each member, five boys and one girl, would take care of his or her own travel expenses and part of mine. So my own expenses would be minimal.

I had never undertaken such an assignment. But neither had I taught university-level German before MEISEI; nor directed a choir of 50 girls before SHOBI. I immediately began writing to my many contacts in Germany for bookings. I also asked the lady in Sangerhausen, East Germany, to proceed with paperwork for visitors' visas. In late 1982 and again in early 1983, I went to Germany ahead of the team to arrange the final details of playing at American and British military bases, etc., and to procure a VW bus and an eight-passenger Citroen. Our Lord made it all possible.

Was I ever excited and thrilled as the group joined me on March 9th! The next day they played on the pedestrian zone of Wittlich, near the Moselle River, my mother's birthplace. (As a young boy, I had great times there, visiting my grandparents.)

I had not planned to have any active part in this tour, other than introducing the group. But at this first appearance, my boy spoke up. "Daddy, why don't you talk to them?" So I did. From that time on, I gave a short Gospel message and a challenge at all the places we visited.

At nearly every stop they played "Lead On, O King Eternal" and other Christian hymns, as well as classical music written especially for the trombone. They played in youth camps, churches, hospitals, jails, by the side of streets, at both British and American military installations, but our greatest adventure was in East Germany. Both vehicles were packed with note stands, instruments and personal belongings. Much to our disappointment, we were not permitted to drive into East Germany. We carried as much as we could, stuffing most of the personal belongings into the instrument cases!

At Gerstungen, the train passed through the barbed-wire and cement fortifications dividing West from East Germany. We were shocked to see the run-down condition of the buildings, and the vehicles looked 30 or more years old. Having heard of the stringent inspection at the border, we could hardly believe it when the customs official didn't ask us to open even a single instrument case.

There were a couple of local teenagers in our train compartment. They scrutinized us and listened to our English conversation. When I addressed them in German, they were surprised and full of questions. I had a great time telling them about the Lord. Although it was a delicate thing to do, I asked them for their addresses, which they freely gave me. Afterwards, I sent them some tracts written in German.

In Sangerhausen, we were met by that dear lady whose daughter had introduced us in Dortmund on my first visit to Germany in 1981. She had taken care of most of the paperwork for us to "go beyond The Wall." I later learned how lengthy and frustrating that process can be.

She fed us as best she could and put blankets on the floor for the team to sleep on. Tim and I had a narrow cot at the neighbor's. It was terribly cold and there was no heat, so I lay down with all my clothes on and just shivvered (two v's for emphasis)!

During the next few days, this lady took us to Bible study groups, youth meetings and various churches. We even climbed the rickety, worn steps of one old church and played from the belfry. We visited All Saints' Church in Wittenberg where Luther's *95 Theses* is now permanently embossed on its door.

Among others sightseeing inside the church was a group of Russian soldiers with their officer. I asked him if I could take a picture of his men together with the girl in our group. His answer was a curt Russian *Nyet* (No).

Everywhere we went, we received additional invitations; we couldn't accept them all. After we had played and spoken at one of the hospitals, a young nurse came running up excitedly, saying I must definitely come to her hospital Bible study group at the Stift Bethlehem (Bethlehem Foundation) at Ludwigslust, about 100 miles farther north — even if the team could not come.

The tam returned to the States June 6th. We had covered close to 1,600 miles in both the former East Germany and the West. I stayed on for about three more weeks, during which time I was also invited to speak to a large congregation on a Rhine River excursion which included lots of good food. The following year I returned to East Germany, especially in order to visit the hospital where the nurse was serving whom we had met while I was with the trombone team. She had arranged meetings with their nurses in training, during which time two of them trusted our Lord. She also had me speak to congregations of nearby churches and especially to their Young People's groups. She then also arranged get-togethers in private homes.

Since then I have gone back there seven times, and when I returned to America and told about it, many folks gave me the names and addresses of relatives or friends in East Germany that they were concerned about and whom they wanted me to look up on my next trip over there.

Thus my contacts have increased from year to year as *these* relatives and friends in turn supplied me with still more addresses. Because of this, during my annual three to four months' travel since 1982, I have never had to stay in any hotel except in Romania. Families there who house foreigners overnight would be severely punished.

Meanwhile, my good wife had a special ministry given to her by our Lord. She visits people in old age homes and hospitals and takes elderly people shopping or to their doctor. She has even stayed at the bedside of the sick for three or four days at a time. She does this whether or not I am home, but when I'm away she has even more freedom to fulfill that calling.

The bridegroom having been one of my students, I was invited as the only "gaijin" (lit. "outside person") to be in this very formal wedding group photograph. Brides frequently wear a western type wedding dress though the ceremonies are traditionally SHINTO.

29

Japan Once More ... and China

AFTER I CAME BACK from the trombone team trip to western and eastern Europe in the spring of 1983, the Mission invited me to visit Japan once more. This was the first time I would take two trips in one year. It turned out that both were extensive.

The Mission wanted me to meet with former co-laborers (most of whom were 10-15 years younger than I) and see how the work of the Lord had prospered. I was also asked to take part in the summer Bible Camp, which gave me wonderful opportunity to again proclaim His Word in Japanese.

An additional reason for rejoicing was the chance to visit our congregation in Utsunomiya, where Shelton Allen and I had ministered before I was married and where I had later lived with Gussie and our children. The present pastor of the church was the one who had confessed on my first day at Meisei University that he, too, was a believer in the Lord. Since then he had graduated from the same Bible school in Tokyo to which Takekawa-san and Ono-san had gone.

I was at that time a member of the Japan-America Society, attending their meetings in Kansas City. When they heard that I was to visit Japan, they gave me a two-fold task to fulfill. They asked me to be their representative to our Sister City, KURASHIKI, in the southern part of the main island of Japan. They planned for me to meet the city elders, including an audience with the mayor. My food and living quarters would be provided. The mayor of Kansas City, my second cousin, authorized me as his personal representative to the Mayor of Kurashiki. He sent the key to Kansas City, a beautifully illustrated book about the city and a letter making the Japanese mayor an honorary citizen of Kansas City.

In Kurashiki I was received with much joy, no doubt because I could immediately converse with them in their own language. Besides presenting to the mayor all my cousin had given me, I also gave him a booklet I had written in Japanese: *Yudayajin To Wa* (Concerning the Jew). It contained a picture of our family (Gussie, myself and the two children) and my testimony: why I, a Jew, should believe in the promises which God had made to our patriarchs concerning the coming of the Messiah, Jesus.

I was well acquainted with a fundamental missionary couple in this city and took the local representative of the Japan-America Society to meet them. I sat up until late at night with my Japanese host family, answering their numerous questions about Kansas City and telling them about the Lord. I reminded them of the missionary nearby who would be able to help them understand Who the living Lord is and how they could get to know Him. I was so happy to be back in Japan! I wished I could have stayed and continued my ministry.

While there I received the joyous news that our daughter and her family would be arriving in Tokyo within a week. They had been visiting various churches in America telling of their call to Japan and were now ready to begin their ministry. I had the thrill of welcoming them at the airport on August 3rd and helping them get settled.

Before I returned to the States, I stayed a few days in Hiroshima where the first atom bomb was dropped on August 6, 1945, at 8:15 a.m., that had killed more than 260,000 men, women and children. The last time I had visited the city was 30 years before, in 1953, when I was still single. I had spoken to some people who had lived so close to the epicenter that they bore ugly welts on their entire bodies. Since then, the city had been rebuilt with beautiful parks, high-rise buildings and wide parkways.

From there I traveled by bullet-train, at that time the fastest in the world, to KYUSHU, the southernmost island of Japan. There I was picked up and hosted by the parents of an exchange student I had met in Kansas City. They drove me around and showed me local places of interest.

While at this location, I thought of visiting another missionary friend in OMUTA, little surmising what this visit would lead to. This missionary told me about a Christian brother in Hong Kong who was continually looking for helpers to take Bibles into the People's Republic of China. He recounted his experience and the blessing it was when he had undertaken such a trip.

I don't know why my Lord immediately created a great interest about this in my heart, and when I shared my feeling with him, I was shocked when he picked up the phone and called his friend in Hong Kong, telling him about my reaction and interest in his need. It was arranged that I should go to Hong Kong as soon as possible, and that he would personally take care of all the details.

I hurried back to our Mission Home in Yokohama, where I had left part of my belongings, and spoke with our mission leaders about this new venture. They suggested I drop in at our mission station in Taiwan (Formosa), which would be on the way. After landing there, I took the bus directly to TAICHUNG. As I stepped off, I was surrounded by taxi drivers looking for a fare. I showed the address of our missionary to one of them, who told me in understandable English that he knew "just exactly" where it was. Half an hour later we finally arrived there, after he had stopped five times to ask for directions. I remained there one day, speaking that evening in a prayer and Bible study meeting, and flew to Hong Kong the following day.

It was extremely hot and humid. The sidewalks were packed with people and the streets jammed with coolies drawing overloaded hand-drawn carts between double-deck busses and taxis, all of which seemed to be pushing each other along.

It was quite a while before I found my way through this maze of hustling and bustling humanity. My friend received me wholeheartedly and took me directly to the Chinese travel agency to see to it that I received a three-day visa to the People's Republic and booked a hotel room for me in Guangzhou (Canton).

Returning to his place, he gave me a rucksack and helped me to put a dozen small Bibles in its very bottom and said, "Put your personal belongings on top and don't fear being detained. Even if the Bibles are found, they would merely confiscate them. However, when you come to the custom official, leave your bag on the floor before the counter and busy him with registering your tape recorder, camera and lens. You will have to have them with you when you return. He may not check your bag, but just send it through a scanner. You can pick it up at the other end and leave the building. If they find your Bibles, they will put them in a bag with your number and return them to you on your way back."

It is not against the law to take Bibles into China. The only objection the government really has is against selling them on the Black Market, since it knows that they are most desirable and are not legitimately available. Of course, the ones I took in were not sold, but GIVEN to faithful and true believers where most desperately needed. During the cultural revolution all scriptures were systematically destroyed. It is not uncommon for pastors of the unregistered or house churches to have only a few pages. There are none at all for the believers in the "congregation." In Hong Kong, a room at the YMCA had been provided for me, and I spent a good part of the night there on my knees. An inner battle raged as to whether I had done the right thing and if it had indeed been directed of the Lord.

The next morning I took a taxi to the pier to board a small ship for the mainland of China. It was a very choppy two-hour ride. Stopped once on the way to take a customs official on board. He stood in front of the rows of passengers, and I felt that he was looking straight at me.

For most of the trip I meditated on God's word. I thought especially about the miracles the Lord performed for my own people in dividing the waters of the Red Sea and flattening the walls of Jericho. Just before we arrived, I read Psalm 136:4, that He ALONE does great wonders ..." which I took to mean *without any outside help!* This gave me such assurance and joy that I had a big smile on my face by the time I walked between the two rows of Chinese border guards in Guangzhou. There they stood in their dark green uniforms with the well-known red star on their caps. I walked toward the section where our travel documents were inspected and on to the customs control.

The lady officer may well have been wondering about the reason for this happy and relaxed traveler in an otherwise so drab and depressing atmosphere. She recorded the serial numbers of my camera, its two lenses and my small tape recorder, a safeguard against selling them on the black market. Then she said, "Have you later?" Since I didn't know what she meant, I had to ask her to repeat it three times before I understood her to mean *calcu*-lator. Evidently a rare luxury item in China. She never once asked what I had in my big bag, sitting on the floor right in front of her; instead she directed me to the conveyor belt, as she did others, where my bag went through the scanner without the Bibles inside evidently having been discovered.

When I picked it up at the end of the line, I was already in the front hall where the booths of the money changers were. My U.S. money, which I had previously changed into Japanese yen, thereupon into Taiwanese yuan and these then into Hong Kong dollars which I had now to change into Chinese fen.

Foreigners do not get the same money notes as do the nationals, but a foreign exchange certificate bearing the imprint, "This certificate can only be used within China at designated places. No request to register its loss will be accepted by the Bank." I found out that any store, shop or restaurant — the ones I went to, at least — will readily accept them and generally give change with the notes the Chinese use.

While looking at all the new and strange sights, I thanked my Lord for having brought me this far. As soon as I had closed the door to my hotel room, I dropped to my knees and poured out my gratitude to my Lord.

It was a beautiful, Western-style hotel, air-conditioned, with tub and shower and hot and cold running water. The inverted drinking glasses were neatly covered with parchment bags inscribed with three Chinese characters. The first one meant simply — *already* — the second one could mean — *extinguished; deadened, disappeared; turned off; neutralized* or *crossed out* — the third meant — *poison virus; venom; germ; harm; corrupt* or *spoil.*

Such is the Chinese language! I'm sure you have figured it out. "Already neutralized virus," or make your own combination for *sterilized.*

My task was to check my baggage at a certain hotel and take the check-stub back to Hong Kong. From there it would be sent to the person who would make the pick-up and distribute the Bibles.

Now free to look around, I thought I was in another world. Chinese music blasted from street loudspeakers, while Chinese street vendors on bicycles and men and women with large-brimmed straw hats carried long bamboo rods with baskets of goods dangling from the ends. As I returned by train to Hong Kong, we crossed rice paddies where men and women plodded behind water buffalo.

Two years later (in 1985) I made another trip for the same purpose, but that one had a different kind of ending.

With my camera mounted on a pole (partially visible at lower left), I tried to convey the terribly crowded condition of the Japanese commuter trains

Dad's bedroom furniture store with our living quarters above them at right.

Father's UN-real estate. Our property as it looked when I visited it (standing in front) as soldier of the U.S. Army of Occupation in November of 1945.

Marlene Dietrich

*As public relations photographer for the U.S. radio production, "Soldiers with Wings,"
I met such participating movie greats as Marlene Dietrich, Hedy Lamar, Dorothy
Lamour and Rita Hayworth.*

In the late 1930s I used this photograph on my calling card with the slogan: "Be it a local wedding, a formal portrait or a recent news event, Bill Baum gets the picture."

As new recruit at the Medical Aid Training Center at Camp Grant near Rockford, Ill. in 1941.

Together with our newly arrived missionaries in November 1952. Mr. Bob Foster, our field chairman, and his wfie are at the left. Our Japanese teachers are kneeling in front.

Photographing a recently promoted lieutenant of the Army Air Corps in Santa Ana, Calif. (1944)

Having to teach the pronunciation of German songs at the Shobi Musical Academy in Tokyo, I didn't think I would have to lead their singing as well, but ——!

Since we sold beds (German: Betten) and our last name being Baum, (English: Tree), our store was known as "Betten Baum", using a tree as our symbol. We also specialized in all kinds of feathers and downs. Thus in the earliest years our horse drawn delivery wagon was accordingly decorated.

One of our interesting show windows to draw attention to our great variety of feathers.

The message on the back reads: "A peak achievement of our bed-feathers factory." We had a special "Dekorateur" (window-dresser) who designed our unusual feather displays.

In later years a big Opel and a Model "T" Ford became our more modern means of transport.

We most happily helped our students with their dramatization of the "Pied Piper". Since Japanese nouns do not have any plural forms as such, we were not too surprised to see them carry this grammatical phenomenon over into English. Also because Japanese words can be hyphenated between any two letters, the left part of their sign read "KILL T" and the right part "HE RAT".

I liked especially to talk to the "down and outers" sitting in front of a church near my home in Dortmund.

Gussie had ways of keeping the children outside until it was time for the Bible Class.

I felt quite privileged to be that close to Japan's famous "Bullet Train", the fastest train in the world at that time.

Above: One of our earliest methods of transportation with Olan Hendrix, from our home office.

Left: Aoyagi-san, our maid, consented to eat with us, if she could do so on a lower table.

Below: "Swany" and I on our most comfortable "beds" shortly after our arrival in Japan (November 1952).

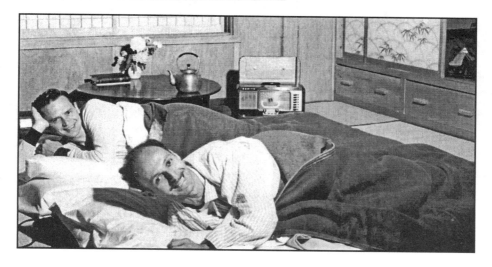

While visiting a family in Russia, I tried on one of their son's uniform.

The fulfillment of one of my dreams: To visit the Great Wall of China.

I was to teach "Simple English" to these tiny tots, but then told them a Bible story (in Japanese) which I was sure their mothers, too, would understand.

Anneliese, Charlotte, Gerhard and Wilhelm (Bill) Baum in the town and country of our birth, Dortmund, Germany, in 1925.

Upon having just graduated from Bible school in my 1950-vintage, wide-lapel "suit-getting suit."

With the Boy Scouts on a bicycle trip to Holland in 1930. I'm the one in front, and the Boy Scout leader, Eberhard Deutscher, is right behind me.

As hospital orderly at Moffet Field, Calif., in 1941, my first assignment after I was trained as a medical aid man in Illinois and before I became a public relations photographer.

"Comparing Noses" with the lovable children of our village. They found my different looks most intriguing.

With Gary Cooper while serving as Public Relations photographer for the Army Air Corps in Santa Ana, California, in 1943

Our growing family during our early years as missionaries in Japan

When Gussie came to visit me, while I was building our church in Kofu (1962), she brought our new son along to check on the progress.

A student of our acquaintance took his own life to pay the debt to his family after having failed the entrance exam to the university for the third time. I (sitting at right) visited the family to comfort them as they were gathered around the box containing his cremated remains.

Above: Some of my university students on a field trip to the nearby zoo, not just to enjoy seeing the animals, but to learn what their names are in German.

At the Japanese birthday party of the girl in the middle (next to me). At the very right is Shelton Allen, our senior missionary with whom I lived in Utsunomiya from 1953 to 1955 after graduating from language school and before either of us was married.

One of our early "ground level" Bible studies in Kofu. Later we used tables and chairs. Gussie played the pump organ, and we had asked a nearby local pastor to come and help us get started.

Not knowing where to stand while photographing a class at the Meisei University, the students suggested: "Why don't you lie on the desk?"

Bamboo grows in abundance in Japan and it is generally used instead of clothes lines and clothes pins. After the laundry has dried, one end of the pole is lowered and the laundry comes sliding down.

"Suffer the little children to come unto ME and forbid them not ..."
WHAT A MISSION FIELD!

One of my German classes at the MEISEI University in Tokyo. I had called the students together to pose for this picture just before a written examination, which I usually conducted in this auditorium which was big enough to have them sit with one seat between each of them, to keep them from cheating. Some of my students evidently were not too happy with that delay.

I started every class praying with my pupils at the Kaetsu Girls Junior High School in Tokyo, 1978-80. Our textbook was exclusively the English-Japanese New Testament provided by the Gideon International of Japan.

I felt pretty "tiny" below the 2,310-foot-high statue of "Christ The Redeemer" on top of Mt. Corcovado in Rio de Janeiro; but was an encouragement to these two survivors of the Hiroshima Atom Bomb Blast in front of the building preserved as a war memorial, and somewhat out of my element standing near the Red Square in Moscow.

Touring East and West Germany with an American trombone team in the summer of 1983. My son stands at the extreme left. I presented a short Gospel message every time they played.

Two of the ovens in which the bodies of the Jews were cremated after they had been put to death in the gas chambers.

The high-class transportation provided for me during my 1989 European trip, at which time I also visited the O.M. missionary ship LOGOS II while it was being refurbished at a wharf in Amsterdam.

I was the High Priest at the Easter drama at our church during the time between my trips abroad.

I took my girls from the LIGHT House along even to the Tiananmen Square, the world's largest, in the center of Beijing.

The girls from my classes at Meisei University especially liked to visit at their teacher's home, enjoying the refreshments served by a perfect hostess.

At my Meisei University German class I always had between 80 and 100 eager students.

These students happily show off their new Japanese New Testaments which were just given to them by the Japanese branch of the Gideon International.

Using every opportunity to witness for the Lord. Here while teaching English at girls' junior college in Tokyo in 1972. (Boys and girls wear school uniforms in Japan from kindergarten through high school.)

As the invited speaker with a young congregation in Osaka Japan, which was especially interested in God's eternal plan for the nation of Israel. The sign in the back reads: "Behold, now is the accepted time: behold, now is the day of salvation." (2.Cor.6:2)

A typical Japanese "low"-key or "ground"-level pastor's conference and fellowship in a Tokyo suburbs.

30

Getting **Beyond** Germany's "Red" Tape

OBTAINING A VISA DIRECTLY from East Germany (the former German Democratic Republic) was troublesome. After requesting such from the East German Embassy in East Berlin, I received four double-sided application cards, all with the same questions. There were the usual birthdate questions, plus places and persons to be visited, their addresses and occupations, relationship to visitor, purpose of visit, beginning and length of stay, border crossing point (if by car, color and license number) and, of course, all personal data plus passport number, where and when issued and length of validity. Very detailed.

I sent these application cards back to East Germany with twenty-eight dollars, a self-addressed envelope and a receipt of the transaction proving I had sent a twenty-five-dollar processing fee for a visa to enter East Germany to the Aussenhandelsbank, A.G., in East Berlin to be "credited to the account of the East German Travel Bureau handling Temporary Visitors and for the Visa of Wilhelm Baum."

The fun was not over yet. To receive that voucher, I had to go to the main branch of a large bank in Kansas City and have them telegraph a specific export bank in New York City, one authorized to do business with East Germany. The charges for this transaction were more than the cost of the visa application.

After about five or six weeks, I received not a visa, but instead only an authorization to pick up such a one at the border. Included was a notice telling me how long I would be permitted to stay (not necessarily the length of time I had requested). An accompanying ten-page booklet explained what I could take into the country and what not and also what I would be permitted to "export" again.

It cited the various border crossing points, the ones by rail and the ones by car for West Germany, for Czechoslovakia, for Poland, for Sweden and Denmark (by ferry), all the countries that bordered on East Germany.

I would have to pay fifteen West German Marks (nine dollars) for the visa at the border, and for every day I intended to stay I would have to exchange twenty-five West German marks (fifteen dollars).

For each West German mark I would receive one East German mark, even though the latter was practically worthless, for one could easily buy twenty or more of them for only one West German mark, but not, of course, in East Germany. It was strictly against the law to import or export East German money (because East Germany greatly desired West German currency).

When I arrived at the border, at first by train, the entire atmosphere was very subdued. I did not converse with the inspecting custom officials. Their arrogance showed that they were in absolute control. I mater-of-factly answered their questions. All passengers had to stand up so that their seats could be opened and examined as well as the hot air ducts above. Looking out the window, I saw soldiers with dogs patrolling the area; others thoroughly inspected the under-carriage of each car (this even yet to a greater extent as I rode back to the West, looking for those who might try to flee the country by hiding there). On subsequent visits I was permitted to enter the country by "motor vehicle."

Within twenty-four hours after arrival, I had to report to the Volkspolizei (the people's police) to have the length of my Aufenthaltserlaubniss (sojourning permit) recorded in my passport. But before that, I had to find a local bank to exchange my twenty-five dollars per day, because the police would require proof of that transaction before they would grant me my respective stay.

The great problem was that the banks were open only on certain days and then only at certain hours, and it seemed to me that the authorities had gone to great lengths to make sure that these didn't coincide with the office hours of the police stations. To this came yet, that the banks, as well as all other places of business in Germany, both East and West, are closed over the noon hour, from about twelve to about two or two-thirty. To add to my frustration, I found that only certain police stations handled visitors' applications, so it took some juggling to get the required business transaction taken care of within the allotted time.

When I finally made it, I found the benches along the walls of the front hall completely filled, mostly with East German citizens (easily identifiable by their dress), though there seemed to be a few visitors from other foreign countries. Trying to befriend one of them, I approached a man from Korea who spoke some German. When I innocently asked him, "Which, North or South?" he looked at me as though there could not be any doubt. "North, of course!" he answered defiantly.

There were doors with signs for Traffic Violators, Car Registrations,

Building Permits, etc. All bore instructions (in German): "Do not enter until green light flashes." My door read: "Besucher-Einreise; Aussreise" (Visitors-Arrival; Departure).

When I headed for the end of the long line in front of it, I noticed the angry look of one of the men sitting along the wall as he motioned me to the end of his bench.

I eventually got into the door, only to find myself standing behind a wooden barrier. I felt like an accused prisoner, facing a stern-looking, middle-aged woman in police uniform. I gave her my money exchange slip and my passport, opened to the page which bore my visa. She matter-of-factly pulled open a small wooden file, took out "my card" (which greatly surprised me), compared my visa number and my time of arrival, and asked me where I was staying.

I gave her the address of the people who had invited me, and she marked it down on the card. If I wanted to stay longer than the allotted time on my visa, I would have to go through the same procedure again. I was amazed that regardless of where I reported, my complete record was always there.

I believe that one's driving record was also checked. The East German police was always watching for West German cars which might be guilty of even the slightest traffic violation. Any fine had to be paid right then and there in Western currency, and it was generally way out of line with the offense. I once had to pay fifty marks when a police car, parked on the shoulder, saw me pass without having dimmed my lights. There was a similar fine for not activating one's turn signal when changing directions and, strangely enough, for activating it when pulling into traffic after having parked at a curb. One was fined also for moving into a left lane on the autobahn to enable another car to more easily enter from one of the approaches.

Upon leaving the country, I again had to go to the police at the last place of stay, asking for a Departure Permit. After having had my record checked and found to be without blemish, my permit was again stamped into my passport. Once I inadvertently asked for an "Auswanderungserlaubnis" (Emigration Permit) instead of and "Ausreiseerlaubnis" (Departure Permit), whereupon I was emphatically and harshly informed that the Deutsche Demokratische Republik doesn't issue such.

At times it took me more than an hour, during which I was sent from one office to another, before my permit was issued. Perhaps it had been suspected that I wasn't just a tourist, as my application had stated, but that I had spoken to church groups on various occasions.

Preaching as such was not permitted for visitors without special government authorization, although I was told that there were no objections to "bringing a word of greeting"; also that there was no time limit for such, but to remember that it was a matter of "just greetings."

I took this to mean that I was to refer to the "folks back home" at various times during my message.

This time (1984) my papers unexpectedly were marked "without motor vehicle," which was a great problem because I had several suitcases and my camera equipment. I had corresponded with the teenager whom I had met on the train when I was traveling with the trombone team and had sent her just half a tract of an interesting Christian testimony, hoping she would wonder how the story ends. She always wrote back, asking for the rest, and she had also asked me whether she might call me "Onkel (Uncle) Wilhelm," which made me most happy.

I had written her when I would arrive in Magdeburg (the former East Germany), and the moment I stepped off the train I heard her voice: "Onkel Vilhelm, hier bin ich!" (Uncle Wilhelm, here I am). It had snowed heavily and it was very cold and windy which, however, did not seem to bother her. I saw some streetcars and a few old taxis, but I didn't want to appear like a soft, spoiled American, so I trudged after her. I lugged my two heavy suitcases and a camera bag through the slush to a bank and then to a police station. On the way she told me she had a new boyfriend and that she was pregnant.

Exhausted, we finally arrived at the police station, only to be told that this one was just for the citizens of West Germany and were directed to a different district. I stopped various times, usually under bridges or in house entrances, to get out of the drizzle and to give my back and arms a rest. My suitcases were filled with slides, object lessons, tracts, German and English Bibles, my concordance, my clothing, and bananas, oranges, chocolate and canned goods.

Finally I suggested we take the streetcar, but my guide only said, "It isn't very far anymore." I was at the end of my strength. Yet only after we had finally and satisfactorily reported at the right "Volks Polizei" (People's Police) did we use the streetcar to go to the parents' apartment. The tracks were in such deplorable condition that the car bounced up and down. It swayed so precariously I thought it would keel over at any moment.

The next day on the way back to the station, the support of the rail gave way, and the car ahead of us sank halfway between the cobblestones and stuck there. It looked like a subway heading towards the underground. A kind motorist took us the rest of the way to the station. When I gave him a bar of chocolate, he acted as though it were a gold nugget.

My next stop was the town of Genthin, a short train ride north from Magdeburg, where the one-armed former employee of Dad's store met me at the station. He could hardly control his joy about seeing me after all these years and all we had been through. I have never before nor since been hugged repeatedly by just one arm. He, as well as others I visited, told me frankly about the limitations they had to endure, especially those pertaining to food.

He said also that the young people who lived near the border liked to watch the television programs from the West. The two state-owned TV programs were full of propaganda which no one cared to see. Strangely, many said they would not want to live in the West (meaning West Germany) where everyone is living such a hectic life, rushing from place to place to get bargains. In their country, all prices were standardized.

While we went for a walk together, I let him talk, "Living in a socialist country such as this," he began, "really has many advantages. We have no pornography here, no drug traffic and hardly any crime, and best of all, absolutely no unemployment. Our state takes good care of us; it pays all of our medical and hospital expenses, and you have seen our nice, well-furnished six-room apartment. We pay only the equivalent of forty-five dollars per month, and heat, water and gas inclusive." He also mentioned how safe it is for young women to go out anywhere after dark without fear of being molested and that life in general was much simpler and quieter. "We may be limited in some ways," he said, "but I have long ago learned to live within them and, believe me, I live here most comfortably and peacefully ."

It was difficult for me to photograph the people I saw lined up in front of grocery stores. I felt they were my own countrymen who had been trapped by Godless Communism, and it was embarrassing to see them in their poverty. I was ashamed of my abundance and quickly put my camera away when I saw all eyes turned toward me. I knew that except for the undeserved grace of God toward me, I would be standing in line with them.

In the fall I traveled even beyond East Germany to Romania. I flew with three young Christian brothers from a local Christian Youth Organization, staying over New Year's Day. The windows of the plane were covered before we landed in Bucharest, but what really surprised me were the gun emplacements at the airport. Having finally made it to our hotel, I awoke at 2 a.m. (because of the time lag) and looked out the window. I saw old women, bundled up in thickly padded coats and head scarves piling snow onto big carts with huge wheels. The women had great difficulty pushing the carts to the nearby sewage holes to dump. Soldiers, generally in pairs, patrolled the streets where very few street lights were burning. In our hotel, as well as in all homes, only one-third of the bulbs were lit because of the extreme energy crisis.

We stayed in Bucharest only long enough to arrange for meetings on the following week — each one of us in a different church — and then we were off again by Tarom, the Romanian national airline (a noisy propeller plane) for Oradea, near the Hungarian border.

We had heard that here was the largest congregation in all of Eastern Europe. Still we were not prepared for what we saw. The brothers who met us at the airport took us to an ordinary-looking row of houses. As we tried to enter the dreary, cold and narrow walkway which led to an enormously large meeting hall, we could barely squeeze past the people to get to the platform in the far corner of the L-shaped building. Men, women and children were tightly pressed together on the benches, in the aisle and along the walls. We were told that some of the 2,000 people there had walked for two hours through the snow and cold and most had arrived one to two hours before the beginning of the service, not to find a seat but to pray. I spoke to them through an interpreter, and afterwards to three different children's classes while the three-hour adult service was in progress.

Each time we left our hotel to go to the homes of the various youth workers for discussions, we noticed a white car following us at a distance. We were never apprehended, but we heard later that one brother we had visited had been interrogated by the secret police. They asked, "Were all your friends Americans? Why were they here? What other homes did they visit? What was the topic of conversation? What plans did you make?" etc.

Persecutions of true believers are very subtle. We heard about a top student in his class who had been witnessing to his classmates and was thereupon refused entrance into college or any other institution of higher learning. He had hoped to become a doctor. A star athlete was dismissed from his swimming team when it was discovered he had publicly declared his faith in the Savior. This was just before he and his team were scheduled to leave for an international meet in the West.

To a Sunday school class of young children I spoke about the beauties of Heaven where our Lord reigns supremely and everything is wonderful and in abundance. Knowing of the scarcity of food in Romania, I mentioned the tree of life which bears twelve kinds of fruit and yields fruit every month. Just then one of the little girls asked, through an interpreter, if the Lord Jesus would let her have an orange if she would ask nicely. We had never touched on that subject in Bible school, but I assured her that all our desires will be fulfilled in Heaven and I was sure the Lord would grant her wish. What a beaming smile she had when I said that!

I became embarrassed speaking to a group of young adults when I challenged them to go and serve the Lord on the mission field. Their leader looked straight at me and said emphatically, "Dear brother, we all are here on the mission field. We ask for no other, for who would win the 23 million people to the Lord if we were to leave?"

I have never forgotten that. The need of Eastern Europe weighs heavily upon my heart, especially now that the borders are open. So long as our Lord enables me to do so (even at 77), I intend to go forth to proclaim His Word. I have still not found a portion of Scripture in which our Lord told His disciples to return and retire when they reached 65.

Christ Himself remained on the mission field of this world until He could say, "It is finished," until His death on the cross for us. Only then did He return to His Father's Home.

When I signed up to become a soldier during WW II, I was not promised a safe return. If I had been concerned about my physical safety, I would not have entered military service. The apostle Paul told Timothy to *"endure hardness as a good soldier of Jesus Christ"* (2 Timothy 2:3). We are admonished to *"fight the good fight of faith"* (1 Timothy 6:12).

And that's what I am doing.

"You Can't Fall Out of Bed". While visiting the home of a "well to do" Japanese family, we were bedded in this large typical tatami room, denuded of any furniture. The flooring consisted of very finely woven rice straw sections tightly fit together on which were placed our foam rubber futons. Our covers were filled with fluffy cotton wadding.

31

I Become a Chaplain

IN THE SPRING OF 1985, I was asked to serve as chaplain in a large Christian home for unwed, expectant mothers about 10 miles from our home. It was called the L.I.G.H.T. House, not only because it was located on somewhat of an elevation, but mainly because its initials proclaimed the purpose of its existence: **Life Is Given Hope for Tomorrow.** The staff was concerned with the physical and spiritual welfare of the girls.

The Home was enormous — a 94,000-square-foot, three-story former convent. It had 50 completely furnished rooms, between 30 and 40 girls, a fully equipped clinic with a staff nurse, a doctor in residence and a fully accredited adoption agency for the girls who did not plan to keep their babies. All young women received prenatal care and instructions in sewing, cooking and the care of infants.

For two years I served as chaplain, working at the Home from nine in the morning until five or six in the evening. However, during this time I also took another Bible delivery trip top China and an extended trip to Germany, Africa and South America.

I ministered to the entire staff and conducted chapel services, but mainly I spoke to the girls individually about eternal issues. This wasn't always easy because many of them came from broken homes and had a most tragic past. Some of them were also rebellious and did not want to hear anything about "religion." I had to look continually to the Lord for patience, love, understanding and, above all, for heavenly wisdom.

One girl made it especially difficult. She came into my office saying, "Hurry up with what you have to say so I can get out of here as fast as possible!"

I was as kind as I could be to her, but she glared at me defiantly. I had thought about her name, Cecilia Markman, and I told her I was intrigued with it. She was momentarily startled when I said it wasn't her first name which interested me, but her family name. She seemed surprised but didn't say anything. So I told her that the first part "mark" conveyed a very painful and seemingly hopeless situation, but the second part "man" was wonderful and promising. The first part speaks of the *mark* which her experience had left on her physically and emotionally — on her heart and her soul. I tried to show my concern and understanding. I assured her that in her own strength and by her own means she would not be able to find her way out of her predicament. I quoted for her Jeremiah 2:22, *"For though thou wash thee with nitre, and take thee much soap, yet thine iniquity is **marked** before me, saith the Lord God."* And Psalm 130:3, *"If thou, Lord, **mark** iniquities, O Lord, who shall stand?"* I explained that sin is not *what we do* but *what we are from birth.*

Then I told her about a particular **MAN** who is able to completely transform her and give her joy, abundant love and grace in spite of all her problems. He would forgive all her transgressions and reconcile her to God, her Creator. I read to her 1 Timothy 2:5, *"For there is one God and one mediator between God and men, the **MAN** Christ Jesus,"* reminding her that her unusual last name encompassed both the problem and the solution.

At that she jumped up from her chair, screaming, "I don't care in the least about what you said, and I don't want to have a thing to do with your religion!" She ran out of the office and slammed the door.

There I sat, greatly disappointed and benumbed. I prayed, "Now what, Lord?" He reminded me I had just implanted the seed of the Gospel into her name and I could safely leave it there. Every time she would introduce herself or write her name, she would "preach" herself God's answer to her problem.

It was lunch time when I saw her walk into the dining room. I said, "Enjoy your meal, Miss *Markman.*" She gave me a blank look. As I was going home that evening, I met her in the hallway. "Good night, Miss *Markman;* pleasant dreams." The next morning I greeted her with, "A pleasant good morning, Miss *Markman.*"

She left the home soon after this incident. The director told me she had come to him, saying she had asked the Lord to save her and wanted him to tell me. She was too embarrassed to tell me because of the way she had acted in my office. She had not been able to get away from what she had heard any more than she could get away from her own name.

32

More Bibles into China

WHILE I WAS CHAPLAIN at the L.I.G.H.T. House, I took a special leave to again take Bibles into China. On my way, I stopped over in Japan to see my daughter, Mary Esther, her husband Mark, and their recently founded congregation for the deaf Japanese. The entire family, including Mark's parents, is involved in this ministry for these young Japanese who are shunned by society. Needing a "family" where they are welcome, they frequently drop in for a meal — unannounced, of course, since they cannot phone ahead. I was amazed and blessed at my daughter's ability to be continually prepared to feed them at the spur of the moment besides caring for her husband and her own three children.

I realized that this was a trait she had inherited from her mother for, knowing my own heart, I seldom could demonstrate such compassion. I could only praise our Lord for such a daughter.

Even though my Japanese had not suffered too much, I couldn't make use of it with her house guests. However, I witnessed a lively silent conversation, as my grandchildren had no difficulty in "talking" with them.

Besides being pastor of the church, Mark has taken on an additional, most demanding task. Some of his young men are in Bible school, preparing for the ministry, and Mark interprets for them and assists them with their homework.

This time I undertook my trip to China with a young Japanese who had once lived there and spoke Chinese fluently. Again we packed our rucksacks with Bibles and headed for GUANGZHOU, taking the same route I had gone before.

We purposely didn't stay together during the customs inspection. He, ahead of me, took his pack off the conveyor belt without any problem. I took mine, but as I was nearing the exit, a lady inspector stopped me and asked what I had in my baggage.

I said, "My personal belongings and a few books."

She motioned me to a table and ordered me to open my bags. She took out the first few Bibles and discussed the contents with an official standing nearby. She told me, "These are Bibles which aren't desired here. Empty your entire pack."

She took them all and put them into a large plastic bag, tagged them with my name and told me I could pick them up on my way back. She gave me one, however, for my "personal use." We returned by train, so the Bibles may still be there, unless the officials have sold them on the Black Market. Perhaps if they did so, and someone had to pay a high price, he might consider it a Book truly valuable. So I don't feel bad about the encounter.

From Guangzhou, we took a train for two nights and a day clear to Beijing, 2300 km away. The "sleeping cars" were divided into compartments made by rods reaching from floor to ceiling. Narrow contraptions, suspended at three levels, served as beds and had to be conquered by rope ladders.

In Beijing, we went by Pedicab (two side-by-side seats, with the propulsion provided by a strong Chinese pedal-person in front) to a housing unit for students, where we stayed. The next day my friend took me through a jumble of narrow back alleys, into a tiny entrance, up a steep, rickety, circular stairway to a small group of believers who met there secretly.

Although my Western face was partially concealed by a recently grown beard, it was advisable I not show it at the places my friend was to make contact to deliver the Bibles. So, leaving him, whose Oriental features might let him pass as a Chinese, I ventured out on my own, first to Tiananmen Square in the center of Beijing.

Many school groups go there on excursions and to have their pictures taken before the huge portrait of Mao Tse Tung. I photographed some of them at this famous Gate of Heavenly Peace, adjacent to the open square, the world's largest. They wanted me to be in the picture with them. So did other nationals and even soldiers of the Chinese Red Army.

From Beijing, I took a three-hour bus ride to the GREAT WALL, where I fulfilled one of my lifelong dreams — of walking on it. It is said to be the only man-made construction (about 3,750 miles long) visible from outer space.

Walking around Beijing, I came upon a working shoemaker seated on a low stool on a sidewalk near an empty lot. I needed to have my heels replaced and waited while he worked, sitting on another low stool near him. Before long, a huge crowd had gathered around us. I felt sure they were not interested in watching *him* work!

I spent considerable time in one of Beijing's most prestigious hotels, sitting in their spacious lounge writing postcards home. The hotel catered mainly to foreign dignitaries, and as the day wore on I found that all chairs at the tables in the lounge were soon occupied. I was asked repeatedly if a place at my table was still vacant, so I met an amazing array of embassy employees, oil prospectors, export managers, news reporters and the like. I spent the day sharing the most important issues in life with them, and obtaining a number of addresses.

Fifty Thrre Years Later! A most nostalic reunion! After much searching while visiting Dortmund in 1980, I was able to find two of my "old" friends, Siegfried Marx and Karl-Heinz Petsch, with whom I went to school in 1927. (I'm pointing to a picture of my students at the Tokoyo university.)

33

KENYA, BRAZIL, PARAGUAY

I HAD WRITTEN A LETTER to the East German authorities saying I was a persecuted Jew who still loved his homeland and would like to visit old friends. When I returned to Kansas from China, I found waiting an authorization for a visa into East Germany "with motor vehicle!" So 1985 marked the second time I undertook two extensive trips in one year.

My loving wife drove me, as usual, to the airport in Kansas City. I was picked up in Frankfurt by a Christian brother who was an insurance adjuster and provided a used Mercedes for me. I drove directly to the East German border, where my car and baggage were routinely inspected. I went straight on to Ludwigslust to the *Stift Bethlehem* (Bethlehem Foundation), the largest charitable foundation hospital under the regulation of the East German socialist government.

To the hospital leadership I gave a slide presentation of our work in Japan. I showed my object lessons, telling how I, though a Jew, or maybe because of it, came to trust the Lord Jesus Christ for salvation, and presented the Gospel using enlarged KANJI cards. This resulted in further invitations, some in nearby communities and others as far away as Görlitz in eastern East Germany at the Polish border and as far north as Rostock, a Baltic Sea city.

Driving across East Germany, I passed a typical shepherd with his staff and his dog. This scene was so idyllic I drove my yellow Mercedes straight across the field to photograph him. He thought I had come from West Germany, and when he found I was an American he was so excited he invited me to his home for supper and to spend the night. I had a great time telling him and his family about the reason for my journey. I have kept in touch by mail and have stopped by every time my ways lead near his small city (Kroppenstedt).

I flew from Frankfurt directly to Nairobi. A Christian schoolteacher friend and his wife from Germany had gone to Kenya to open a mission station. Now he was having a Bible conference at their station at Eldoret and had asked me to be a teacher. My friends picked me up in their VW bus, and we drove 365 km over one of the roughest roads I have ever traveled. It was, in fact, the ONLY road to their station, a nine-hour trek across a barren, desolate land where giraffes and zebras roamed the countryside.

The next day we visited a village where a horde of happy little African children in dirty, ragged attire welcomes us at the entrance of their compound with its grass-roofed huts with walls made of interwoven straw plastered with cow dung. Some children were carrying a baby brother or sister on their backs. But they were singing the praises of the Lord in songs they had learned in Sunday school! I recognized the tunes immediately, though I couldn't understand the words.

My guide, one of the African brothers from the Bible conference, suggested I tell them a story, which he interpreted. What shining eyes and eager faces my audience had! At a nearby hut, he asked me to pray for a disfigured old mother with ugly, oozing sores on her legs.

They eat bland-tasting corn mush three times a day, that is, when there is enough to go around. In fact, that is what all the children said they would like to eat when they get to heaven: LOTS AND LOTS AND LOTS of it. Without question, we will meet a great number of these folks in Glory. They will no longer be clothed in filthy rags, nor will their faces be marked by signs of malnutrition.

In one of the African churches on the following Sunday, my message, spoken with German accent, was translated into *Swahili*. What a mission field!

I have already mentioned my ministry at the L.I.G.H.T. House. One of my sisters in Christ there had a daughter living in Durban, South Africa, with her Jewish husband. Recently this daughter had trusted the Lord for salvation and so, shortly, did her husband. Hearing this good news, my co-worker wrote them about me and of my plans to visit Kenya. They called her, asking whether it would be possible for me to come to Durban for a few days as their guest, to enjoy fellowship and to answer some of their questions.

I found that I could fly straight south from Kenya to Johannesburg and then get a direct flight across the south Atlantic to Rio de Janeiro. I could visit my older sister in Rio without having to fly back to Europe first. Durban was only an hour's flight from Johannesburg, so I could visit my friend's daughter on the way, so to speak. I jumped for joy, thanking my Lord for another open door.

The daughter's Jewish brother-in-law and his Jewish wife met me at the airport in Johannesburg (Jo-burg, as it is commonly called), helped me with my transfer to Durban and invited me to lunch. As soon as we were seated, they asked what I thought about "those new religious ideas of *those two down there.*"

With limited time between planes, I chose to talk and not eat. After sharing some of my own experience with them, I explained that the brother was now more Jewish than ever before and that upon his Gentile wife were now bestowed all the promises given to Abraham and his offspring (Galatians 3:16, 29).

As we parted, the best of friends, I sensed their amazement. It seemed similar to those who said, "We have seen (heard) strange things today" (Luke 5:6). I went on my way rejoicing that my trip to South Africa had already been worthwhile.

There followed three most enjoyable and challenging days in Durban with my new brother and sister in Christ (the children of my L.I.G.H.T. House co-worker). I prayed with them and at times was hard-pressed to find the answer to some of their simple yet profound questions such as: "Did Judas have to betray Jesus in order to make our Salvation possible?" and: "Why did God choose the cross, would another method not have accomplished the same?"

Breakfast was served by a Zulu maid on the straw-thatched veranda beside the swimming pool of their Mediterranean-style home. Just beyond lay the Indian Ocean, sparkling in the balmy South African sunshine.

We watched the sharks performing acrobatics a few yards beyond the foaming waves that pounded the rocky shore and heard the distant sound of the A-Di-Da bird, named after the cry of that giant sea gull. Having just come from the barren plains of Kenya with the deprivation and despondency which marked the village I had visited, I was in culture shock.

After Kenya, this seemed like a veritable Paradise. The veranda was part of my host's tropical garden — palm and banana trees, along with mangoes, gualas, papayas, litchis and wild figs. Animals with strange-sounding names as fervet monkeys, mongeese and meercats made fleeting appearances.

Best of all, before I left this place of bliss, my Lord gave me the additional, unexpected joy of speaking at length with the African servant and hearing her ask the Lord Jesus to come into her heart.

It was already dark when my plane touched down in Rio de Janeiro. I was amazed at the comparatively short hop, eight and a half hours, that had propelled me — oops, I came by jet — from South Africa to South America in such great comfort. My sister, Anneliese, accompanied by one of her three maids (one or two maids seemed to be the norm in Rio for middle or upper class families), met me at the airport. Her husband was out of town when I arrived.

Restrained from openly expressing my thanks to the Lord for my safe arrival and the privilege of seeing my sister again, I felt unfulfilled.

Knowing how she felt toward my faith in the Lord Jesus, my inner unrest continued as we wove our way by taxi to her home, a double-sized eighth floor apartment two blocks from one of Rio's famous beaches.

Even after greeting my brother-in-law the next day, I felt like a stranger, though in the home of my immediate family. It was a painful realization of the Truth of God's Word: *"A prophet is not without honor except in his own country and among his own kin"* (Mark 6:4).

I asked about my niece who lives in a different part of Rio. My sister said I could not contact her since it was Friday evening, already past sundown. She would not pick up the telephone until after the end of the Shabbat, that is, after sundown the following day.

It seemed that the entire family had, to a greater or lesser degree, reverted to traditional Judaism to counteract the decision of one of their own kin (me), who had become apostate by converting to the "Gentile religion." In her quest for true Judaism, my niece had become deeply involved in *Cabala,* an occult religious philosophy developed by certain rabbis, based on a mystical interpretation of the Scriptures.

With the rest of the family I attended her private *End of Sabbath* observance. I watched the candlelight ceremony, chanting of Hebrew prayers and sipping of the wine. I took the opportunity to quote some of our Old Testament Scriptures, telling her how much I believed all that our prophets had written, and their fulfillment in the New Covenant which God had promised to make with our people (Jeremiah 31:31), but there was no response.

From her top-floor apartment balcony, I could see both ways: on the inside, the scene I have just described. Outside was a full view of the 98-1/2-foot-tall white stone statue of *Christ the Redeemer,* famous landmark of Rio de Janeiro on the summit of Mount Corcovado. It was brilliantly illuminated with arms fully extended, forming a cross, the head inclined ever so slightly, the gaze encompassing the teeming multitudes below — much as Christ must have done when He prayed over Jerusalem hundreds of years ago. It was a heart-rending experience.

My next stop was in Paraguay, the outworking of one of my first trips to Germany. When I first met dear brother Richert of German Mennonite background, he and his family had come out of Russia, where like David Klassen, he had been repeatedly interned because of his faith. At that time they were planning to re-locate in Paraguay. They were concerned to remove their children from the evil of the affluent and unrestrained Western society and return to the simplicity of their former way of life. I found such simplicity and wholesome fellowship with that family with its six children that I was drawn back to them again and again. I became interested in their undertaking and how they would fare in such an uncultivated land. So I had kept in touch, especially with their son, Cornelius, and they had repeatedly invited me to come and visit them. A stopover in Paraguay fitted perfectly into my return travel route.

It was only a three-and-a-half-hour flight from Rio to Assuncion, Paraguay's capital. (Most of the people there did not even know that it means ascension.) Moving from the coolness of the airplane cabin into 96 degrees was quite a shock, and I was ready to turn right around. But I knew that our Lord had a few more lessons for me to learn, or at least to be exposed to.

Cornelius met me at the airport, and we went by taxi through a neglected part of town to the bus terminal. After a four-hour wait, we started the five-and-one-half-hour ride, squeezed between potato sacks and chicken cages. I had ample time to decide whether my nausea was caused by the stifling heat or the ethnic fragrance.

We finally got off near a small community. Cornelius told me to wait by the side of the road while he went first for his motorcycle, parked nearby, and then for the family car. The car was so well camouflaged with a thick layer of red dust, inside and out, it was barely distinguishable from the red, rutty road on which we were driving. Close to midnight, it was still hot and sticky with no breeze. It was pitch dark since there was no moon, at least not on our side of the clouds. We finally stopped near the fence at the outer part of their property.

Soon the father came running toward us, holding high his kerosene lamp with one hand while embracing me with the other. I got kissed, too, on both cheeks. Then I was "shone" the way to the house, and through their primitive quarters to the room where I was to spend the night. I was under a mosquito net, and even the slightest breath of air would have been welcome. Taking the light with them, I was left literally "in the dark" as to the direction of the outhouse. How glad I was that our Lord has given us five senses, so if any one becomes inoperative one of the others can take over.

I have been in homes where the chimes of a clock would awaken me every hour, sometimes every fifteen minutes. I could always stop the pendulum before retiring. But how do you stop a rooster determined to announce the Paraguayan morning at seventeen minutes to four, including Sundays and holidays? Unless by having had that specific bird for supper the day before!

The days at the colony had to begin *very* early, for there was no electricity. Our Lord Himself showed the need of taking advantage of the light, though He was mainly conveying a spiritual Truth: *"I must work the works of him that sent me, while it is day; the night is coming when no one can work"* (John 9:4). That is doubly applicable to the folks in that colony, where every minute of daylight must be utilized. I guess even the rooster must have been indoctrinated.

None of the farms I visited had running water. It had to be pumped from a well by an oil or gasoline engine or hauled up by hand. To take a shower, I was directed to a cubicle made of old crates. A small drum hung down, from the bottom of which sprouted the spraying end of a watering can. Before filling it, I heated the water to the desired temperature on the kerosene stove in the kitchen. They suggested that I be through with my shower before all the water would run out. Guess I would have been "through" with it, even if I hadn't been *through*. I pulled the water canister to the top by a rope. There was even a cock by the shower head so the showering would not begin prematurely.

The colony I was visiting consisted of homes, each with an adjacent fenced farm, three to five km apart. The farmers were of Mennonite or Amish descent, a cordial and lovable people with an admirably simple lifestyle, implicit trust in the Lord and total commitment to their calling.

I could scarcely comprehend that the houses, garden and farms had been literally hewn out of the jungle. As I admired one beautiful, well-cared-for property, the owner pointed to the primeval forest at the far end of his field. "I was not able to get into that wilderness except with a sharp machete and a big axe," he said. Looking at the ground, he added, "That, over there, is what this place where you are standing looked like twelve years ago."

He proudly showed me his latest acquisition, a Yamaha gasoline generator, rigged up to the motor of his wife's wringer-type Maytag washing machine.

The children played with the dogs and cats, or with "the wagon Daddy made." Children also helped milk the cow or feed the chickens if they are old enough. Okay, so how old do the chickens have to be to be fed? I meant to say that when the children are old enough, they would feed the chickens. Then when the chickens are old enough, they will feed the children!

At the time I visited, it had not rained for many weeks. The ground and the crops showed the effects of the excessive heat and drought. This could hardly be said about their abundantly fruitful families. The great need for rain was the main prayer request at the Bible study I attended in a "nearby neighbor's" home, about two kilometers away.

While the father "opened the Word," his wife and eleven children, the oldest one 14, sat quietly attentive on wooden benches placed against the bare wall. The bluish flame hissed at the end of a long thin pipe sticking out from a propane bottle in the middle of the floor. It cast an eerie light over our gathering, adding to the already stifling heat in the unventilated room. I had great difficulty enduring this but, to my amazement, it seemed not to bother the others in the least.

A few days later I was on my way back to the good old United States. I sat, contented and comfortable, in the modern jet of the Paraguayan Airline, reveling in its refreshing coolness. I reflected upon my stay among these down-to-earth people of our Lord and what I had experienced in their midst.

The loudspeaker announcement jarred me rather abruptly out of my thoughts. "Please put your seats into the upright position ... in a few minutes we will be landing at Miami International Airport ..." I had come back to *reality* — or — would that now not be the right word to use?

For a while I was glad to be back at the L.IG.H.T. House, not having to live out of my two suitcases. Yet, soon I was no longer satisfied just to remain at home.

34

NOT EXACTLY UNAFRAID

I HAVE OFTEN BEEN ASKED why I feel constrained to go, especially now that I am "retired" from missionary service (as though one could ever be that). Why do I still head out pretty much on my own, into the neglected and needy socialist countries? I even ask myself that question, and I'm not sure I can come up with a good answer. Maybe it is because I look at the Word of God as primarily a missionary book, beginning with Abraham. The first of our patriarchs, the one who received God's command to get out of his country, away from his kindred and his father's house into a land God would show him, and that I, being his offspring, sense a similar, peculiar calling to make His statutes and judgments known among the nations (Deuteronomy 4:5-8).

Our prophet Isaiah spoke of One Whom the Lord had called for a light to the Gentiles to *"them that sit in darkness out of the prison house"* (chapter 42:6, 7). This passage speaks prophetically of our Messiah, the Lord Jesus Christ, Who in turn has said, *"— as my Father hath sent me, even so send I you"* (John 20:21).

When God in times past had a message to convey to a heathen nation or even to a Gentile individual, He usually used a Jew: Moses to Pharaoh; Daniel to Nebuchadnezzar; Jonah to Nineveh; Peter to Cornelius; Philip to the Ethiopian eunuch; and Paul to the Roman jailer at Philippi.

Thus I started out again in the fall of 1986, the fourth time that I headed for Eastern Europe (in addition to West Germany) since I had "retired" from Japan. The same family who had done so before again supplied me with a vehicle. This time even a 1981 white Mercedes.

My feelings when approaching the border of a socialist country are difficult to describe. I was alone, without anyone to talk to or to pray with, apprehensive even entertaining doubts as to whether I should proceed into the "unknown." I was uncertain what a socialist border guard serving an oppressive dictatorship might do to me who was from a capitalist country.

I had been told that thorough spot checks would be made periodically; if I should happen to hit one of these, I could expect a delay of up to eight hours. These checks could entail an examination of every piece of luggage, including the clothes on one's body. A search of a vehicle could include removing the car's interior paneling and, if contraband were suspected, even the tires.

I had inquired of one who had gone that way before, which is usually a good thing to do. Yet, that time at least, I wished I hadn't. This Christian brother told me to be sure I didn't have any letters with me from "over there," nor any addresses on paper; to memorize them if at all possible. If I should not be able to do that, to hide them securely. Not too comforting an advice. I might have had more time to contemplate upon this had it not been told me in Vienna, my very last stop before crossing into Czechoslovakia. You can imagine the battle that raged within me as to whether I should really go ahead with my plans. Or were they God's?

It was then I remembered God telling Gideon that the number of Israelites he had was too great to go against the Midianites lest they say, "My own hand has saved me" (Judges 7:2). So he was to let all those return home who were fearful and afraid, and 22,000 did so.

At that time, Gideon had an army in which every two Israelites would have to fight nine Midianites. One Israelite for every four and a half Midianites, if you can visualize half a Midianite! But he ended up with only 300 fearless men against a mighty army of 135,000 — making it one Israelite *and the Lord* for every 450 of the enemy!

As for me and my apprehension, that was all it took to dispel it. I scribbled the addresses for Czechoslovakia and Poland real small into my notebook, since they were difficult to remember. The rest I wrapped up, along with my letters and most of the literature I had brought along. From a neighborhood post office, I mailed them to a pastor friend whom I planned to visit after my return to West Germany.

As it turned out, every one of my border crossings was so UNeventful that I had tears in my eyes every time — tears of relief and tears of thankfulness to my Lord. I never had to open more than one of my bags, and I was asked very few questions.

At one control point, I saw a customs official dump out the contents of all the suitcases of one large family and thoroughly examine *every item*. I was conscious that the same God Who won the battle for Gideon was the One Who saw me safely through those border crossings.

Through one of the nurses in East Germany (whom I had been privileged to lead to the Lord), I made contact with a pastor in Prague. Twice already I had visited him and spoken in his church, showing slides

172

from Japan while he interpreted for me. On this trip, he called for me a pastor in BRNO (Brünn), and I went there to speak to a group of attentive young people. They took me on a trip around town and sent me to BRATISLAVA near the Czech/Hungarian border. From there a Christian brother took me to many of the surrounding communities to speak and show my object lessons.

At a tiny village called Nesvady, we visited a home where a huge portrait of an attractive young girl hung in the living room. When I asked about her, there came an unmistakable expression of grief. My friend told me quietly she was the daughter of the family and had recently become a nurse. After she professed Christ as her Lord, her husband went to the hospital where she worked and shot her.

I drove without an accident or a breakdown 6,057 km (3,764 miles), staying in 34 homes throughout West Germany, Austria and three Socialist countries. It must have been during the night that a souvenir hunter spied my Mercedes Star, a specially desired memento before the borders opened and foreign cars were no longer a "novelty." He was not too successful though, for in breaking it off, he left part of the ring surrounding the emblem, thus leaving me a "memorial" to look at for the rest of my journey.

When Takekawa-san came unexpectedly to introduce me the the girl he met at Bible school, we read the Bible together concerning God's standard for husband and wife and having prayed they left most happily.

35

TO THE BLACK SEA

MY LONGEST, MOST EXTENSIVE and unquestionably most exciting odyssey began on August 15, 1987. This time I had at my disposal a 1982 Nissan, which had been used to pull a car trailer. It showed unmistakable signs of wear inside and out, so I was a little apprehensive when I first saw it. Though it had already traveled over 90,000 km, it proved to be one of the most reliable cars I had ever driven. I traveled without a single mishap, not even a flat tire, 9,519 km through two western countries, West Germany and Austria, and five socialist nations, Hungary, Romania, Czechoslovakia, Poland and East Germany.

My purpose for going was two-fold: to share the Good News of the Gospel and to learn how God's people were faring where governments ignored our Lord and were keeping their people in bondage. I wanted to tell them they were not forgotten by their American brothers and sisters in Christ and share Eternal Truths which would encourage them in the midst of hardships and persecutions. When I was with them, I experienced their lack of basic nourishment, so I often shared our Lord's account of Lazarus and the rich man. He who had nothing but continual hunger and pain longed for and obtained eternal bliss, while the one who had everything lost it all. In eternity he began to beg from the one who had once been the beggar.

One Saturday afternoon before I left West Germany to drive to the East, I went to a street meeting with some members of a church in Amberg, close to the Czechoslovakian border. The main business street was closed off to traffic so the citizens could safely stroll and shop. I stood beside a table with Christian books and tracts and spoke in German, presenting my object lessons. My friends also conversed with those who stopped to watch me perform.

Here I am, I thought, *having barely set foot on German soil after many years of wanderings and manifold experiences — a Jew who once knew nothing of God's Love and Grace, proclaiming the wonderful message of the God of the Jews in the land and to the people that once sought to annihilate them.*

It was a thrilling experience!

Prior to leaving West Germany I met a rather well-to-do businessman who had formerly lived in Romania. Knowing well the plight of his countrymen, he had obtained through wholesale outlets large amounts of canned goods and other non-perishable foods such as powdered milk, soups, coffee, cereal, sugar and flour. Besides that, he had an abundant stock of dry goods, shirts, pants, socks and gloves and even a variety of plastic toys. All these he would give freely to anyone willing to distribute them among the believers beyond the border.

When I went to see him, he loaded my car with more than I thought it would hold. After he finished, the rear springs were nearly bent onto the axles, and I was afraid they might break.

The load included yard goods and plastic shopping bags. "They are one of the most desired items over there," I was told. Only after I arrived did I realize the un-exaggerated truth of that claim. Everywhere I went people asked, "Do you have any plastic bags?" They were the most desired items, second only to the food.

Every nook and crevice of the trunk and a good part of the car's interior was stuffed. As I traveled down the road, I felt like the proprietor of a general store on wheels.

Another interesting event occurred in Völklabruck, Austria, a small idyllic community amidst lush pastures and beautiful, snow-capped mountains. I always considered the opportunity to view all this scenery one of the many fringe benefits of traveling for my Lord.

I was on my way to visit a missionary couple with whom we had been in missionary re-training in Brooklyn in 1964. Passing a small chapel, I saw a group of people waiting for a wedding party to come out. I stopped to take some pictures. I didn't want to squeeze through the crowd, so I was looking for a good vantage point when I noticed a family watching from their roof garden across the street.

The man motioned me to come up, and when I nodded, he came down to greet me and took me up with him. He introduced his wife and daughter, and they all watched as I took the pictures. He asked where I was from and where I was going, and I took the opportunity to give a short testimony.

As I wondered what their reaction might be, the lady asked, "Have you had any lunch already?" You can't imagine how happy I was. I'd been on the road quite a while, far away from my family and, well, lonesome. I was hungry and could easily have gone to a restaurant, but I was waiting, as I usually did, until I arrived at my scheduled stop for the night to enjoy the fellowship around the table with brothers and sisters in Christ.

I was yearning for a family to talk with, and my Lord performed one of those miracles He has done all along my journey. I had to control myself to give a reserved answer, Japanese style, making sure I didn't sound too restrained. By then she had already asked me to have a seat at the table. She even excused herself that the family had already eaten and then brought me a wonderful meal: first soup, then roast beef with gravy, fried potatoes, a vegetable and, for dessert, plum pie, typical European style, like Mother used to make! My thankfulness to her was small compared to that which I express to my Lord.

After that they said to me, "Why don't you call your missionary friend in the nearby village before going there?" When the aged father answered the phone, he told me that the family was away for the weekend. Not knowing me, he didn't invite me to come over. It was mid-afternoon by then, and I didn't think I could make it to the next stop near Vienna. Besides that, I really wanted to see this nearby brother. I guess my disappointment must have been quite apparent.

As I hung up, my host, without hesitation, said, "If you'd like, you're most welcome to stay here until your friends come back." Not once had I been made so welcome by total strangers, ones I had met by chance. They even suggested that I call my wife in America at their expense so she would know I was in good hands and not to worry. Naturally, I was thrilled to do this. I was overwhelmed. It was one of the brightest days of my entire trip, Saturday, August 29, 1987.

In the evening we were sitting leisurely in the spacious living room. It seemed like the perfect opportunity to express my gratitude to the family by entertaining them. With the words, "Let me show you how we visualized things from the Bible for the Japanese children," I opened my bag and began to demonstrate. I had barely begun when the wife said, "Wait a moment, I'm sure some of our friends would like to see that, too. Please wait until I call them." Pretty soon some of the neighborhood mothers came with their children.

It was an unexpected gathering, but exceptional. I had not shared the Word of God in German for a very long time, and I was rusty in quoting verses from memory. Their laughter as I stumbled through them added to the relaxed, congenial atmosphere. Yet the way of Salvation was being told them in their language. I have always wished that my American brothers and sisters in the Lord could have looked in here — as well as into many other situations into which our Lord led me. I soon realized these folks were Catholics, as are most Austrians, and I went with them to their church on the following day (Sunday).

On Monday, I visited my friends in the neighboring village and went on to Vienna. I stayed two nights in the local Child Evangelization Office, then went on to Glivice (Gleiwitz) in Poland, arriving there on a Friday.

Here was located the Sister Church of a Methodist Church near my home in America, so this was another one of my contacts — and I never knew how they would turn out. After threading my way through the confusing streets and making many inquires, I arrived about noon at a huge, ornamental, typically European structure. I was not able to raise anyone, not by ringing the bell, shouting, nor by rattling the big iron gate. Beside the door there was a sign announcing English language classes from three to five p .m., Monday-Friday. I copied the phone number and walked down the main business street in search of a telephone. This, I thought, was an internationally known and understood word, but even though I went to a number of shops with my closed fist to my ear as though I was holding a receiver saying "hello," all I received were blank stares and a shaking of the head.

Some words were more difficult to express by trying to act them out. For me, the most frustrating one was TOILET, especially when there was a time element involved. I found out it is not an internationally understood word. The simplest thing would have been to have a friend who knew Polish write the word beforehand. Then I could have just shown it when the need arose. I was fortunate to have some tissue in my glove compartment. Waving it in the air might not have been very ethical, but I found it to be most effective.

After I walked six or seven blocks to the railroad station, I found a whole row of telephones. Now it was a matter of finding someone who would convey my message to the party on the other end, that is, after I would succeed in conveying my request to the conveyer.

I finally found such a one; he spoke some English, but there was no answer to his efforts. Walking back to my car, I contemplated whether I should wait around for three hours until the English classes would begin, or drive to my next destination. I thought to try the bell once more, and EUREKA! A young man came down and opened the door. I asked to see the pastor, and whether he understood me or not, he took me upstairs where a kind, elderly man greeted me most cordially. He spoke no English and only a few words of German with a heavy accent which was very hard to understand. It took quite a while to explain who I was, where I came from and why. After about an hour or so, his wife brought lunch, a very thin milk soup.

In the meantime I was able to figure out that he leased his large facilities to an English Institute. The four paid instructors who spoke fluent English were members of his church.

This was my cue to show him one of my object lessons which I always had in my pocket. I think he caught the hint, because after a while he took me downstairs to meet the teachers. What a relief that was. Now I could make myself understood again, though I was very amused to realize that their accent sounded very much like mine.

They told me that as far as they knew, none of their students (about

250, divided into four classes) were believers and that they, as hired teachers, were not permitted to talk to them about the Lord. After I had shown one of my object lessons to them also, they thought it would be a great idea to have me present some of them to the class as part of the day's English instructions.

One of the teachers would interpret my presentation into Polish so that all would be sure to understand the spiritual application.

When she introduced me by telling the students that they were now having the rare privilege of hearing English as spoken by a "native American," I thought for a moment to correct her, but not wanting to embarrass her, I just smiled and began.

The students sang some Polish folk songs for me in appreciation and afterwards some of them came up to try and practice their English.

36

INCIDENT AT THE BORDER

ON THE WAY to the Romanian border, I again spoke with some folks who had recently returned from "across." The reports were similar concerning vehicle inspection. But they also told of the exorbitant amounts of customs duties charged for food and even for used clothing, and of waiting periods of four to six hours while every item was minutely examined and evaluated. Again, they suggested not to have any sermon notes, which would identify me as a missionary or preacher, and warned against having addresses or letters. This would not present a problem to me so much as it would to those whose addresses were found.

I was at a real loss again. I could not even pronounce the names of the places in which my contacts lived: Cisnadiora, Splauiul, Tapioszole. I felt particularly sorry for the people who lived in Hajduszoboszlo, a town in Hungary just a little north and east of Puspöckladany. Again our Lord made a way; throughout my trip I never ceased to be amazed at His provision. Before I went across the border, I stayed with a family whose visitors from over there were returning shortly. They were its citizens and would not be searched as foreigners would be. They offered to take all my addresses with them. I would pick them up after I came across. All I had to remember was one name and address — theirs. I made that easy for myself by writing portions of it on different pages of my notebook — in JAPANESE!

The nearer I drew to the border, the more I thought about all I had heard. I had no one to talk to but the Lord, no one to lift my spirits or encourage me. Also, the Scripture portion that came to my mind was not too reassuring:

"... which of you, intending to build a tower, does not sit down

*first and count the costs, whether he has enough to finish it?
Otherwise, after he has laid the foundation and is not able to
finish it, all who see it begin to mock him, saying, This man began
to build, and was not able to finish" (Luke 14:28-30).*

Isn't it strange, the different portions of God's Word that come into
one's mind? I wondered if I had what it took to complete what I had set
out to do? Also, I asked myself, "Has the Lord really directed me in this
way? Maybe it would be better to turn back — but then, what would my
friends at home say, those who knew of my plan, if I came back without
carrying it out? And what about all the food I had with me to take across?"

I felt very much alone there in that car, far away from home with a
fearful situation before me.

*"... the people are strong who dwell in the land, and the cities are
walled, and very great; ... the Amalakites dwell in the land ... and
there we saw the giants ... and we were in our own sight as
grasshoppers ..." (Numbers 13:28-33).*

I even remembered the words of Ronald E. McNair, a physicist who
perished in the Challenger tragedy: "You can only become a winner if you
are willing to walk over the edge." But then again came the words of our
Lord in reassurance:

*"My peace I give unto you ... let not your heart be troubled, neither
let it be afraid ... I will never leave you nor forsake you ... The
Lord is on my side; I will not fear what man can do unto me.*

With these thoughts I approached the Border Inspection Station and
its flashing red lights: the customs officials in their respect-demanding,
well-fitting uniforms; the soldiers with their machine pistols leisurely
slung over their shoulders; the foreboding watchtowers; the massive
cement abutments supporting the heavy steel barriers; the high barbed-
wire fences. An intimidating array. If these could succeed in instilling
timidity and fear into a person, the dictators would have little difficulty
in subjecting, controlling and exploiting him.

The first officer who approached me was very businesslike, asking
for my passport and visa. He walked slowly around the car and then told
me to drive forward to a large stone table and unload everything from
the inside of the car and the trunk. I saw other travelers already doing
the same, and opening all their suitcases. For me, that would be a major
undertaking. Three stern-faced customs officials stood by, and as soon as
I opened the trunk lid they looked inside and saw the carton filled with
one-pound bags of coffee. It seemed to particularly interest them, but to
bribe a customs official could prove to be disastrous. Yet there was nothing
against my saying, "If you would like one, help yourself."

They did. Each one took a pound and quickly stuck it under his coat.
I slowly started to take out my suitcases, the first one being the one with
my object lessons. By that time, I had become more relaxed and
encouraged. Being somewhat of an extrovert and nearly always ready for

a challenge, I thought to try to distract them from checking all my baggage, especially from going through my entire food supply.

I took out three different lengths of string and very "innocently" turned toward them, saying, "Have you ever seen this before?" I began to manipulate the strings so they ended up being the same length. The result surprised me nearly as much as it evidently did them. Their stern looks suddenly changed to child-like curiosity. Evidently forgetting their primary responsibilities, they excitedly called to some of their colleagues, "Look what this man can do!" and asked me to show it to the others also.

By that time, some of the other travelers, hearing the happy laughter of the guards and their expressions of surprise, came to see what was going on. Soon also some of the more distant soldiers came, still carrying their weapons.

While I was showing them another trick, someone called the head inspector, who now came running up, so I went through my routine once more. He asked if I could teach him how to do it, and realizing that I was now on the winning side, I took great pains to explain it to him. When he tried it, he came pretty close to succeeding. His men were smart enough to applaud and congratulate him. He beamed with pleasure, and for a moment I toyed with the idea of taking a picture of this most unusual gathering. I quickly changed my mind, remember the strictly enforced rule against using a camera at, or anywhere near, a border or military installation. Also, I didn't dare overdo a good thing lest someone should detect deceit in my behavior, with possibly very unpleasant consequences. They might have decided I was trying to cover up something I should not be taking across.

At last, the head inspector had to live up to his trusted position. He sent them all away, glanced into the window of the car and the trunk, asked quite perfunctorily where I was going, if I had anything to declare and about how much food I thought I had.

I told him I was going to visit friends, that I had nothing to declare and I really didn't know how much food I had, maybe 25 pounds or so. He told me to close the lid and motioned to one of his men, who stamped and returned my papers, raised the heavy barrier and waved me on! I could hardly believe it.

You can't imagine the great thrill and the relief to have passed a usually very vexing and frustrating border crossing without any difficulty. Here I was, even though in a land with an ideology so vastly different from mine, a language and customs completely unfamiliar, yet I was "on the road again."

The first thing I invariably did was thank my Lord and ask Him for guidance in this strange new land. The only familiar sights were the steering wheel and the dashboard. They had accompanied me from the time I had left my close Christian friends and gave me a certain amount of security while the scenes on the other side of the windshield were continually changing. The spiritual exercise of casting myself completely onto my Lord took on an entirely different meaning as I was *all alone,* far away from home and loved ones. How *in*sufficient I was.

The sights I never tired of seeing were old-fashioned rack wagons with huge loads of hay, drawn by horses or oxen. Often the wagons were filled with families, from grandparents to small grandchildren, but sometimes all young people, waving and shouting at me. Little children played beside the road. When I stopped, they came running up asking for a bon bon (the French international word for candy) or for gum.

Families oftentimes walked from one village to the next, the father carrying an old suitcase in each hand and shouldering a big knapsack. The mother struggled with a big bundle of clothes in the one hand, holding on to one of the smaller children with the other. The older ones walked behind, trying to keep away from the big noisy trucks that were passing them.

It was hot and dusty, no houses for miles around and a long way to the next community. Whenever I could, I stopped and took them along. On this trip, three or four was the most I could carry because my car was stuffed with so many things to "deliver to the saints." How I wish you could have heard the excitement of the children and seen the expressions on the faces of the parents as they tried to express their gratitude.

Often flocks of sheep took up the entire roadway. As soon as I stopped, my car was surrounded by the entire herd. I was engulfed in a sea of moving wool. The shepherd, his dog and the quiet countryside completed the picture of perfect peace and tranquility. It seemed I was no longer in a socialist country but in one like ours, a land the Lord has made, amidst the animals typifying people for whom He gave His life. I must confess, I had a great longing to remain and share my life and the message He had laid upon my heart.

Driving in Europe, even in its eastern countries, proved to be most nostalgic. It reminded me of the Europe I had left as a youth. I felt as though I had swallowed a time capsule instantly propelling me back 50-some years. Cobblestone streets made the signs *Langsam Fahren* (Drive Slowly) quite unnecessary. Wall-to-wall housing edged the streets, beautiful flower boxes adorned many windows, some windows with featherbeds partially hanging out for airing. In front of one house, a truck had dumped some coal and the people were busy shoveling it into buckets. Steep tile roofs graced the houses; smoking chimneys and chimney sweeps (sweepers) with their traditional black top-hats and long ladders completed the picture.

Housewives carried shopping bags, some rode their bicycles, others leaned on them, leisurely chatting with neighbors. Children trundled big wooden hoops down a sidewalk; farmers cut their grass and grain with a scythe, periodically stopping to rest and to sharpen their blades with a grindstone. Nobody seemed to be in a hurry.

I saw no familiar Chevys, Fords, Buicks or even Toyotas, but rather very cheaply built, noisy, smelly and old-fashioned looking cars with strange-sounding names: DACIA made in Romania; SKODA from Czechoslovakia; TRABANT and WARTBURG from East Germany; LADA, VOLGA and MOSKWITCH from the former Soviet Union. Some of them had a two-stroke engine like some motorcycles have, and that's what they sounded like.

Many were stranded at the side of the road in various stages of breakdowns, largely due to the use of a very poor grade of motor oil. Like so many other commodities, the good quality oil was appropriated by the government "for defense purposes." Also, since high grade oil is essential for the production of oil paint, most of the houses and installations remain unpainted, accounting for their drab, run-down appearance.

Not knowing all this, I had not taken any oil with me. After much searching I was able to locate two quarts of not only very high grade, but also very high-priced oil, imported from a capitalistic country. Amazingly, I didn't need it. I traveled over 9,000 km, and my dip stick still registered FULL. No doubt, its source and supplier was the Same One Who had sustained the oil for the poor widow at the time of Elijah.

Road maps, most of which were from AAA Club in Kansas City, were my constant companions. None of these showed the smaller towns I intended to visit. Strangely, there were no maps available in Romania, not even in the capital, Bucharest.

37

FRUSTRATED IN ROMANIA

ROMANIA WAS THE MOST TRYING, the most difficult and the most needy country of all those I visited. The U.S. Congress had denied Romania the Most Favored Nations trading status, considering it one of the worst violators of religious liberty in the world.

One pastor told me that after he had repeatedly been refused building material to renovate his church, he was unexpectedly approached by the Security Police. They told him that they had decided to grant him all the material he needed if he would cooperate with them.

Their request was not one of spying for them, but to merely inform them once or twice a month what was being preached from the pulpit, who the visiting speakers were and what they said, as well as what he would overhear others say concerning the government. He refused and thus never received the requested building material. Not only that, but he has been continually harassed since that time.

Another pastor, after having eventually been granted permission to build an addition to his church extended it nine inches beyond the official permit limit. His entire building was leveled to the ground.

This was my second visit to Romania. I again saw the effects of the energy crunch. The homes I visited were very poorly lit. While I was talking with a Christian brother on the street in front of a large housing complex, he called up to his wife, hanging up laundry on the third floor balcony, to remind her not to forget to fill up all the containers with water. Then he turned to me and said, "You know, it will soon be five o'clock and then all the electricity, including that to our pump, will be turned off."

Wherever I went, things were in utter disrepair. Nothing was being fixed, whether light switches, faucets or door locks. In the hotel where I stayed the desk clerk, after assigning me to my room, said, "Simply pull the door open just before you come even with the third floor, which you can see through the side panel and the elevator will stop."

After a few tries, which included the second floor and a half and the third floor minus one-fourth, I came close enough to be able to step up. My next problem was in trying to unlock the door to my room. I couldn't do it regardless of how hard I tried.

I was wondering what the key to this mystery might be and went back down, barely stopping before I reached the cellar, and asked the desk clerk how to handle the door. (The puns came naturally).

He went back up with me and we both climbed out together. He too tried unsuccessfully and then gave me a room on the fourth floor. I made it the first try. The toilet had much in common with the others I saw. The seat was fashioned somewhat like the upper part of a thin plastic shell, and by reason of its fragile material and lack of reinforcement was cracked in several places. One's weight would tend to widen these crevices, so that upon arising (or trying to do so) one would feel strangely and painfully restrained. The water canister suspended above (and often it was that, rather than fastened) leaked. I would then find myself unceremoniously sprinkled, much against my religious conviction!

Heat, or rather the absence of such, was another problem. In offices and apartments the temperature rarely rose above 50 degrees.

In that country there is (or was) a waiting list from 15 to 20 *years* for new cars. Available used cars are much more expensive than new ones, and replacement parts are virtually non-existent. Yet one can buy any American or Western European car if one can pay with Western currency.

There is/was also a thriving — but very expensive — Black Market. If a person is a land owner he receives no coupons for meat. Otherwise, he gets five pounds per month. Even that is seldom, for there is rarely any to be had, *unless he can pay with Western currency.* Then, strangely, there is no limit! The same goes for fruit and dairy products. There really is an abundance, but it is for export only. *Unless you pay with Western money.*

I was told that Nicolae Ceausescu (the nation's ruler at that time) had once been a shoe cobbler who had brought food to the Communists when they had been imprisoned years before. After they came into power, they rewarded him by giving him the highest office in the country. At the time of my visit in 1987, he had held that position for 22 years. He had made Romania the poorest and most repressive member of the socialist bloc. Whenever he visited a locality, meat, vegetables and fruit, including oranges and cheeses, which the people otherwise would never get to see, suddenly appeared in the shops and at the marketplaces, disappearing just as rapidly when he left.

From the very outset, I had been asked to speak at more churches, home Bible studies and children's meetings than I thought my strength would allow. Yet the more I poured out my heart to these spiritually starved people, the more places were found for me to minister. When I told them I had planned for only nine days in the country (for which I had to exchange ten U.S. dollars per day), they begged me repeatedly to extend my visa. I finally gave in and agreed to apply for another ten days. To get an extension, I had to go from Faragas (where I was then) to Bucharest, around 300 km. Due to other commitments, I had to go as soon as possible, so I left the next morning at four o'clock.

Navigating through the hustling, bustling traffic of the teaming metropolis that was Bucharest was unsettling, to say the least. It was a more frustrating experience than I encountered in any of the other capital cities in Eastern or Western Europe, or even in the Orient. By the time I found a parking place I was exhausted. I squeezed into half a parking space, the front end of the car extending over the sidewalk.

I set out to call the Christian family I had met when I was there before, but none of the public telephones was in working order. I had never seen public telephones in such deplorable condition. The booths were filthy, the walls scratched up and the phone boxes partially bent out of shape as though someone had tried to tear them off the walls. Each receiver was anchored to the box with a massive chain. Holding it would certain discourage a caller from talking very long.

I began my odyssey to obtain a visa extension. I thought the American Embassy would be a good place to inquire about the procedure and it wasn't too far to walk. The iron-fenced compound was guarded by Romanian Militia who, after sufficiently scrutinizing my passport, opened the electrically operated gate.

Once inside, I was frisked by an American Marine guard and asked to fill out a questionnaire: passport number, place of birth, nationality, home resident, purpose of visit; then told to have a seat. And all I wanted was to know where to get a visa extension! We in America have little appreciation for the complexities and frustrations the Eastern Europeans are subjected to in completing what is, to us, a simple task.

After I had duly awaited my turn, I was ushered to a window where a lady asked me what she could do for me. When I told her, she gave me a mimeographed map showing where all I would have to go, beginning with a place at which I was to exchange my money ($100 — for ten days). Once there I was told that they didn't accept Traveler's Checks. "Try the bank down the street."

The lady at that bank took my checks, looked at them and said: "Just a moment," talked to the manager, than gave them back to me, saying: "I'm sorry, we are not familiar with these that have AAA printed on them. Why don't you try our main bank?"

(No doubt, the "Triple A" Auto Club, in making them available to its members without charge, had them printed in this way for advertising purposes.)

Down to the main bank I went. Strangely, there was no waiting line, but none of the five ladies idly sitting there paid any attention to me. I waved my checks at them. Ever so slowly, one of them moved in my direction. I stuck my checks out at her before she could walk past.

She reached under the counter, matter-of-factly pulled out and laid in front of me a lengthy form, starting again with passport number, place of birth and down the line. I felt like saying, "Look lady, I'm NOT running for Congress. I just want to exchange some money." But I kept nice and quiet and proceeded with the task.

When I had finally finished (again), she told me to wait, for it would take a while. So I *whiled* away my time *while* waiting for a *while*. After waiting a very long *while,* not knowing exactly by what standard a Romanian *while* was being measured, I went back to ask if she had forgotten about me. She said my request was being processed and it would take a *while* longer. I didn't ask for a definition, nor if it was an extension of the former *while* or the beginning of a new one.

Finally, I was called. Instead of receiving my money, she gave me a little yellow disk with a number on it. "Wait over there." She pointed to a row of benches which looked like those in a classroom. I joined about 20 other disk-holders who were watching for their numbers to light up above the first of the five windows at the far end of the hall. The other four windows remained unoccupied and the "lights" above them unlit. I knew that the numbers would have to light up about 20 times before I could expect my number in lights, so I just remained seated for a *while* longer. I was well rested and ready for my next adventure when I finally saw the light.

Now at last, with cash in hand, I was well on my way (I thought) and headed down the street.

A person might have been embarrassed if he had followed me through the crowds as I tried to find my way to the next place on my not-too-detailed map. I would periodically stop someone, shove my map under his nose while pointing to the spot marked with a circle. Then I'd give him a questioning look, shrugging my shoulders and making an outward motion with my hands, palms up, thus trying to say in body language, "I don't know where this is, do you?" Frequently the reply would be a similar gesture. It must have been amusing to see two people standing there, shrugging their shoulders at each other.

Sometimes I'd receive a lengthy dissertation, at which I'd nod my head as though I understood. I'd try to remember in which direction and sequence the arm was extended and the hand was pointing. Time after time, I arrived at what I thought was my next destination, only to be told that my request would be handled in a different government office. Each time, my papers were examined by the police. They invariably stood guard in front of each building entrance. Large numbers of people were always standing in line, crowding the hallways or milling around within the building compound. None of them could tell me where to go.

At last, I came across a guard who directed me to what appeared to be a private dwelling. It had evidently been taken over by the government, and it took some inner persuasion for me to go in. I came to a wooden winding staircase with a sign pointing up.

The steps creaked as I slowly dragged myself up to the second floor. There, right in front of me, was a small room with a partition in the middle. Two openings were cut for "windows." Behind them stood two men; only three people ahead of me. When it was my turn to inquire, I could hardly believe my ears. This was indeed *the* place which would issue my extension. They asked for my passport and told me the issuing fee was 150 *lei,* about $12. As I began to count it out, the man said he couldn't accept cash. It would have to be paid by a voucher, obtainable at a nearby bank. He gave me an address about 15 to 20 minutes walking distance.

By that time, my mind had pretty much slipped into neutral, or beyond. I headed for the bank, moving more mechanically than consciously, showing my slip to soldiers and policemen standing guard at various corners.

At the bank at last, I automatically joined the line in front of the only window where people were being waited on. There were two additional windows with clerks on duty (?), visiting with each other and frequently engaging the one behind "my" window in their discussion. I wondered if the conversation centered on the great virtues of a socialist society.

By the time it was my turn in front of the window, it had become coffee break time behind it. The line moved over to the next window, during which I lost my place. Eventually I did get my voucher, and eventually also my long-sought extension.

I began backtracking to my hotel. After a block or two, I felt a sudden, excruciating blow to my chest. I could hardly breathe. Sweating profusely, I leaned against one of the buildings, unwilling to believe that anything like this, whatever it was, could happen to me. I also had pain in my left shoulder and arm, so I was pretty sure it was either a heart attack or something very close to it.

That was September 17, 1987. A day to remember!

After the pain had subsided to a degree, I managed to get to a cafeteria where I ate what I saw others eating. Evidently their stomachs were differently constituted, conditioned or constructed than mine. I became violently ill, but finally managed to drive to the home of my Christian friends. Fortunately they were at home. They gave me some medicine to soothe my stomach and said it would quiet my heart also. Then they saw me safely to my hotel. There I went on my knees by my bed, before the Lord, pleading for strength to go on.

When I went back to my car the next morning, I realized I had left my key in the ignition. All the car doors were locked and the windows tightly closed. The night before I had left my zipper case containing my money and other valuables, including my extra keys, with my friends for safekeeping. So when the daughter came by bus to my hotel as we had arranged, we went by taxi back to her home. There we realized I had put the zipper case into the trunk of my car as well. Now everything was securely locked up.

We called the father at work. He came with wire, pliers, screwdriver and whatever else he thought might be useful to open my door. In front of the hotel, scores of people watched us "breaking in" to the foreigner's car. The crowd offered plenty of advice, and we were eventually able to remove a rear window panel, reach in and unlock a door. After that we were able to find a shop which could put the window back in.

I still had frequent chest pains, so the father offered to ride along to Constanta, my next destination, a 280-km trip farther east, at the Black Sea. His daughter, who spoke English fluently as well as Romanian, came along to interpret.

When I arrived, I called a Christian brother, who said he was expecting me and to come right over. When I got to his place , he was gone. The wife, who couldn't speak German as he did, had a hard time explaining his absence. After about an hour, he returned. Breathless and triumphant, he held up four chicken feet and four scrawny chicken wings, saying he had heard there was chicken being sold down the street. He had hurried down and after standing in line for over an hour, he was "still able to get some."

In their country, soldiers guarded potato fields at night to keep people from stealing them. In some areas farmers sold their potatoes one by one. Yet there, in some areas of Romania, with mere subsistence a daily struggle, I found the greatest desire for spiritual nourishment. It was there also that I enjoyed that most selfless hospitality.

Those beloved folks would share what little they had and would often make great effort to find difficult-to-obtain ingredients so they could prepare something extra special, such as a pie or some fruit cobbler.

In Constanta, I spoke to a packed church. But the most wonderful experience there was the thrill of leading a teen-aged Romanian girl to the Lord. She had come to visit in the home where I stayed, being distantly related to my host. Though we needed to converse through one who spoke both languages, her transformation was genuine and so was the joy, yes, and even the tears. I recalled it was said of the Lord, he "must needs go through Samaria ... (John 3:3). I had wondered why I felt I had to travel that far, almost as far eastward as I could go, and now I knew.

I headed south a short way, along the coast of the Black Sea toward Bulgaria. For a while I toyed with the idea of covering the 500-plus km across it and be in Istanbul, at the doorstep of Asia proper. Yet in my heart, I felt otherwise. I knew our Lord had set the boundary and I was to return.

The brother who had gone after the chicken wings was so concerned about my health that he insisted on riding back with me from Constanta. At Bucharest, we dropped off the father-daughter team and went on another 300 km or so to Faragas. From there, another Christian brother took over. He drove my car all the way back to Oradea, near the Hungarian border, a distance of nearly 400 km. I was more concerned about these men going so far out of their way for me than about my own physical condition.

At one place we stopped to visit a pastor friend. Hearing of my problem, this precious saint tried calling every doctor in town. He sought help for me without success, until at least he remembered an acquaintance whose neighbor was a doctor working in a local hospital.

Arrangements are not as easily made there as they are here in America, especially for "Western capitalist foreigners." It was nearly midnight before I was unobtrusively whisked off to the hospital for an electrocardiogram. Upon arrival, I waited anxiously for those in charge to grant me clearance. I was thoroughly looked over and discussed, and I didn't understand one word. The pastor and two friends interpreted for me and put me at ease.

Finally they took me to a room and had me lie down on a wooden table covered with a brown rubber sheet. A nurse tied two itchy strings around my chest. From a nail in the wall beside me, she unhooked four wires, on the ends of which were soldered four square pieces of tin. These she slid under the strings at four places. I heard the buzz of a funny-looking box beside me; and when the result had been inspected, they said I had angina pectoris, because of extreme emotional stress or possibly from overeating. I was sure it wasn't the latter.

My friends suggested I return home by the shortest possible route, leaving my car and flying from the nearest international airport. But my pains were only sporadic, and I now had an ample supply of Romanian nitroglycerin. I decided to keep on going — as it turned out, 53 more days, 5,000 more kilometers, spending nights in 31 different places.

I did not, however, continue on in Romania to the many places I had been invited. Instead, I headed for Hungary. I needed to go through there anyway to get to the West, unless I went through Russia, or south through Yugoslavia, for which I had no visa.

In Ziliz, Hungary, I was again asked to extend my stay, also in Hanusovice, Czechoslovakia, where for each additional day I would have had to exchange $26.–. If I had been well, I surely would have considered it as I would have in many of the other places where I had been invited to extend my stay. Then there would have been no telling when I would have returned home, for there are never-ending opportunities to proclaim God's Word in the East.

38

I VISIT AUSCHWITZ

WHILE ON MY WAY THROUGH POLAND, I stayed in the home of a pastor who invited me to visit one of the most infamous and inhuman, if not one of the most barbaric, concentration camps of the Hitler era: Auschwitz.

It was the one-time Reichsführer SS Heinrich Himmler who, on April 27, 1940, had given the order to establish the Auschwitz concentration camp, Oswiencim in Polish, named after the small village nearby.

The first prisoners sent there were Poles, Soviet prisoners of war, political prisoners and members of the resistance. From 1942 Auschwitz was transformed into the biggest center for the mass extermination of European Jews. Their names ceased to exist, and they were known only by the numbers tattooed on their left arm. The sanitary conditions were deplorable. Lice, because clothes could not be washed, hunger, rats and insects brought on malaria and other epidemics resulting in hundreds of agonizing deaths.

Even while still in Germany, we heard reports about people who had been hauled off, even in the middle of the night, to early concentration camps where forced labor, beatings, starvation and not infrequently ensuing agonizing death were the order of the day. These reports struck horror and indescribable fear to our hearts, causing some of our friends to early commit suicide at the very dread of possibly being sent there. At Auschwitz there were no established rules as in other camps; permitted behavior was taught with the help of a stick. Auschwitz became the symbol for the slaughter in all the camps because of the intensity of the fury let loose there, primarily against the Jews. Here it was that millions of Jews were gassed, shot, beaten, starved to death or killed by phenol injection, their bodies burned or buried like so much garbage.

Now it was Saturday, October 31, 1987. I had spent the previous night in the home of a Christian family. How sick I was! My stomach pain as well as my heart had gotten me up various times during the night. Repeated doses of nitroglycerin did not eliminate my misery. Perhaps in my subconsciousness I had an instinctive dread of what I was about to see and hear.

I was startled by the presence of many touring busses and groups of visitors from all over Europe. Guides met us, ready to tell the story and answer questions. Above the foreboding iron gate were the deceptive words, *Arbeit Macht Frei,* "Labor liberates." I saw in my mind's eye the thousands of my people, including some who had been my close friends and relatives. As I soon learned from the guides, the captives were told by their captors that the only way they could ever hope to leave this place would be by the smoking chimneys of the crematoria.

At an International Monument just inside the camp, on plaques written in perhaps 15 languages, I read: *Four million people suffered and died here at the hands of the Nazi murderers between the years 1940 and 1945.* At various places throughout the rest of the camp, pictures and displays with texts in Polish, German, English and French offered mute but graphic evidence of the unthinkable horrors of those days.

Faces were solemn and voices were hushed. Visitors stared, expressions bordering on unbelief. A heavy pall lay over the entire encampment. As I heard and read the stories that day, a question repeatedly pierced my spirit: why had my Lord saved me from being one of the four million who had perished here?

The rows upon rows of weathered-brick buildings had, before Hitler's invasion of Poland, been the barracks of the Polish Army. Under the Nazis, SS (Storm Squadron) men in the sentry towers had kept a round-the-clock vigil over the entire area. Throughout the nights, powerful searchlights had continuously probed the double row of electrified barbed-wire fences which still enclosed the camp.

I stood at the ramp where the cattle cars, jammed with their human cargo, had been unloaded. Many arrived already dead, suffocated because they had been packed in so tightly they couldn't breathe. They had often been without food or water for as long as two weeks, some of them coming from Norway, France or Italy, and being re-routed or held on sidings to let wartime priority trains go through.

A Nazi officer would check each "shipment." Those he deemed fit to work would be sent to the right. Those who were not, usually old men, old women and children, except for twins, were sent to the left. (Twins were "rescued" by Dr. Josef Mengele, doomed to participate in his diabolical genetic experiments to develop a "pure" race.) Those accounted unfit, an average of 70-80 percent, sometimes as high as 90 percent of the shipment, were immediately surrounded by SS men, told they were going to the showers and for disinfection, but marched off to the gas chambers.

Each of these chambers could hold 1,500 to 2,000 people. I climbed onto the roof of one and lifted off the square wooden lid from one of the openings. It was through this hole that *Cyclon B* pellets were dropped into a bucket of acid, generating the lethal gas used in exterminating the prisoners. Nearly fifty years later, just the thought of that gas made my own breathing difficult.

The belongings of the murdered were sorted and sent to the Third Reich for use by the WEHRMACHT (Army) and the civilian population. The SS did not even stop short of desecrating the bodies of the murdered victims. Searching for gold, they broke out teeth and cut off fingers with rings. Women's hair was cut off and recycled for cloth and mattresses. After being ground up in special bone mills, human bones (even ashes) were used for fertilizer.

Removing the bodies from the gas chambers to the crematoria where they were burned was done chiefly by Jewish prisoners of the countries from which the current transport had arrived. They were called *Todeskandidaten,* candidates marked for death. That meant they would live only so long as they were needed to carry out their task. To isolate them from the other prisoners, they were quartered separately and made to sleep in their clothes with their hands and feet chained. In the event of refusal to carry out this work, they were immediately put to death. (This happened to 435 Greek Jews who, because of their refusal, were sent to the gas chambers on July 22, 1944.) Bending down to look into one of the ovens, I tried to visualize the bodies being shoved mercilessly into them, but my mind refused, unable to comprehend the hideousness of this thing.

Sometimes the crematoria could not keep up with the vast numbers of bodies that had been gassed. Bodies were then burned on pyres with layers of 2,000 corpses each alternated with layers of kindling. The fire was kept burning by pouring waste products of refined petroleum or methanol on the bodies, as well as by the fat of the burning bodies.

To be sent into the camp upon arrival at Auschwitz instead directly into the gas chamber was a cruel twist of fate. It would have been more merciful in the long run to be gassed right away. At four a.m., the block warden would rush into the room and, with shouting and beatings, drive everyone outside for roll call regardless of the weather. Breakfast consisted of half a liter of bitter liquid they called coffee.

In columns of tens, the captives were marched off for 12 hours of labor without any time to rest. SS guards drove prisoners relentlessly with shouts and beatings. The SS dogs, specially trained to attack people and capable of causing serious injury with their fangs, were the terror of the inmates, especially of the women.

Some SS guards, desiring a few days' leave, frequently ordered a prisoner to go beyond the guarded perimeter. Claiming the prisoner was trying to escape the guard would shoot him down.

Daily time at forced labor was measured by the number of those killed. Work stopped only once for a "meal" consisting of soup often made with rotten vegetables. Returning to camp, the crews (prisoners) carried, dragged, wheeled in barrows or pulled in carriages any murdered fellow prisoners and those who had been injured by clubs or dogs. Inmates burdened one day with the bodies of their fellow sufferers knew that the next day might be their last and that their colleagues would be bringing them back for roll call.

During roll call, everyone, we were told, had to be accounted for. The actual number present, living or dead, had to agree with the records. Another function of roll call was the execution by hanging of anyone who had tried to escape, especially if it was a bold or a renowned try. These executions were aimed at terrorizing the prisoners, to convince them of the senselessness of any attempt to escape. Two mobile gallows were kept in the courtyard of Block 11. The yard between Block 10 and Block 11 was notorious as the place of execution, or the "wall of death." The wall, painted black, was built of wood and insulating board. At the foot of this wall, sand was sprinkled to soak up the blood of the victims, who were always shot naked, regardless of the season of the year. A van took the still-bleeding bodies to the crematorium, leaving trickles of blood as it went.

As I looked at the execution wall in the courtyard of Block 11, I imagined myself standing there before the SS guards. In my heart I sensed the burst of gunfire and wondered what might have been the last thoughts of the victims. Indeed, what would I have thought and felt just before being abruptly ushered into eternity?

The executions were only a small part of the horror. They, like the gas chambers, were terminal, putting an end to the torture of the victims. Beatings were another story. The right to beat a prisoner was enjoyed by every SS man and by every prisoner to whom a specific function was entrusted, from the camp senior to the block hairdresser. Beatings were performed with clubs, rifle butts, pipes or whips and occurred spontaneously, spur of the moment, relentlessly, without warning, 24 hours a day.

Attending to physical needs at the wrong time resulted in blows from clubs or rifle butts. So did trying to trade a gold tooth for a piece of bread. At night, the inmates often awoke to the sound of sharp rifle fire aimed at those who could no longer endure the terror and had tried to throw themselves against the electrified wires to commit suicide.

Flogging was an "official" punishment administered with a stick or a whip, not to exceed 25 strokes at a time. In actuality, it depended on the mood of the supervisor. Inmates were strapped to the whipping block, flogged and released, usually unconscious. They would receive the remaining 25 strokes at a later time, in some cases all at once. Our guide explained that the inmates had to count aloud each stroke as it descended.

If the victim made a mistake, the strokes began all over again. Most blows were aimed at the kidneys, resulting in agonizing death.

Feeling unworthy, I touched the whipping block, the instrument of many of my kinsmen's most excruciating sufferings and death. It was like touching something sacred.

A source of particular horror in the camp was execution by starvation. I saw the cell in which inmates had been entombed, awaiting this slow, torturous death. To avenge the escape of a prisoner, the camp commandant would, during roll call, choose ten or more prisoners at random. These were drawn from the block in which the escapee had lived or from the *Komando* in which he had labored. These ten would be locked in one of the cells of the basement of Block 11. Receiving nothing to eat or drink, they would suffer an excruciating death in the course of a few days, perhaps a fortnight.

Ten men for every one who had escaped! I had to prevent my mind from picturing their dying. I was afraid I would lose my mental balance.

Camp inmates who became too ill to work were initially sent to the euthanasia center in another town. Later, a continuance of this action was the liquidation of the sick at the camp itself by phenol injections through the heart. I saw the room where these injections were given. Human language has no words to help me describe the hideousness of that crime. I felt as though the needle was piercing my own heart.

The SS medical tams made the most horrifying contribution to the genocide operation — the so-called medical tests. They used prisoners to test effects of liquid war gases, mustard and phosgene, when applied to the body. Symptoms were recorded and photographed. Prisoners died in progressively increasing agony.

Tests were carried out over a period of years and ranged from Rasher's low-pressure, high-altitude experiments and his study of the effects of freezing parts of the human body to Mengele's ghastly "twin experiments." Any SS doctor of reasonable authority could order whatever human samples he desired.

By the end of 1944, as the guns of the Russian front drew closer, the prisoners who were considered "the most dangerous witnesses" were evacuated first, followed by another group of 60,000 a few days thereafter. Dragging themselves more than walking under the ever-ready guns of the S.S., those who fell behind were mercilessly gunned down on the spot. The entire evacuation route was marked with the bodies of the slaughtered.

Left behind in the camp were those too sick and too weak to walk. They had been scheduled to be liquidated, but time had run out for the executioners. Auschwitz was liberated on January 27, 1945, by the 60th Army of the First Ukrainian Front.

If there is such a thing as part of one's self dying when seeing such a place, then that is what happened to me when I visited Auschwitz. I don't believe there are any words in any human vernacular to begin to describe the extent of the inhuman atrocities committed there. And had it not been for the foresight and the forethought of my dear parents and for the kindness of Mother's dear cousin and her husband, the Berkowitz family of Kansas City who enabled my brother and me to come to America just in time, we would both unquestionably have perished in a concentration camp.

While I can never forget to thank them for all that they did for us, my praise and thanksgiving does foremost belong to my Heavenly Father, who, no doubt, had His Hand upon me even then. Wherefore I can do nothing else but to serve Him the best I know, for the rest of my days here on earth.

39

THE ROAD BACK

RETURNING FROM AUSCHWITZ, I passed a group of young men and women in colorful traditional Polish garments. They were grouped on the steps of a church, serenading a newly married couple. The men were wearing red velvet hats, squared at the top and each with a feather sticking up. The girls were dressed in white embroidered blouses with high frilly collars and puffed sleeves; white aprons covered their colorful skirts.

This was a welcome counterbalance to the melancholy gloom I had felt at Auschwitz. Here was love, joy and hope for a happy future. I got out of the car, mingled with the merry crowd and began shooting pictures with my video camera. Though they all looked at me, perhaps wondering who I was and where I came form, no one asked me any questions. I don't know what or how I would have answered if they had.

Sometimes taking pictures was a delicate undertaking. On our way to the concentration camp, the pastor with me had stopped at a general produce store. I wanted to take some pictures, and he asked the cashier who referred us to the manager, a rather stout woman. She asked the purpose of my pictures. My friend told her I was from the West where it is believed there is a great lack of basic nourishment in Poland. He said I was surprised at the abundance and variety even of meats and canned goods. She was elated and gave me absolute freedom to photograph anything I wished. I sensed, however, that some of the employees and even some of the customers were not as much in favor of it.

As I was looking through the viewfinder, I noticed a sales clerk at the meat counter who was waiting on a policeman. The clerk was calling his attention to what I was doing. Seeing his angry look, I immediately stopped and quickly headed for the door and to our car. He caught up with me before I got there, grabbed my camera from me and angrily demanded what right I had to take pictures there. (At least, that's what I understood him to say.)

My pastor friend said, "Let me handle this. I know how to do it." He fearlessly confronted the policeman saying, "I'd like to know by what authority you can so rudely take a camera away from such a peaceful visitor? There are no signs prohibiting picture taking." He added that we had specific permission from the proprietor to do so.

The policeman appeared startled. Trying to save face and still holding my camera, he asked us to follow him back into the store to see the manager. When she told him she had indeed given us permission, he looked satisfied. Then, using that little bit of prestige left to him, he asked to see my passport. Opening it, he pulled out the two long accordion-type extension pages, with the various stamps and seals accumulated through the years of traveling. He became confused and didn't know where to look. He nodded and handed it back to me, together with my camera, mumbling something that sounded like an apology. He stuck out his hand, both of us shook hands with him, and that was the end of it.

I drove on through Poland to the cities of Ciescyn, Biasco Biala and Jelenia Gora, and I even learned to pronounce them. I was lovingly received by brothers and sisters in Christ, who took me to meet others of their fellowship. Though we had trouble understanding each other linguistically, we had no problem communicating *heart*ily. The miracle of *blood relationship* in various countries, regardless of language, has to be experienced; words cannot adequately describe it.

I was now in western Poland near the border city of Görlitz, at the Neisse River which forms the natural border between Poland and East Germany. Since both countries were members of the "Eastern Bloc," the border was comparatively lightly guarded. The contents of my trunk were hardly looked at, the same as when I was there the year before. I was again pleasantly surprised at the courtesy of the customs officials in comparison to those on the borders between East Germany and the West.

My German had come in handy during my travels in the Eastern Bloc countries, but now that I was in East Germany, I reveled in the fact I was "back home" in language on a regular basis. I stayed with members of a local congregation in Görlitz, spoke there and showed object lessons to young and old. I went with a group of very fundamental churches — and there really are such — to a special outing. I was so sick I spent the time doubled up in the back seat of a pastor's car.

Next day, the pastor's wife, a nurse, went with me to a doctor in her hospital. The equipment for the EKG certainly was superior to that in Romania, but I was still wondering why an electrocardiogram, though spelled with a "c," is called an E K G, even in German.

The doctor told me that thus far only the vessels leading to the heart were causing the problem and that the heart itself had not yet been affected. The pastor's wife suggested, "Why don't you give him a pound of coffee for his kindness, rather than money." Was he ever overjoyed!

Now that I felt somewhat at ease concerning my heart, I went on to speak to student nurses at Leipzig, from where they called their sister hospital in Halle, and I went there as well. On the way, I stopped off at places where I had been on former trips, including Sangerhausen, the very first place in East Germany I had visited with the Trombone Team in 1983.

I also went to see some of the relatives whom people in West Germany and America had asked me to look up. I always liked that particularly well as it gave me a legitimate entrance into homes and family situations. It was natural to talk about my background and why I was on this journey.

I drove west all the way across East Germany and then north within a few kilometers of the Baltic Sea, and finally into the Federal Republic of West Germany.

Leaving East Germany proved to be more hectic in many ways than entering it. The authorities were on edge about Fluchtversuche, literally escape tries, and were always on guard. For a mile or so before the actual border both sides of the road were lined with high barbed-wire fences. The porcelain insulators were reminders that the wires were electrically charged. Warning signs told the exact distance before the border and also the distance to the last "free," meaning *unchecked* exit.

After a few hundred yards I came to the advance control point. A preliminary check of my papers was made to ascertain that I had a legitimate reason for being within the restricted zone. Had I not had these papers, I would have been suspected of trying to flee the country and be immediately arrested. Those who live within that zone must carry special identification cards. For security reasons, these are issued anew every few weeks and are continually checked by patrolling border guards.

I neared the second flashing red warning light and a sign: Halt! Grenze! (Stop! Border!) *Do not proceed beyond this point unless signaled to do so!* There was a guard talking to the driver in the car just ahead of me. Expecting to momentarily be next, I (American style) let my car inch slowly forward. The guard immediately barked at me: "Don't you know RED when you see it? Do you generally go through RED traffic signals? BACK, TO WHERE YOU BELONG!"

When it was my turn and my papers had been sufficiently checked, I was directed to proceed to the inspection ramp. There again my passport was taken. When the guard came back with it, he went inside the car, pounded on the seat cushions and on the backs of the rear seats. He told me to open the hood, the trunk and the gas tank cap. Having looked at the engine, he pushed the baggage around in the trunk so he could inspect every part of it. He stuck a flexible rod into the gas tank as far as it would go. After all, I might have concealed a person in a reconstructed tank. Then he took a small long-handled, tilted mirror on wheels with lights on both sides and pushed it at different places under my car. I was tempted to ask what he was looking for, or whether he had lost a coat button. But everyone knows that guards are the undisputed master, at least they were at that time. Every traveler was really at their mercy, so I kept my attempts at humor to myself and just looked completely blank until it was all over.

After all that, there was one more stop. The guard looked at me and back at my passport photo. He said, in German, "Guess you didn't have a beard when this was taken." Then he disappeared with my passport. I shall always wonder what they do with it during all the time they take. Sometimes I wondered if they would really return it.

When he finally came back with it, he leaned far into my car window, looked at my small coat pocket and said (and these were his exact words): "Sie haben da so einen schönen Kugelschreiber, darf ich den haben?" (You have there such a nice ball-point pen. May I have it?")

I was astonished at his forwardness. Thus far no border guard had ever asked me for anything. I'm pretty sure it is strictly against the rules, but I wasn't about to ask him of it. That pen was an advertising pen, given me by my brother-in-law, but it wrote extremely well so I offered him another one from my glove compartment. He said, "NO! I'd like to have that one!"

Whether intentionally or not, he was holding my passport out toward me as though to say, "Do you want to have it back or not?" So there is now an American ball-point pen, advertising a Kansas Oil Transport Company, adorning the gray-green uniform of an East German border guard. Or maybe just his inside pocket.

His parting words to me were, "Danke schön" and "Auf Wiedersehen," and as I was driving off he called out, "Fahren sie vorsichtig" (Drive carefully).

40

RUSSIA

WITH THE GUARD'S farewell words ringing in my ears, I drove carefully, as he had admonished me, straight south, toward Herford and Bielefeld. I was still having bouts with my heart and, in retrospect, even though I felt somewhat better at times, I probably should not have tackled this next venture.

I had been put in touch with the director of a mission with a far-reaching ministry behind the Iron Curtain. It had always been my dream to one day preach in Russia, especially since my wife's ancestors came from there. When I told my desire to the director, he leaned back in his chair and asked me to tell him something about myself — my upbringing, salvation, mission board, mission field and my specific ministry there.

After a while, he asked a question I had not anticipated. "If I should help you to go to the Soviet Union, will you contribute anything worthwhile to offset the possibility of creating problems, not for yourself but for the believers you will visit, just by your being there?" Slowly he added, "The believers in the Soviet Union are very fearful of a visit from a foreigner if they do now know his background and the purpose of his visit."

I didn't know what to say right away. But after I told him of some of my travel in socialist countries and my experiences and ministry there, I seemed to have gained his confidence.

He told me of a mixed group of about 12 believers, German Mennonites born and raised in Russia. Fluent in both Russian and in German, they had been repatriated and now made their homes in Germany. They were going back to Russia to visit relatives and friends; I would be the only American among them. Everything would be arranged through a certain travel agency, even the obtaining of my visa. All I would have to do is meet them at the airport at the appointed day and hour. In the hotel of our final destination I would meet a person called "Jason"; he would be my guide.

I asked how "Jason" would be notified and how I would know him. The mission director just gave me a warm, reassuring smile. I had no difficulty finding those repatriated brothers and sisters in Christ at the Frankfurt airport. We flew to Moscow, and there began an ordeal.

Travel here in the Untied States is so uncomplicated and unrestricted that we can scarcely comprehend the rigorous transactions required when traveling abroad, especially as it once was in Eastern Bloc countries. When I had arrived in West Germany, they barely glanced at the cover of my American passport and waved me through to customs, where no one really looked at my baggage. Here, in great contrast, I first had to wait in a long processing line and then go through passport control and customs. Altogether it took nearly one and one-half hours from the time we arrived in Moscow. (I have since learned that international travelers are told, when booking flights to Moscow, to allow six hours between their incoming flight and their outgoing one.) Not only were all the contents of my bags thoroughly inspected, but every bit of my German, as well as my American money, was counted and recorded, even my traveler's checks and all my loose change.

The flight from Frankfurt to Moscow had taken three hours, crossing two time zones. It was about eight p.m. when we arrived and three degrees below zero centigrade (18 degrees F). Though I was feeling rather weak, I was thrilled to be in what I called "my last frontier," the last of the six socialist countries I visited on this trip.

I was the first of our group to clear customs, and I found myself in the huge arrival hall of the largest of Moscow's airports — there are five or six of them in that city! What a conglomeration of the world's populace, languages, outfits and smells. I went to one of the somewhat official-looking persons and inquired about our guide. He asked to see my travel documents and soon came back with a guide I will call "Galina," a girl with dark blond hair and a pleasant smile. She was probably in her late 20s. I saw other Intourist guides being assigned to their respective groups, which they had to accompany wherever they went until their return to Moscow to depart the country.

Galina was multilingual, as they all must be. She spoke perfect German and Spanish and, of course, Russian, but only a few words of English. While we were waiting for the rest of the group, I asked her about her family, how long she had been working as an interpreter and guide, about her experiences with other visitors and her plans for the future.

She said she thoroughly enjoyed her work, but that she didn't like to be away so much from her husband and her daughter. Then she asked me about my family, my travel and my occupation. That gave me the opportunity I had been looking for to tell her about having lived in the Orient and the reason for it. She listened very attentively and helped me with exchanging my money and buying postcards. Throughout our time together, I had other occasions to speak to her about the things closest to my heart: the gospel of our Lord — what Christ has done to save us from our sin. She was convinced, however, that Socialism was the only religion needed to solve all the world's problems.

It was well past nine o'clock when all the group got through customs and Galina took us to our "private" bus. While most of my travel companions were speaking to her (in Russian), I gazed at Moscow's wide boulevards and the rows upon rows of high-rise buildings. After an hour or so, we arrived at a second-class Intourist hotel, were ushered into an empty dining room and served rice with boiled chicken, dark wholesome bread, half a boiled egg with a dip of delicious black caviar (a Russian specialty), cake and tea. It was all good, but I was still hungry when we were finished. Then back to our bus for another hour's ride through snowy, slick, very wide and nearly deserted avenues to another airport.

It was past midnight when we arrived there. Guards were patrolling the huge entrance gate. One of them came into the bus to look us over, talked to Galina and left to open the gate, or so I thought. But we just sat and waited. The others waited patiently, seemingly familiar with this custom which had become an intrinsic or inherent part of their culture. I ventured to ask Galina why the delay. With an understanding smile, she explained that the responsible Intourist official would have to be informed of our arrival so we could be cleared. (After three months of traveling in the Eastern Block, I should have already learned that much!) During all this time, the heater of our bus was having a hard time combatting the outside temperature.

At last a female official arrived. The two big wings of the gate swung ceremoniously open, and we drove to a small, unpainted and unfriendly-looking building at the far end of a huge airfield. There, in a barren makeshift waiting room, our papers were again checked, our baggage weighed, and we waited some more.

When it was two a.m., Galina ushered us out into the dreary darkness of the icy tarmac. We followed her, not knowing which of the many planes parked on the sprawling expanse would be ours. As best we could tell, none of them had any steps pushed up against them.

There were other groups from different directions converging at the far end upon the same plane we were approaching. On the side were the Russian letters for Aeroflot, the name of the national Russian airline. I don't remember where the steps eventually came from, but they did arrive. I was shivering, as were all my companions, and anxiously waiting to get inside. But — at the bottom of the steps, one on each side, stood two ladies in their official uniforms and their fur hats. They again inspected the papers of everyone and were evidently in no hurry to get us in out of the cold.

I was pretty numb when, finally, with the rest of the large group of travelers, we were pushing and shoving our way up the slippery steps made of metal grating. Holding on to the frozen handrail didn't help much!

There were no reserved seats, so it was up to each individual to squeeze himself into the first available seat. Most of the citizens of that nation, at least the ones on that airplane, were larger than I. I was hard-pressed (!) to fit into the narrow space next to a woman of such mighty stature she should have paid for two and a half seats. I had quite a time to keep my knees from pushing the seat ahead of me out of its moorings.

The upholstery was torn, the seat belts frazzled, the floor filthy and the baggage compartments above the seats were just open shelves. I found a seat by the window so I wouldn't be clobbered if things should come tumbling down. There seemed to be no limit to the amount of baggage one could take inside; some passengers piled theirs onto their laps.

About an hour into the flight, the flight attendants began to serve breakfast. Their stern and unfriendly manner left no doubt as to who was in complete charge. Since they "carried a lot of weight," it would have been difficult to "get by them" when they were in the aisle. It was amusing to watch them trying to pass each other.

There were no carts from which to serve the passengers. Each tray was carried individually from the pantry to the travelers. Since the plane was filled to capacity, I was amazed at this inefficiency — and mighty hungry when I finally received my tray, which I had to balance on my lap because the tray table was broken.

My breakfast consisted of half a slice of very hard black bread, half a cold, clammy, greasy chicken drumstick cut (or rather sawed) exactly through the center of the bone lengthwise, and a dip of cold rice with some matching frozen peas. For dessert, each of us received a very stale, hard cookie with a dab of dried jam in the center and a small yellow unripe apple full of bruises. I think they call them drop apples here. Mine must have bounced a few times!

Throughout all my missionary journeys on airlines, both international and domestic, even including Romania and the People's Republic of China, nothing really shocked me as much as the poor and terribly neglected conditions of air travel in what was then the Soviet Union. Especially the food, the service and the inside appearance of their planes.

Upon arrival near Alma Ata, four hours' flight from Moscow and spanning three more time zones, we were directly bussed to our Intourist hotel and assigned to our rooms. (Intourist hotels are — or were — assigned by the Russian government to house, feed and otherwise accommodate international travelers.)

Shortly after I got to my room, "Jason" introduced himself. He spoke English quite well, but was most secretive about his work. Repeatedly, while I was talking to him, he put his finger to his lips and pointed to the two "sprinklers" at the ceiling. Again, I should have remembered from my time in Romania. Until then I had only read about those mysterious and well-disguised devices called bugs.

After a while, Jason suggested we go for a walk, during which he told me about arrangements he'd made for a meeting with a German-speaking congregation. As we were passing certain people or when he noticed someone walking close behind us, he lightly touched my arm. We stopped talking or changed the subject. He pointed out cars parked at certain intervals and called my attention to those slowly driving by.

When we were in our room and he wanted to talk about details of meetings, he would motion me into the bathroom, turn on both water faucets and, bending low over the sink, spoke to me in a whisper.

He told me when to be ready, and later that day, looking toward the sprinklers, he said with a smile, "Well, let's go to a movie tonight!" When the time came, he called a taxi and had the driver drop us off at a nearby theater. After ascertaining that our "shadow" was evidently satisfied and had left, we walked to a nearby bus stop and joined others waiting on benches there.

Jason kept looking at his watch. After a while he said, "Now we shall go!" We walked around the block and through a few side streets. Suddenly, per previous arrangement unknown to me, a car dove up alongside us and stopped. My friend opened the door and told me to quickly get in. The driver greeted us very warmly and we drove off.

Jason told me we were leaving town. Though I knew it was against the rules of Intourist (the travel organization through which we had come), I felt sure Jason knew that also.

The road soon became very muddy and bumpy. Before long, we arrived at a high wooden fence. Our diver got out, quickly opened the gate drove through and just as quickly closed it again. This was the home of a most hospitable family with seven children. At the beginning, the smaller ones stayed at a respectable distance, eyeing me curiously and wondering what sort of man it was who had come (as they had been told) from faraway America. After I spoke to them in German, they loosened up and became quite excited. We had a simple meal with delicious homemade bread and then went together to the church.

It was a very plain structure, also surrounded by a high wooden fence. The inside was fairly large with rows of very coarse unfinished benches and a simple rostrum behind a low railing. The place was full when we arrived with Jason. We went to sit at the front, next to the leader of the congregation.

He greeted me most cordially, though I sensed some reservation. I was feeling silently scrutinized and, as we say here, checked out, by everyone in the place. Later I found out it was only at Jason's persuasion I was allowed to come. They did not know very much about me, including my convictions about the fundamentals of the faith.

They asked Jason to speak first and to introduce me. It was then I remembered what the mission director had told me about the fearfulness of the believers there. I told them how a Jew can come to know the Lord personally through his Old Testament Scriptures. I said I felt my heart closely knit with theirs, whose faith is founded on the same precious Truths, and told them how happy I as to be now in the land of my wife's ancestors. (Her grandparents were German Mennonites from Russia.) After I finished, they asked my wife's maiden name. When I told them it was Thiessen, they all laughed, because that is a name quite common among the Mennonites there.

After the service they remained in their seats and asked me to tell how I, a Jew, had come to know the Lord. From my seat in the front row, I spoke to them for about 15 more minutes. They asked so many questions, they decided to continue at the home of one of the believers for those who would like to come.

There I met with about fifteen men and two ladies. They sat on a divan, a piano bench, a couch and some folding chairs while I answered questions about Judaism and told them about my missionary work in Japan and my ministry at the L.I.G.H.T. House.

I was curious and asked them about the problems they faced as believers in their country, but their answers were very vague. Believing I was among those "of like precious faith," and enjoying the unrestrained fellowship of heart, I felt free to ask also about the persecution and imprisonment of some because of their faith. There was no answer. Even though I rephrased and repeated my question, there was absolute silence.

It took me a while to figure out that even among so-called believers there may be informers, those actually working for some government agency. I was in a country where no one dared to wholly trust even his closest friend. Reading about this is one thing. Being painfully involved in it, quite another.

I arrived back at my hotel at one o'clock that night and lay awake for quite a while thinking back upon my life in Germany as a youth during the Hitler era. I, as a Jew, also had to be careful where I went, what I did and how I spoke, to not give occasion against myself to those who sought it. In a measure at least, I could feel with those dear brothers and sisters deep behind the Iron Curtain. Thank the Lord, things at this writing have begun to change.

41

MY HEART GIVES OUT

AFTER MY RETURN to Frankfurt from the Soviet Union, I felt pretty well for a while, and my friends booked me for speaking engagements in three cities. In the first of these, on November 20 (1987), I began to feel very sick as I was on my way to the evening service. I sat on a front seat during the preliminaries, hoping that my condition would improve by the time I was to speak, but instead it worsened. I was helped out of church and barely made it to bed, falling onto it with my clothes and shoes on. My other meetings were immediately cancelled.

That night I thought my heart would jump out of my body, and I expected to meet my Lord at any time. In the morning my host called a doctor. He took my pulse and suggested I get an EKG at a hospital in nearby Bonn. I was sure I knew what the result of such a test would be and thought I might still be all right until I could return to the States, scheduled for nine days later. I felt sure it was a heart attack or the closest thing to it.

I stayed in bed another day until the pain had somewhat subsided, and on the following day drove 120 kilometers to the small community where "my family" lived — the ones who had provided the car and had lovingly adopted me. At their insistence I went with them to the local doctor. Having examined me, he ordered me to head straight to the nearby hospital. He picked up the phone and told them to expect me momentarily. He didn't even want me to go by the house to pick up some of my things.

I did stop by the house, mainly to call my wife (in Kansas). I really didn't know what to say to her in order to not alarm her. I had not yet told her one word about my condition, not in any of my letters nor my frequent phone calls. So I just told her I felt sicker than ever before and that I was going to a hospital for a thorough examination.

She no doubt guessed the severity of the situation when I added I would very much like her to come to me. I told her how to go about getting her passport renewed, where to get traveler's checks and through which agency to make her travel arrangements. Then I headed for the hospital.

They immediately put me into Intensive Care, intravenous tubes in my arms and a number of sensors all over my chest. As it turned out, I had angina pectoris, blockage of the main arteries to the heart.

The following day they transferred me to the ward, a room with three other patients, where I remained for the next two weeks. I was impressed with their excellent treatment and care, even giving patients a choice of tasty meals. The all-inclusive charge was $194 per day. There was a phone by my bed, and Gussie called every few days. I had told her I'd always be "at home!"

They took two sonograms, a number of X-rays, even of my stomach, and repeated EKG's to check the effects of the medication. Over there, X-rays are called Röntgen Strahlen (Röntgen Rays), after their German discoverer, Wilhelm Röntgen. I was amused to see we had the same first name.

I improved rapidly, and as I gained strength began a new phase of ministry, Hospital Evangelism among the doctors, nurses and especially the patients in my room.

I had never been hospitalized before, and now it had happened in the land of my birth. Members of my adopted family came to see me, also some of their congregation to whom I had ministered. Their men's choir performed in the hall outside my room. One Christian bother played the guitar, sang and gave his testimony to us patients.

Gussie arrived on December 8th, the last of my 16 days in the hospital. We left the place together, spending the next two weeks at the home of my, now our, family, who gave Gussie an extra warm welcome.

Besides the fellowship and splendid meals, we enjoyed afternoon "Kaffee," pie and tarts of all sorts. We were impressed anew with the many kinds of wholesome and delicious German breads, which we remembered from our missionary days there (1965-67).

I stayed home most of the time to recuperate, but Gussie did some shopping and some sightseeing with the lady of the house. We both loved the German countryside, especially watching an old shepherd and his sheep, Gussie's favorite animal.

On our last Sunday there, we all took a trip to the Moselle River. High among the vineyards we ate in a typical German restaurant overlooking the river. I was so thrilled to be back "home" again, and especially happy to have my dear Gussie with me, though it took nothing less than my heart attack to get her there.

We returned to the States three days before Christmas. After the New Year I had a thorough examination, including a heart catheterization, in one of the local hospitals. A part of my heart muscle had been affected and one of the main arteries leading to it. An operation was not considered advisable, but rather a treatment with medication.

I began three months of rehabilitation, treadmill, exercycle, daily walks and a fairly strict diet. Instead of going on a missionary journey abroad the following year, I ministered at home in prisons, youth rallies and mission meetings.

42

AFTER A YEAR'S PAUSE

THE DESIRE TO HEAD OUT again for my Lord continued to tug on my heart. So in the fall of 1989 I took off for Europe again, where I was provided with an old but road-worthy Mercedes.

I first visited my hometown of Dortmund. Each time I walked again the old familiar streets I once roamed with my bicycle as a youth, I felt as though I had never left. As usual I went to see the present owner of Father's former store and called some of my former classmates.

I lived with a pastor friend in Dortmund's suburbs and again had the opportunity to speak to his congregation. Going on to Amsterdam, I saw the museum at the house were Anne Frank and her family had been hidden, cooped up in that small space for so many months. Many young people were milling around the city square. Most of them were addicted to drugs, for which the city is in disrepute. I spoke to them, and then went to the harbor, where the newly bought LOGOS II of the Operation Mobilization lay at anchor being completely refurbished. I spent a whole day watching the international crew at work and spent the night in one of the recently completed cabins.

Then on to the small town of Hückeswagen where an all-city festival was in progress, and an evangelistic effort was part of the goings-on. They had erected a stage, from which I showed object lessons and spoke to the passersby. Then a youth choir sang and dramatized the gospel story. At a retreat center near Stuttgart which was located amidst beautiful green pastures, I ministered to a large group of senior citizens. Heading south toward Switzerland, I was driving close to the French border, so I went across and had a great visit in the home of a French exchange student Gussie and I had met the year before in Pennsylvania. That was something: rejuvenating the French I had learned in school as a teenager in Germany.

In Kandern in the Black Forest near the German Alps, I stopped again at a retreat, this time in conjunction with the Evangelistic Outreach of the Jantz brothers. I stayed with the family of Dr. Hartmuth Sünderwald. He is a genius, a personal "buddy," and had been a member of the mission with which we had served in Germany in 1965, a long time before he earned his doctorate. At that time he had come to me with a "romantic interest," and I strongly encouraged him to marry the girl who is now his wife. So it was a joyous interlude.

Nearby in Switzerland, among the most beautiful mountain ranges, lush meadows and idyllic hamlets, I visited relatives of one of my close friends here in Kansas City. How attentively the young granddaughter and her girlfriend listened, intrigued by the story of blind Bartimaeus.

Early the next morning I crossed the Alps into Italy. Passing Milano, I went to Vincenza to a missionary couple whose address Dr. Sünderwald had given me. They had a German co-worker with whom I rode to Venice, and it seemed there were more foreigners in the "Water City" than native Italians. We rode the water taxis, and I had a great time telling Japanese visitors why I had lived in their country for so many years.

I felt that my Lord had directed me step by step. Humanly speaking, I could have questioned my movements. Why, from way down south (Italy), did I go way up north again into what was still East Germany, shortly before the reunification?

The lady customs official was exceptionally kind, thanking me for marking down the exact number of felt-tip pens I was taking as gifts. When I wrote down the manufacturer's serial number of my telephoto lens (so that upon leaving they could verify that I hadn't sold it), she asked what that was. I had her look through it on my camera, and she called one of her colleagues to do the same. Both of them shook their heads in amazement.

When she saw my video camera, she asked if I had any exposed film in it. When I admitted that I did, she said, "Then we have to play it and see it." I was surprised and asked if they had any such apparatus, to which she answered, "We here have everything; come along and see." (*Everything but telephoto lenses,* I thought to myself.)

I went with her to a little room and watched as the frustrated technician produced nothing but a snowy image. They both were rather embarrassed. She said, "I guess you use a different frequency over there," which is indeed the case. She stamped my passport and let me go.

In Eisenach I visited the in-laws of a nurse I had met when speaking in one of the hospitals. These people didn't know me, but when I explained the connection, they remembered that their daughter-in-law had spoken of me. The clergyman at the Lutheran (German) state church there was a vicar (parish priest with limited authority), and when I told him about my ministry in Japan, he arranged for eight of his trainees in Kirchendienst (church ministry) to come over. We had a great meeting in his living room that night. Our Lord opened one door after the other for me to proclaim His Word.

The Autobahn to Leipzig was, as most roads in East Germany, full of chuck-holes. Because of its deplorable condition there were many detours over not-much-better side roads through many small communities. I was always glad when I had conquered them. In Leipzig I visited many believing families and their fellowships, most of them in their homes because the German State Church (Lutheran) does not recognize them. Officially they are not permitted.

On the way straight north from there to Ludwigslust, I got myself into a very precarious situation. Someone had given me sandwiches to eat along the way, and I was looking for a wide spot in the road where I could stop and eat. Watching on the right side of the road, I finally found one, stopped and began to unwrap my lunch. I glanced around to my left, only to discover I was opposite the big gate to a garrison of the Russian Occupation Forces. Realizing that any car, especially a Western one, would arouse suspicion parked right there, I quickly re-wrapped my sandwich and prepared to drive on. A German motorcycle policeman drew alongside, demanding to know what I was doing there. I knew it would sound foolish to say, "I wanted to eat my lunch," but I had no other answer. He asked for my passport and my driver's license. I showed him my international one, which I get every year for ten dollars at the local auto club. I also had my permanent German driver's license which was issued to me in Dortmund on July 1, 1933, with my picture when I was 18 years old. He copied my license number and told me to leave the place as fast as possible. It was still 300 km to Ludwigslust.

I later asked a local Christian brother what the result of such an encounter might be. He said they would check a nationwide computer system to see if I had been guilty of similar misdemeanors, whether I was a military member of an enemy nation working in civilian clothes. If so, all border posts would be immediately notified. If not, nothing would come of it. Anyway, from that time on I drove more circumspectly, that is, "around-lookingly."

In Ludwigslust, I passed a Russian garrison. Here, a few years before, an American Intelligence officer had been shot by a Russian guard at a Russian maintenance facility when he tried to take a picture of a Russian tank through a window. His jeep driver was prevented from going for help; he bled to death.

Each time I go to East Germany, I visit the large charitable foundation hospital in Ludwigslust, speak at the Bible classes of the nurses-in-training and visit the families of some of them who live nearby and one of my children in the faith (though our Lord has no grandchildren). Another nurse's family lives in nearby Grevesmühlen, and

I visited them before crossing the border to West Germany at the most northern part of East Germany. Later, their daughter, the nurse, wrote me of her "first in her lifetime" trip to a free country.

She and her husband had ventured across the recently opened border into West Berlin. They were impressed with the clean, colorful houses in contrast to East German drab, neglected buildings. She said they felt like beggars going to the bank to each receive their 100 West German marks, then to a supermarket. So overwhelmed were they in seeing all the things that could be purchased, they stood in utter unbelief. They finally indulged in … an ice cream cone.

Another Christian brother in the East told me of the time he and his wife crossed over for the first time and entered a supermarket. The wife stood transfixed, her mind unable to grasp what her eyes beheld. Her face turned ashen; she ran out into the street and vomited.

While with a Christian family in Leipszig, the man told me how blessed they had been with the presence of a missionary from Malmö, Sweden, who spoke to them. I had, of course, asked for the address. Now that I was close to Denmark with Sweden just across a bit of the Baltic Sea, I thought to venture forth in that direction.

When covering great distances, I generally look for stopover places en route with brothers and sisters in Christ. I had no such in Denmark, and I did not think I could make it all the way to Sweden before the end of just one day.

Being on the ferry to Sweden reminded me of our Pacific crossing to and from Japan, and I enjoyed being on the water again. I felt a little lonesome though, so I looked for someone to talk to. I was between two countries, not knowing exactly where I was going, although I knew with Whom. I checked the two fashionable restaurants of this eight-deck ship, but most of the passengers were eating or reading or sleeping on the comfortable deck chairs.

Passing the cosmetic concession in the ship's shopping arcade, I decided to ask the salesgirl what language she would use with such an international clientele.

"Either German, Swedish or English. And I also speak some Danish." Stopping for a moment, she added with a smile, "And Japanese."

Wow! I could hardly believe my ears! Her mother was Japanese, her father a Swede, and she had studied in England. She didn't say where she had picked up her German. When I spoke to her in Japanese, her eyes lit up, "Where did you learn that language?" she asked. When I told her of my missionary activities, she suddenly said in Japanese, "I too believe on the honorable Jesus." I knew then that it would end my search for a place to stay while in Denmark! She gave me the address of a believing brother in Copenhagen, where I spent that night, taking another ferry the next morning to Malmö, Sweden.

Once there, I called a distant cousin who had moved there at the time of Hitler. They treated me royally and drove me all over town sightseeing. When we sat together in the evening I showed them from the Jewish Scriptures what the prophets had said about the coming Messiah. They were very open, but not convinced.

The missionary whom I visited interviewed me and wrote an article with pictures for a Swedish Christian magazine. He arranged for me to speak to two classes in the local Christian school, and my cousin came along. Since I spoke in German, which was translated into Swedish, both of which my cousin, of course, perfectly understood, he heard the Word of God presented twice.

I returned to Germany by a different route, aboard an overnight ferry — one of the largest I've ever seen. It was newly built, 530 feet long, the length of one and one-half football fields. Two of its ten decks were for passenger cars, another for trucks, holding a total of 550 vehicles. One could shop at a big supermarket or a boutique, enjoy the swimming pool or one of the two saunas. The ferry had a passenger capacity of nearly 1,800, including 1,150 in cabins, each with a shower and toilet. There were playrooms for children, a table tennis room and solarium, besides eight conference rooms, four restaurants and a salon bar.

I walked all over that ferry and took video pictures before finally going to my cabin late that night. The next morning, after we docked, I headed directly for Frankfurt, 500 km farther south. Rather sadly, I returned my trusty Mercedes to its owner. I had driven it 6,975 km (4,335 miles) during my 49 days abroad, having spent the nights in 27 different homes, including one on a ferry.

Back in Kansas, new challenges awaited me, among them performing a bilingual wedding ceremony of an American Marine sergeant and his Japanese bride. I had to prepare a 45-minute lecture to be given at the local Japan-America Society on "Japan, Its Customs and Its Teachings," including Shintoism and Buddhism (somewhat out of my line).

Besides these, there were bi-weekly rehearsals for eight performances of an Easter drama in one of the largest churches (1,700 seats) in our area. In a cast of 60 (and a 150-voice choir), I played the high priest.

I was also translating more of my English Bible studies into German for my ministry over there, especially those dealing with the People of Israel, the proof of the Trinity in the Old Testament, prophecies concerning the Messiah, and our Lord's continual dealing with my people.

I diligently continued my correspondence with my contacts in Europe, which again led to new invitations. All this work is needful; yet doing it cannot compare with the thrill — the blessings and the fulfillment — which our Lord is pleased to bestow upon me when I actually serve Him abroad.

43

THIS TIME, A TWO-SOME

IN THE SPRING of 1990 I had met a Christian physician who had discontinued his medical practice to serve the Lord another way. He was now challenging other doctors, nurses, laboratory technicians and hospital employees to give themselves to the spiritual welfare of their patients as well as to their physical needs. He ministered through the Hospital Christian Fellowship and had traveled widely in the Orient, Africa and South America. Not having yet been to Europe, he had asked about the possibility of joining me.

At the end of August, I went to Holland to meet him. Together we visited missionary Van Der Bijl, better known as Brother Andrew, *God's Smuggler,* and drove to northern Germany. We dropped in on a young Christian brother whom I had met at a tent campaign. He had scribbled his address on a piece of paper and I'd stuck it carelessly into my pocket, not ever hoping to go there.

He and his friends could hardly believe we had come. Their first question was. "How long can you stay?"

We stayed five days, were generously cared for, had a youth meeting every night, spoke at an old age home and a neighborhood high school and showed object lessons on the street.

In Bremen, we went to a missionary conference. In connection with that, we attended a large meeting where Joni Eareckson Tada spoke to many handicapped people in wheelchairs. We also visited the German *Bibel Schule* in Brake. In Dortmund, my hometown, I interpreted for my doctor friend at a small but filled Stadt Mission (City Mission) meeting. I interpreted also in private homes and wherever we visited because the doctor spoke no German. Interpreting constantly from English to German and vice versa proved that my brain wasn't quite as nimble as it once had been.

Traveling together for five weeks, we ended up in Berlin on October 1, the day before the official reunification of Germany. We went to the famous *Brandenburger Tor* (Gate), where I bought a piece of "the Wall" and a Russian soldier's fur cap, of which many were sold by the returning Russian occupation forces. After the good doctor returned home from there, I headed for Dresden, then on to Prag, Brno (Brünn in German), Bratislava, Vienna and Ungenach, in Austria. After that, I drove back to West Germany, having been used of our Lord in all these places.

On the German Autobahn, speed limits, for all practical purposes, are not observed; yet driving became second nature to me. I stayed at or below the 120 km/hr line (75 mph), but some cars buzzed past me at 200 km/hr (125 mph), weaving in and out between huge trucks with trailers. Many of these are from Holland, France, Italy and now even from Czechoslovakia, Poland and Hungary. I found myself continually watching my rear view and side mirrors, and I have not had a single accident during the thousands of miles I have traveled. That is a real miracle which I didn't and don't take for granted, but daily thanked my Heavenly Father for.

I particularly liked to pull in at the large refueling/rest stops. Not only the huge trucks and the large touring busses stopped there, but I often saw U.S. military convoys, giving me an opportunity to talk to the soldiers about the Lord. They took me for a German National because of my accent and frequently complimented me on speaking English so well.

In Selm, adult Bible class members asked me to stay and give some personal counsel. I reluctantly stayed until noon the next day, realizing that family problems are international. I usually ended up just listening and praying with the individuals rather than "helping" in any way.

In Bünde it was a ladies' luncheon, and in Schoppen I was just in time for the children's hour at a youth retreat center.

As usual, when it finally came time to return to the States, I experienced an inner battle. So unbelievable are the many opportunities over there — opportunities to be of help.

When November 13th arrived, the 104 days and 8,202 km I had traveled and the 43 different homes I had visited became only a cherished memory.

44

INSIGHTS

1991. THIS TRIP was getting a delayed start. With over 180,000 km on the odometer, the engine of "my" 1980 Audi-200 was getting a complete overhaul. While I was waiting, I visited nearby communities, spoke in two widely separated localities (one on missions, the other an evangelistic effort), led a teen-aged boy to the Lord and spent a week at a camp with 150 young people. They all pitched in to erect their own tents and the ones for the "kitchen" and for the meetings. I was aware that my youth was long past, but I had a great time speaking to the group and to individuals privately.

I again visited the official in the city hall of Dortmund. I told him in more detail than before of my faith in the Jewish Messiah and my willingness to tell this anywhere he thought it would help the "Fellowship of Christians and Jews."

He looked puzzled for a moment and confessed that none of the other Jewish visitors had ever expressed such thoughts. He said he was not very religious, but suggested I write a letter about my intentions and background (education, occupation and experiences during the Nazi reign), to be submitted to the City Council. He thought they might consider inviting me to speak at various high schools for a week or two, not only in Dortmund but in nearby communities.

Now *I* was puzzled. I was wondering what my education and so on during the Nazi reign had to do with telling them about the Lord. I was even more perplexed when he said the city would provide transportation, meals and hotel accommodations and would also give me an honorarium. Things became very clear when he added that my presentation would have to be about the many things that had happened to us Jews during the persecution and not my personal viewpoint of religion. I wasn't quite ready to accept such an assignment, though no doubt it would have given me an opportunity to weave the message in.

What surprised me most was his emphatic statement of the need for a very honest, frank and unbiased representation of all that had taken place. Their concern now is that the youth of today has only a limited knowledge of that era. The government wants the young people fully informed of Germany's darkest and most shameful past so that such events may never be forgotten and never occur again.

His bold assertiveness astonished me. He said that anyone, especially one in an official capacity, who would speak lightly about these atrocities would lose his position. Indeed, Philip Jenninger, president of the West German Federal Diet, speaking to the entire assembly, quoted a phrase which was interpreted as minimizing Germany's dreadful past. Although that was not his intention, he was immediately dismissed from office. No amount of intervention from his colleagues was able to get him reinstated.

Germany today publishes articles such as "Lest We Forget." I was given a thick volume, distributed in cooperation with the city's archives division. Entitled "Lest Any Grass Ever Grow Over It" it contains eyewitness accounts of people who lived through the Holocaust.

The well-known phrase by George Santayana, "Those who cannot remember the past are condemned to repeat it" is indeed taken very seriously in Germany today.

In a nearby town I was staying with a loving Christian family. One evening while riding with them in their Mercedes, my host asked when I had last spoken with my wife. As I was trying to remember exactly when it was, he handed me the receiver of the phone between us, saying, "Here. Do you know the number?"

I've been acquainted with quite a few of the latest innovations, but until then I thought it impossible to speak to a person from a moving vehicle. Here I was, somewhere among the forests and fields of the sprawling German countryside, talking to a person clear across the European continent, then across the Atlantic and across the great expanse that is America, out in the middle of Kansas! I was thrilled to hear her voice and to tell her where I was calling from.

From there I headed directly for the former East Germany, now known as *Die neuen Bundesländer* (The Land of the New Federations), consisting of five additional provinces or regions. I spent most of the next three months in those regions which for the previous forty years had been completely closed to any form of evangelism. According to the Communist dogma, "Religion is the opium of the people."

I had planned to visit many of those whom I had met in previous years. Then it had been needful to go through the long, weary, troublesome and rather expensive process of obtaining a special visa. But now, with the borders wide open, I experienced from the very outset that the people where I had thought to stay for a day or two literally begged me to remain two weeks or more.

One of these towns was the very small community of Serrahn in the province of Mecklenburg, in the most northern part of the former East Germany. Men from all walks of life who had become addicted to alcohol lived together at a large compound. Here they were cared for and rehabilitated by working at a nearby farm. They are taken along to sing or to give their testimony at other nearby rehabilitation centers. I held chapel services for them every morning for two weeks, and in the afternoon or evenings I went with some of them to special meetings at old age homes, jail services or home Bible studies, including those in Rostock, 80 kilometers farther north on the Baltic Sea.

There were similar arrangements for ministry in Leipzig and Schneeberg in the most southern part. I was able to speak at schools and youth meetings also. The people had such deep spiritual hunger, I could hardly get away from the continued requests in the now wide open former East Germany.

In a little village school in Prützen, after I had spoken to them, the teacher of the senior class grabbed my arm with both of her hands. "We really don't want to let you go!" she said.

The students presented me with flowers and drawings dramatically depicting the trauma of their inner struggle to extricate themselves from the shackles of the socialist ideology.

Soon after my return to Kansas City, I wrote a very detailed letter to the city official in Dortmund. I sent a clear explanation about what I, as a Jew, believe and why. A few weeks later I received a short reply. Another former Jewish refugee had already been contacted to visit the schools in the following year, but there might be an opportunity for me to be invited to do so at some later date.

I am sometimes being put on the spot when asked about the virtues of America. While I still think it is the greatest country on earth, I also have to be honest concerning its pitfalls and vices, but mainly its godlessness. I am a Jew, and as such, a defender of the Truth of the Word of God, which clearly states, "The wages of sins is death" (Romans 6:23). Whether sins of an individual, an organization or a nation, it is a law of God that has never changed.

When my people wandered away from the God Who had formed and led them, the nation was split. It wasn't long before it was carried into captivity. The judgment of God fell, and Israel was scattered.

Rome, the Eternal City that they said would last a million yeas, fell in 410 A.D. without a single battle. Sin had done its evil and deadly work. Sin and sinful practices had eaten out the heart and core of the Roman way of life before the vandals ever came.

In his book, *The Rise and Fall of the Roman Empire,* Gibbons lists five reasons for the fall of Rome:

First, the rapid increase of divorce;
Second, the craze for pleasure;
Third, the building of giant armaments while the real enemy was within;
Fourth, demoralization of the people;
Fifth, retrogression of religion (that is ungodliness).

In American today, the same five things are at work as a cancer, eating out the very heart and core of the American way of life as we have known it to be. But this cancer is also spreading around the world. It is, in fact, the cancer of the sinful human condition, and I have found it wherever I go.

Yet, in my travels, when I continually hear comments like, "Can't you stay a little longer? We have so many other places for you to go;" "How can we get in touch with you?" and "When can you come back?" my leaving there becomes most difficult. It is especially so since that is the country of my birth and my upbringing. I was delivered not just from the wrath of the Nazis, but in order to come to know the One who delivered me from sin and eternal doom.

How can I do else but go back with a heart full of love and compassion and the message of Salvation? Go to these people who have for so long been blinded, deprived of the very essence of Truth for their eternal welfare.

Thus, at this writing, I'm preparing to go forth again.

THE LAST OF MY MISSIONARY TRAVEL REPORTS

During each of the following eight years I was "back on the road" again, and I want to share with you just the last of my missionary travel reports, dated July 28 to October 27, 1999.

From the dubious position of an instructor to that of serving as a chaplain and finally to that of a traveler on the road again for my Lord and with all this to you all, by means of this letter.

It really began when I heard about the COMMUNIVERSITY, a non-academic adult education program, affiliated with the University of Missouri in Kansas City, of which all classes are non-credit and all teachers are unpaid volunteers. Just right for me, I thought, and signed up to teach German, Japanese and Messianic Judaism. There were an average of 14 students in my classes which I always began with a short devotional thought and with prayer and ended by handing out tracts. In the spring I began making the rounds among the sick and their visitors as a volunteer chaplain at the Shawnee Mission Medical Center, often using as a natural "opening" that it is good to be lying down, for that makes it easy to "look up." I engaged doctors, as well as nurses, in conversation as I met them in the halls. On July 29th, though having passed my 84th birthday, I headed for Germany again, the land of my birth and upbringing, an old Jew who had been ostracized from there as well as his family with loss of all their possessions under the Nazi reign, but who had been reconciled to God through the Messiah, and therefore also completely to those who once sought to annihilate him.

I was given the same 12-year-old Citroen again that I had driven last year, and not too long thereafter I found myself standing on the street in Dortmund, not far from the house we once called "home," introducing myself as the little Jew that once used to live there and telling everyone who passed by of the greatest Jew who ever lived.

The present owner of Dad's former store invited me to lunch, but I preferred to talk rather than eat; yet, as many times before, he "heard, but understood not" why I had come back.

Then 'way down south to Ludwigsburg to speak at an Israel-Friendship-Circle — there are many of such now in Germany, to reach our Jewish friends with the Good News about the Messiah and to intercede for them at the throne of Grace.

Traveling the German Autobahn was a constant challenge, a dare and a threat, for most cars couldn't wait for me to get back into line after I had passed a slower-moving vehicle, flashing their lights and then swooshed past with speeds of 160 to 200 km/hr. I generally stayed behind those huge trucks for safety reasons, for they by law are not permitted to drive faster than 80 km/hr, though they often go up to 100.

At Wildberg in the beautiful Black Forest for a Bible conference for senior citizens was my next stop, and as always at such gatherings I received many invitations to visit and speak at their churches or home Bible studies. At a Children's Retreat Center in Sinsheim I showed my gospel object lessons, and they dressed me up to represent Moses for their Bible story time. On to a city fair at Wermelskirchen where whole families sat outside for "Kaffee and Kuchen," the typical German afternoon refreshment time, while a mixed choir presented gospel music, during which time I tried to think of something interesting to say for my periodical spots on the program.

My next contact was a family in Everode which I had last seen about eight years before in Görlitz, the German Democratic Republic. At that time I was considered a most rare visitor, for not only was I a person from the West that had managed to get across the border, but I was an American, a German-born Jew, a believer in the Messiah, and beyond that, I had been a missionary in Japan.

Though I'm usually received "with open arms," this time it was with most affectionate "tight hugs." After I was made to "feel at home," I was told that they already had taken the privilege of offering my services to their pastorin — who soon would be coming over to meet me.

A lady pastor is the custom in many German Landeskirchen, which are the old-type state-supported Lutheran churches, of which all good

Germans must be a member and who have their church tax automatically deducted from their salary. Since their services are very liturgical and ritualistic, I met the dear lady with some apprehension.

She, however, was quite congenial, dressed in jeans and a sweatshirt and carrying her two-year-old daughter. Her husband, I soon found out, had a secular job, not having studied "theology." She then explained that she had a pre-confirmation class planned for 10 to 12-year-old children which I was to "instruct." Not having had time to find out all that would be involved, I told them who Jesus is, how I made Him to be not only my Saviour, but the Lord of my life, and then I explained to them the difference.

I'm sure that none of them had ever heard it as I told it to them, and the dear pastorin was so impressed that she asked me to speak at the senior citizens meeting two days hence, for which I decided to stay though I had planned to leave the next day. After that, she even invited me to conduct her Sunday morning church service, but I had to move on.

Since I'm a member of the Japan-American Society here in Kansas City, whose sister city in Germany is Hannover, I wrote to that organization and was invited to a typical Japanese luncheon at their city hall. It was attended by a representative of the mayor and by the local head of the Japanese committee. They also allowed me time to show how I proclaimed the Gospel in Japan by means of my object lessons. Then I was put up in a home of a precious Christian family whose wife was a Japanese and the husband a German.

It was so much fun to hear my mother-tongue spoken with a typical Japanese accent. We laughed a lot as I spoke to the children in Japanese and they answered me in German, and then again the other way around. There in Hannover I also spoke at a home for alcohol and drug-addicted young people, somewhat out of my realm.

From there nearly 500 km south to Mosbach, the headquarters of the Operation Mobilization, to attend a most thought-provoking strategy conference on Jewish evangelism stressing the timeless truth that the Gospel is to be proclaimed to the Jew first.

Little did I think when I left for Germany that my travels would extend beyond its borders, but at a missionary conference near Bielefeld, I was invited to come along with a dear Christian brother to that turbulence-experienced part of Yugoslavia, called Croatia in southeastern Europe, which stretches from the rivers Mura and Drava in the North all the way to the Adriatic Sea in the South and to the Danube River in the East. We covered the 1,000-km stretch during a 14-hour ride at night, so that I could only see the misty outline of the Austrian mountain ranges in the faint moonlight.

At dawn we reached Maribor, the capital of Slovania, and about an hour later the little village of Puscine, near Varazdin. During the day I visited a small dental clinic on wheels which made the rounds to the refugee camps. The families there live between tiny makeshift partitions made of old cardboards and of old blankets in dilapidated old tenement houses or in vacated factory buildings with often only one bed for a family of four and a small hot plate to prepare their meager meals. They come from Serbia and Bosnia where their homes had been destroyed.

I spoke through an interpreter in a small overcrowded room with many looking in through the doorway, and I made my way back to Germany again by night. The leading of our Lord never ceases to amaze me. A dear family in Hannover with a special love for Israel invited me to come with them to Jerusalem for the yearly celebration of SUCCOTH, the Jewish Feast of Tabernacles, which was sponsored by the International Christian Embassy of Jerusalem. It was attended by more than 3,000 visitors from all parts of the globe, and the program consisted of a magnificent orchestra as well as of lectures, spectacular performances with singers, actors and dancers from Israel, Africa and the U.S. Riding the huge city busses to the gatherings at the congress hall on the outskirts of Jerusalem, I was squeezed in between young men and women in uniform, many of which had their machine pistols on their lap or slung over their shoulder. In the streets I saw numerous decorated booths where the most orthodox Jews were celebrating with eating, singing and dancing. There were also the booths of many messianic organizations represented in the halls adjacent to the auditorium making public their various ministries. One especially caught my interest. Its mission was to reach the very poor and homeless Jewish people, many of whom had just recently come from Russia and only spoke that language. This organization gathered them from the streets and even from under bridges to bring them to their makeshift center, feed them and give them a place to sleep.

I spent two days and two nights with them, sharing the same big hall in which these poor people were stretched out on mats on the floor while I was privileged to sleep on an old sofa.

During my travel I also had many sessions with a young man who was determined to end his life. He felt that there was no other way out because of his extremely wicked past, and no promise which I showed him from God's Word seemed to alleviate his obsession.

I had many other "long personal talks," including with those who sought the Lord's will for their lives. One poor girl had narrowly missed being "sacrificed" by her masters after she had allowed herself to get involved in the occult.

So I'm mighty glad to be at home again after three months "on the road," having covered over 4,000 km and having stayed in more than 20 different places.

To our Lord be all the glory and the honor and my extreme thankfulness for having protected me during all this time and, above all, for having given me the great privilege of making Him known.

Appendix

APPENDIX

"Reichskristallnacht" (The [State's] Night of Broken Glass), Nov. 8-10, 1938

On October 28, 1938, the Germans who thus far had encountered only very limited opposition to their antisemitic strategy began a thus far unheard-of brutal aggression against thousands of Polish Jews who had lived in Germany for many years. Hitler's brown-shirted Storm Troopers indiscriminately grabbed not only innocent little children off the streets, but spared neither the aged nor the sick, forcing them by the thousands into trucks and box cars heading for the Polish frontier.

There they were ordered out and given over to their own fate. Finding no protection from the bitter cold in the open "no man's land" between the two boundaries, these Jews sought out empty railroad cars and broken-down, unheated shacks. Since the Polish government was taking no responsibility, they lived on whatever they could find in the field, and many of them starved or froze to death.

In the meantime, the world at large had taken notice of the deplorable condition of this human tragedy and of their extreme hardship, especially of those who were suffering most severely in the vicinity of Zbaszyn.

Among the multitude of human misery was the Zindel Grynszpan family which had lived in Hannover. Their seventeen-year-old son Herschel had shortly before fled to France. Hearing that his own family was among the deported ones, he was so overcome with grief and anguish that he bought a pistol, intending to kill the German ambassador in Paris, Johannes von Welczeck.

At the embassy, however, a lesser official named Ernst vom Rath (pronounced vom raht ['a' as in 'garden']) was sent out to speak to him. Herschel, mistaking him for the ambassador, fired, mortally wounding him.

It was one of those tragic ironies, for even while vom Rath was walking toward his death, he was under investigation by the "Gestapo," (the secret state police) for his well-known opposition to Hitler's antisemitic policy.

The moment the shots were fired, however, his "fallacy" was forgotten, and he was proclaimed a martyr for the "Führer." When he died in the

233

morning of November 9, 1938, the German government security forces, under orders from its police chief, Heinrich Himmler, began a systematic, spontaneous orgy of looting over 7,000 Jewish establishments and willfully burning some 200 synagogues while the police stood idly by.

Hundreds of shop windows were smashed, littering the streets which gave the disaster the name "The Night of Broken Glass" (Kristallnacht).

An unknown number of Jewish homes were ransacked, and practically all male Jews between the ages of 18 and 65 were arrested, deceitfully told to be taken into "Schutzhaft" (protective custody).

Diplomatic reports stated that 20,000 were hauled off into concentration camps, some of them brutally beaten, so that many of them perished before they arrived. Jews were forced to walk barefoot on the shattered glass that littered the streets. One eyewitness tells of a men who couldn't walk fast enough to please his captors because of heart trouble. His fellow prisoners were ordered to drag him face downward, tearing his flesh until his features became an unrecognizable bloody pulp.

The German newspapers, after the death of vom Rath, boastingly proclaimed that the consequences of the assassination would be of such enormous consequences that no Jew dare to underestimate their extent.

Beyond that, the editorials sought to agitate its readers by stating that there were thousands of Jews within the German borders who owned stores and shops in unending numbers on the cities' main streets, that they dominated great entertainment centers and owned huge housing complexes for which they charged exorbitant rental fees, while as "alien parasites in our land" there were among their clan those who would stir up other nations to war against our great fatherland and others again would assassinate our highly esteemed officials.

During the night, storm troopers repeatedly arrested all the men who stood in long lines awaiting the opening of the American Consulate.

One American consul wrote that when he saw the Nazis attacking and beating the Jews in front of his consulate, he was "unable to bear the assault" and asked for police intervention. He further wrote that "the Jews of Germany have suffered such incomprehensible vacillations that would seem unreal to one living in an enlightened country during the twentieth century if one had not actually been a witness to their dreadful experience.

There is even yet today much speculation as to who ordered the assassination. From the very beginning there were rumors that Grynszpan was a subtle tool of the Nazis who were well known for being unscrupulous and deceitful in finding a legitimate way for a renewed and more extensive way of persecuting the Jews.

(We may well remember Hitler's untrue charges when he accused Poland of having deceitfully attacked the German radio station at Gleiwitz on the Polish border, thereby giving a "legitimate excuse" for the surprise invasion of that country on September 1, 1939, which cast the entire world into the second World War.)

Certain records which were found later clearly revealed that in anticipation of the Kristallnacht raids, new barracks had been built in the concentration camps of Sachsenhausen, Dachau and Buchenwald, which had stood empty until that fateful November night, and rumors freely circulated that these were being made ready for the Jews, thus showing clearly that preparation for the razzia had been well planned in advance.

Another proof that these camps had been built many months before was that, while they were yet in their planning stage, one of the officials of the "Reichswirtschaftsministerium" (the government offices of economics) took the chance of sending a "most urgent warning" to one of his "befriended Jewish families," telling them that yet before the middle of November "the most terrible things" would befall every Jew in greater Germany.

A report dispatched from England stated that the German public was quite aware of the existence of these early built concentration camps and that everybody in Weimar knows of Buchenwald and could readily indicate the direction in which it is located, although no one dared to mention the word "Concentration Camp."

It was from this dreaded spot that families of those interned there have at times received a short official notification that the particular inmate had died on a certain day, that he had been cremated and that the ashes could be obtained for a required payment of three marks (1.20).

The brutality of the "Kristallnacht" did not come to an end when the last pane of glass had been shattered.

On November 12, the German government ordered a "money atonement fine" of 1,000,000,000 marks (approximately $4,000,000,000) for the death of vom Rath and ruled that every Jew was responsible for the repair of his destroyed property. The repair would have to begin immediately. Furthermore, no Jew was allowed to collect any insurance on his loss.

Six million Jews perished during the holocaust; yet Germany again today has a Jewish community, one that is, however, a tragic shadow of its former self.

AN ILLUMINATING TRUTH

In the course of my photography after I had trusted the Lord Jesus Christ for my salvation, I came across an astounding biblical principle.

In my early photographic activities I was not aware of this, though I *was* acquainted with its basic principle which is light-writing. The word *photo* (from the Greek FOTOS) means light or illumination, and the word *graph* (from the Greek GRAFOS) means writing or script. Thus, a *photograph* is in the truest sense of the word a light-writing — the light passes through the lens making a writing on the film of *exactly* that which it sees.

In my work I would frequently be asked by a young bride to retouch her photo a little, so a mole or a wrinkle or some small blemish wouldn't be so visible.

Now, the word *retouch* comes from the French RETOUCHER, and it literally means to touch or handle again. Thus a retouched photograph is one that is no longer factual — it no longer corresponds to the truth. It therefore is a falsification, or to say it bluntly, a lie.

Our Lord Jesus Christ, the personification of the TRUTH, said of Himself: "I am the way, THE TRUTH and the life ..." He also said: "I AM THE LIGHT of the world."

Since He, the True God and Creator of all mankind, knows what is in His creation, even as a manufacturer would know what is in His product. God gave us an *un*retouched photograph of ourselves as He, THE LIGHT, sees it, "For the Lord seeth not as man seeth; ... the Lord looketh on the heart." (1 Samuel 16:7).

It's not a very pretty picture, it's full of wrinkles and blemishes. *For from within, out of the heart of men proceed evil thoughts, adulteries, fornication, murders, thefts, covetousness, wickedness, deceit, lasciviousness, an evil eye, blasphemy, pride, foolishness: all these evil things come from within and defile the man* (Mark 7:21-23).

Shocking, isn't it? But rather than to deceive ourselves by depending on a "retouched" image, how great it is to trust Him who not only gives us a new nature now, but who one day "shall change our vile body, that it may be fashioned like unto His glorious body" and be conformed to the very image of the Son of God.

JAPANESE DESIGN

I have noticed that in Japan nearly all of the diagonal designs on their neckties run in the opposite direction from those here in the West, that is, from upper right (where the knot is) to the lower left, while ours run from the upper left to the lower right, since we also write that way. In Japan even their diagonal wallpaper and curtain designs run from upper right to lower left. The average Oriental would feel uncomfortable and unnatural if it were the opposite.

It seems his mind is programmed from right to left. The Japanese, as well as the Chinese, write that way, starting at the upper right of a page, then straight down in rows, moving from right to left, until the last character is at the bottom on the far left.

Traffic in Japan moves on the left side of the road, so the Japanese look first to the right and then to the left when crossing the street, whereas we do it the opposite.

I have a necktie made in Japan, embroidered on the diagonal with the words FAITH, HOPE (and) LOVE. Since it would look strange or not quite right to them if the letters were stitched from left to right, and because the words couldn't be spelled backwards, the manufacturers solved the problem by placing the words as pictured here.

Thus it was written from "right to left" and from "top to bottom" and yet in a way it could be read from left to right.

I tried to make a spiritual application of these differently designed ties by first showing one or two of each type of design. But since my illustration involved a play on the English words RIGHT and LEFT, I could tell it only to English-speaking audiences in Japan or when I came home on furlough.

I sometimes made my presentation at American military bases in Japan, explaining that the upper part (near the knot) was to represent Heaven and the bottom part, this earth.

On the Western tie I started at the lower RIGHT, which I said spoke of people such as those mentioned in Proverbs 12:15, "The way of a fool is RIGHT in his own eyes." Or, "There is a way that seems RIGHT to a person, but the end of it is the way of death." Sometimes I referred to Judges 21:25, when "there was no king in Israel, everyone did that which was RIGHT in his own eyes."

Then I told of the consequences of self-RIGHT-eousness by pointing to the top of the tie, the heavenly sphere, where the lines go to the LEFT. I told of the time in which all nations shall be gathered before the Lord:

"— and He shall separate them one from another, as a shepherd divides the sheep from the goats, and He shall set the sheep on His right hand, but the goats on His L E F T ... (and say to them on the L E F T) Depart from me, you cursed, into everlasting fire, prepared for the devil and his angels" (Mat. 25:32-41).

In other words, if a person considers himself all RIGHT "down here" without the Lord, when he gets "up there" he will come to the realization that he has been LEFT. Taking the Japanese tie on which the diagonal design runs from the upper right to the lower left, I would also begin at the bottom (LEFT), and tell the story of the fishermen by the sea of Galilee who, when the Lord Jesus called, "straightway LEFT their nets and followed him."

So also did Levi, the publican, who sat at the tax collector's table. Of him it is written that "he LEFT all, rose up and followed" the Lord. So did the Samaritan woman who LEFT her waterpot at the well, going into the city telling everyone she had met the Messiah.

I pointed to the top of the tie where the diagonal design went toward the RIGHT. I said that all these had LEFT their earthly belongings to serve the Lord, so in the day when he separates the sheep from the goats, he will set them on His RIGHT, and "they will have the   R I G H T   to the tree of Life and may enter in through the gates of the city" (Rev. 22:14), the eternal city of glory. Even to this day, I meet Christian friends who tell me that they still remember my "Necktie Sermon" though they don't recall what else I had said.

THE UNITY OF GOD

Just about every Jew knows by heart the verse of Deut. 6:4 and can readily recite it in Hebrew: "Sh'ma Yisroel Adonai Elohenu Adonai ECHOD." His entire conviction, I might even say his entire psychological and emotional stay, is founded on this one and only verse of its kind in his Bible.

It concerns the ONE-ness of God. I firmly believe that our God in His infinite wisdom has used this verse to preserve His people from being assimilated by the many heathen nations among whom they lived over the centuries.

Even though this Hebrew word *Echod* is considered as meaning ONE, it is in reality a word that represents a "combined" or a "united" ONE-ness. It may be quite well understood in the account of Genesis 2:24, where we read: "Therefore shall a man leave his father and his mother, and shall cleave unto his wife: and they shall be ONE flesh," (Bosor *ECHOD*); there are TWO, yet living unitedly before God as ONE.

Even more amazing is the use of this word *Echod* in Numbers 13:23 and 24 which tells about the men who went to search out the land of Canaan and cut down "a branch with ONE CLUSTER of grapes" (Enawb Escol *Echod*), signifying a "joined" or "linked" ONE-ness, for the ONE cluster consisted of many grapes.

There was a time (Judges 20:1,2) when *"all the children of Israel went out and the congregation gathered together as ONE man (Iysh Echod) from Dan even to Beersheba ... 400,000 footmen that drew sword."* Here the 400,000 men are sets forth as being knit together as ONE *(Echod)* combined and compound reality. The same ONE-ness is again mentioned in verses 8 and 11.

Why is it, then, that my people do not recognize this true and intrinsic meaning of the word *Echod?* The reason is that they have replaced it with another Hebrew word for ONE, namely *Yachid,* which signifies an "absolute" or an "indivisible" ONE-ness, as we find in Genesis 22:2 where God said to Abraham, *"... Take now thy son, thine ONLY son (Ben Yachid) ... and offer him ... for a burnt offering ..."*

It may be even clearer in Judges 11:34: *"And Jepthah came to Mizpeh unto his house, and behold his daughter came out to meet him ...; and she was his ONLY child; beside her he had neither son nor daughter." (Yachid* — an unquestionable and *absolute* ONE-ness.)

How, then, did this change from *Echod* to *Yachid* come about? Until about 800 years ago, Jews in general did believe in the tri-unity of God; but around that time (1135 A.D.) there was born in Cordova, Spain, a great scholar named MOSES MAIMONIDES, popularly known among Jews as "RAMBAM," a contraction of "Rabbi Moses Ben Maimon." He was called the "Jewish Aristotle," for he was not only a philosopher but a physician, an astronomer, ardent Talmudist and a prolific writer. He introduced the scientific and rational spirit into the study of Judaism, and his system of religious philosophy forms the basic foundation of Judaism today. As the result of this, we have today the difference between the Reformed, the Conservative and the Orthodox way of Jewish worship.

This great Jewish scholar Moses Maimonides wrote in the 12th of his "Thirteen Articles of Faith" which even to this day are incorporated into the "Book of Daily Prayers," published by the Hebrew Publishing Company, this well-known creed: "I BELIEVE WITH PERFECT FAITH, THAT THE CREATOR, — BLESSED BE HE, — IS ONE " *(Yachid,* an ONLY and ABSOLUTE ONE).

Amazingly and strange as it may seem, our Jewish friends read and quote the verse in Deut. 6:4 correctly as "ECHOD" (a combined Try-Unity), but while doing so they *think* YACHID (an ONLY and ABSOLUTE ONE) as proclaimed in the creed of Moses Maimonides. And thus they renunciate, in their mind, the Tri-Unity of God.

KANJI on Being HOLY

One of the most interesting Japanese language characters which illustrates and clearly visualizes its basic meaning is the character for HOLY. This ideogram consists of three parts or *radicals:* EAR, MOUTH and DEPENDENCE.

As I studied it, I thought how Mary, mother of our Lord, typified or personified every aspect of this ideogram. She was not holy in the sense that she had no sin; she too had to trust the Lord for her salvation. But she was certainly devout and consecrated, fitting the description in 1 Peter 3:3-5. We read (in part):

... the ornament of a meek and quiet spirit, which is in the sight of God of great price. For after this manner in the old time the HOLY women also, who trusted in God, adorned themselves, being in subjection unto their own husbands.

In this respect, we read in 1 Peter 1:15 *concerning every one of us:* *"... as he which hath called you is HOLY, so be ye HOLY in all manner of conversation."*

The first of the three radicals in HOLY is the one for EAR 耳 . It may have evolved from the drawing of the human ear 𦔮, with which it has a certain similarity. The EAR is thus one of the most important parts of our body as a prerequisite to obtaining HOLY-ness as our Lord would have it. The EAR is needful to HEAR the Word, the instruction of our LORD.

Psalm 78:1: *"Give EAR, O my people, to my law, incline your EARS to the words of my mouth."* Isaiah 1:2: *"Hear, O heavens, and give EAR,*

O earth; for the Lord has spoken; ... Eight times in the Gospels we read, *"He who has EARS to HEAR let him HEAR,* and *eight times* in the Book of Revelation: *"He who has an EAR, let him HEAR ..."*

Having heard, then one is faced with the need for a response *for* or *against* what has been heard. The Bible contains examples of both kinds. Nehemiah 8:2, 3: *"... and the EARS OF ALL THE PEOPLE WERE ATTENTIVE unto the book of the law ...* Zechariah 7:8: *"And the word of the Lord came to Zechariah saying, Execute true judgment and show mercy and compassion ... but they REFUSED TO LISTEN, and pulled away the shoulder, AND STOPPED THEIR EARS, that they should NOT HEAR."* So either response is possible. The point is that THERE IS A RESPONSE NEEDED TO THAT WHICH THE EAR HAS HEARD.

Responses, as they are these days, were foretold to Timothy by the apostle Paul: *"... the time will come when they will not endure sound doctrine; but after their own lusts they SHALL TURN AWAY THEIR EARS from the truth ..."* (2 Timothy 4:3, 4).

Mary was not one of these; she inclined her EARS DILIGENTLY to the angel Gabriel when he told her she would bear the child Jesus (Luke 1:30, 31). That her EARS WERE ATTENTIVE to the angel's proclamation is apparent from her honest question: *"How shall this be, seeing I know not a man?"* After the angel's assurance that the Holy Ghost would come upon her and the power of the Highest would overshadow her, her response was instantaneous: "Behold the handmaid of the Lord; be it according to your word ..." Her MOUTH uttered her response to what her EARS had heard.

So we come to understand that the MOUTH follows the EAR in its importance for being HOLY. Our Lord desires an answer to His voice to us. It is just as clear in the Japanese ideography.

The present symbol for MOUTH may have begun with a drawing like this 👄 , perhaps simplified to this ⛝ , and eventually to this ☐ , its present form. Mary had heard with her EARS , and replied with her MOUTH.

Have you ever considered what might have happened if Mary had refused to give herself to the Lord *completely* and *unreservedly?* I recall the time God used a Christian brother to speak to me about going to Japan as a missionary. It was a momentous decision. In saying YES, I completely turned over the reins of my life to HIM. The entire course of my life was changed.

This brings us to the final radical of the character for HOLY.

It looks like this: 壬 . I don't know how it came into being, but it exactly represents Mary's decision because it only has value when *joined with another radical.* For instance, with the radical for *man* or *person* 任 , it conveys the meaning of DEPENDENCE and encompasses the idea of ENTRUSTING SOMETHING TO SOMEONE or TO LEAVE SOMETHING IN SOMEBODY ELSE'S CARE or even to GIVE OR

RESIGN ONESELF IN COMPLETE SUBMISSION. As it is with all Japanese and Chinese characters, it also can mean *duty, responsibility* and *obligation.*

I was amazed to find it used with the character for *woman* 女 placed right in front of it = 妊 , in which case it means *pregnant,* LIVING IN EXPECTANT DEPENDENCY. At such a time, a woman is indeed completely cast upon her CREATOR, Who alone can form a human body and bring about the miracle of birth.

What thoughts must have gone through Mary's mind after she had given herself to her Lord in utter DEPENDENCE! We can be fairly sure she knew the mockery, the disdain and the sneers she would have to endure. This did not take place in our present-day society; it was A.D. "1." She, a respected, God-fearing and undefiled young woman, was suddenly found "with child." Whether she tried to explain her encounter with the angel we do not know, but even Joseph, until God gave him a dream, had decided to put her away privately. What an unspeakably high price to pay (humanly speaking) to bear the Lord Jesus in one's body.

Thus, from the example of Mary, the Nazarite maiden, we learn the complete picture of the meaning of the word HOLY: 聖

The EAR which inclines toward the voice from Heaven 耳 ;
The MOUTH which declares our readiness to obey Him 口 ;
The body in dedication and utter DEPENDENCE upon Him 壬 .

It is this *absolute dependence* which Paul exhorts in Romans 12:1, 2:
I beseech you brothers (and sisters), *by the mercies of God, THAT YOU PRESENT YOUR BODIES A LIVING SACRIFICE, **HOLY,** acceptable unto God, which is your reasonable service. And do not be conformed to this world; but be transformed by the renewing of your mind, that you may prove what is that good and acceptable and perfect will of God.*

Consider the significance of this. That which Mary experienced and demonstrated bodily has a spiritual meaning which Paul graphically describes in 1 Corinthians 4:15:
For though ye have ten thousand instructors in Christ, yet have ye not many fathers: for in Christ Jesus I HAVE BEGOTTEN you through the gospel.

Paul was saying that through his preaching to the folks at Corinth he had given them life (a new creation) by the power and in the name of the Lord Jesus Christ (2 Corinthians 5:17).

I believe he went one step farther when he wrote to the young believers in Galatia: *"My little children, of whom I TRAVAIL IN BIRTH again UNTIL CHRIST BE FORMED IN YOU."*

Paul's desire was not only that Christ may be formed in us, but that we be HOLY as HE, our Lord is HOLY, and that through our UNION WITH HIM, we, as did Paul, would bear other Christians, that is to say, spiritual children to the glory of HIS name.

THE GOSPEL A LA CHOPSTICKS

As time went on, I looked for more and more ways to convey the message of salvation by means of language or customs that were typical Japanese. My thinking was that if I could attach eternal truths to the things that a Japanese would see or use in his daily life; these truths would keep on speaking to him even after I was gone.

As I continued to study my KANJI characters, I came across one for *chopstick.* It closely resembled another more complex character which conveys the meaning of *person,* except that it had the contracted symbol for *bamboo* on top. I was able to remember *chopstick* by association as a *bamboo person.* In former times — so I was told — people cut sections of the bark of a bamboo tree lengthwise into short sticks and used them even as they use chopsticks today.

This gave me the idea of using different kinds of chopsticks to typify different kinds of people and to have chopsticks illustrate various Biblical truths. So whenever I saw a chopstick, I sought for a spiritual application.

It all started one time in a restaurant. I noticed that people received a simple unfinished chopstick with their orders of rice. At first sight, it looked like only one stick, but having been partially chopped or slit lengthwise, it needed only to be completely broken apart.

My first thought was that these chopsticks had once been a part of a living tree which had to be *cut off* and *die* in order to meet man's need, even as our Lord was. The verse I used was Isaiah 53:8, *"He was cut off out of the land of the living, for the transgression of my people was he stricken."*

The chopsticks had to be broken (apart) in order to be used, and so was our Lord, for in breaking the bread with his disciples he said: *"This is my body, which is BROKEN for you."* A person, too, must be *broken* before God before that one can be used for His glory. Psalm 34:18, *"The Lord is nigh unto them that are of a broken heart and saves those that are of a contrite spirit."*

In using chopsticks, one of them is firmly gripped and held in place while the other one is used somewhat like a pincher and is scissored against the immovable one. In that way, solid pieces of food can easily be lifted (raised up) to the mouth.

Our Lord is *the immovable One,* the One who "changes not" (Malachi 3:6); the *"same yesterday and today and forever"* (Hebrews 13:8). People must be brought to Jesus in order to be *raised up* "in that day" (John 6:40). Andrew found his brother, Simon, and brought him to Jesus. In Matthew 9, people brought a man sick with palsy to Jesus, whom He thereupon *lifted up.* And thus I had my application.

I would show some expensive chopsticks made of highly polished ivory, the kind that might be used for special guests. But though they are very "high class," they can be used only as are the simple, cheap ones in a restaurant which are discarded when the guest has left and the dishes are taken up. If the fancy, highly polished ones had been dropped or otherwise had become soiled, I would rather eat with the plain and ordinary ones which the restaurants use.

Our Lord can use only clean vessels to serve Him. Isaiah 52:11, *"... be clean you who bear the vessels of the Lord."* And Hebrews 12:11, *"... let us lay aside every weight and the sin that so easily besets us ..."*

Another similarly expensive chopstick is made of ebony. This kind is not to be washed with soap and water lest its lacquer-like finish loses its luster. These should only be firmly rubbed with a soft, dry cloth. In demonstrating this, I would briskly rub such a one, explaining that my fingers got hot, for friction crates heat; yet at the same time they would also increase in lustre and beauty. The apostle Paul experienced this "friction," for he wrote: *"Thrice was I beaten with rods — once was I stoned — in perils of waters — in perils of robbers."* And even in perils of his own countrymen.

Even Stephen's face was seen by the council who accused him, as if it had been the face of an angel and he displayed the beauty of his Spirit when he was about to be stoned: *"calling upon God — crying: Lord, lay not this sin to their charge."* And Romans 5:3: *"— we glory in tribulation also, knowing that tribulation worketh patience."*

I also showed chopsticks made of a *mixed* substance, that is, the top was made of wood and the bottom of plastic. My Scripture verses were Proverbs 30:5, 6: *"Every word of God is pure* (unmixed with human ideas) *... add not to His words, lest He reprove you, and you are found to be a liar."* And Deuteronomy 4:2, *"You shall not add to the word which I command you, neither shall you diminish anything from it ..."* (Also Revelation 22:18, *"... If any man shall add to these things, God shall add to him the plagues that are written in this book ..."*)

Then I used three pair of plastic chopstick with identical delicate inlay, one black, one white and one transparent. I told them God loves black people and white people, but that He is most pleased with *transparent* people — those who have nothing to hide before Him. David prayed (Psalm 139:23), *"Search me, O God, and know my heart; try me, and know my thoughts and see if there be any wicked way in me ..."* Also 1 Samuel 16:7, *"... for the Lord sees not as man sees; for man looks on the outward appearance, but the Lord looks on the heart."*

With small chopsticks that little children would use, I quoted Luke 18:16 and 17, *"... let the little children come to me; forbid them not; for of such is the kingdom of God ..."* And *"... whosoever shall not receive the kingdom of God as a little child shall in no wise enter therein"* (Luke 18:17).

Not all chopsticks are the same length, and it sometimes happens that someone gets two that don't match. I'd show such a pair and quote 2 Corinthians 6:14, 15: *"Be not unequally yoked together with unbelievers; for what fellowship does righteousness have with unrighteousness? And what communion does light have with darkness?"* Or Amos 3:3: *"Can two walk together except they are agreed?"* I sometimes referred to Deuteronomy 22:10, *"You shall not plow with an ox and an ass together."* The reason is that they not only pull differently, but the ox is a clean animal while the ass is unclean.

Also, I would show my audience three long metal "chopsticks," making them wonder who would eat with such. They are *not* used to eat with, but are used like tongues to pick up or to re-arrange cinders in the charcoal pots which the Japanese in the country used to heat their rooms. I would show these metal ones which don't burn.

Then I'd tell the story of the three friends of Daniel: Shadrach, Messhach and Abednego, who for the testimony of our Lord dared to defy the king's order to bow down to idols. They were consequently thrown into the fiery furnace, but *"upon whose bodies the fire had no power, nor was an hair of their head singed, neither were their coats changed, nor the smell of fire ... on them"* (Daniel 3:27).

KANJI: THE SON OF GOD

Here is another interesting illustration in which Japanese language characters convey biblical truths.

In 1 Samuel 13:14 we read, *"The Lord hath sought Him a man after His OWN HEART."* (See top character on opposite page meaning "SELF" — or one's own). When combined with the one (below) for "HEART," it spells "BREATH ·character at bottom).

The One chosen after our Lord's "OWN HEART" was David, from whose offspring our Savior came. *"The book of the Generation of Jesus Christ, the son of David, the son of Abraham"* (Mat. 1:1).. In Luke 1:35 the angel said to Mary: *"The Holy Ghost (Spirit) shall come upon thee"* (the word SPIRIT is the same as BREATH).

I-1-36 (p. 83)	JI SHI	self; oneself
自	onosuka (ra) naturally; spontaneously onozu (to) **mizuka (ra) in person; oneself** yori (inverted order) from	
	自分	jibun (14) oneself; yourself; himself
	自然	shizen (534) nature
	各自	kakuji (614) each one; every individual

I-2-8 (p.158)	SHIN	core; wick; center
心	**kokoro**	the heart (mind)
	kokoro (suru)	to be attentive; take care
	心持	kokoromochi (90) feeling; sensation
	中心	chūshin (20) center
	心配	shimpai (n.v.) (354) anxiety; uneasiness

III-11 (p. 73)	SOKU	to leave off; cease
息	**iki**	breath
	iko (u)	to rest
	musuko	**son**
	消息	shōsoku (508) communication; news; movement
	息子	**musuko** (34) **son**
	休息	kyūsoku (n.v.) (45) rest

INSPIRATION means GOD-BREATHED). Jesus thus was the Child of the Breath of God upon Mary who enabled her to bear the Son of God or literally the child of God's BREATH, His BREATH CHILD. In the Japanese ideography, when the character for "breath" is combined with that of "child" it becomes BREATH CHILD, pronounced "musuko" (see where the two lines merge), and means: "SON."

III-11 (p. 73)	SOKU	to leave off; cease
	iki	breath
	iko (u)	to rest
	musuko	**son**
息	消 息	shōsoku (508) communication; news; movement
	息 子	**musuko** (34) son
	休 息	kyūsoku (n.v.) (45) rest
I-1-16 (p. 29)	SHI	viscount
	SU	
	ko	**child; son**
	ne	1st zodiacal sign; the rat; north
子	親 子	oyako (324) parent and child
	女 子	joshi (33) female sex
	椅 子	isu (2154) a chair

246

THOUGHTS ON — WHY THE HOLOCAUST

The Holocaust is over, and six million Jews lie in nameless graves. Why did I subject you to these inhuman brutalities which we Jews had to endure? Why did our God permit it? Is there a lesson to be learned? What could it be?

It's amazing to read about the glorious blessings which God has promised to our people in the Book of Deuteronomy (28:1-15) of our Bible, the *Tenach*. Blessings so renowned that the Gentile nations would stand in awe, saying, *"Surely this great nation is a wise and understanding people; for what nation is there so great, who has God so near to them ..."* (Deuteronomy 4:6-7). But there's a prerequisite to all this. The passage begins, *"And it shall come to pass, **IF** you hearken diligently to the voice of the Lord your God ..."* The possibility was that the people could choose to hearken or not to hearken to the voice of Jehovah.

Being a true believer in the God of Abraham, Isaac and Jacob, and in His infallible Word, THE BIBLE, I must concur with and concede to the graphic description of the actual waywardness and sin of my people. Our prophets, Isaiah, Jeremiah and Ezekiel, frankly wrote about it: — and this is what God said through them:

ISAIAH 1:2-6

2 *Hear, O heavens, and give ear, O earth: for the Lord hath spoken. I have nourished and brought up children, and they have rebelled against me.*

3 *The ox knoweth his owner, and the ass his master's crib, **but Israel doth not know, my people doth not consider.***

4 ***Ah, sinful nation, a people laden with iniquity, a seed of evildoers, children that are corrupters: they have forsaken the Lord, they have provoked the Holy One of Israel unto anger, they are gone away backward.***

5 *Why should ye be stricken any more? Ye will revolt more and more: the whole head is sick, and the whole heart faint.*

6 *From the sole of the foot even unto the head there is no soundness in it, but wounds, and bruises, and putrifying sores: they have not been closed, neither bound up, neither mollified with ointment.*

ISAIAH 1:11-15

11 ***To what purpose is the multitude of your sacrifices unto me? saith the Lord:** I am full of the burnt offerings of rams, and the fat of fed beasts; and I delight not in the blood of bullocks, or of lambs, or of he goats.*

12 *When ye come to appear before me, who hath required this at your hand, to tread my courts?*

13 ***Bring no more vain oblations;** incense is an abomination unto me; **the new moons and sabbaths, the calling of assemblies, I cannot away with; it is iniquity, even the solemn meeting.***

14 *Your new moons and **your appointed feasts my soul hateth:** they are a trouble unto me; I am weary to bear them.*

15 *And when ye spread forth your hands, I will hide mine eyes from you: yea, when ye make many prayers, I will not hear:*

JEREMIAH 2:9-13

9 *Wherefore I will yet plead with you, saith the Lord, and with your children's children will I plead.*

10 *For pass over the isles of Chit'tim, and see; and send unto Ke'dar, and consider diligently, and see if there be such a thing.*

11 *Hath a nation changed their gods, which are yet no gods? but **my people have changed their glory for that which doth not profit.***

12 *Be astonished, O ye heavens, at this, and be horribly afraid, ye very desolate, saith the Lord.*

13 ***For my people have committed two evils: they have forsaken me the fountain of living waters, and hewed them out cisterns, broken cisterns, that can hold no water.***

EZEKIEL 5:5-9

5 *Thus saith the Lord God: **This is Jerusalem:** I have set it in the midst of the nations and countries that are round about her.*

6 ***And she hath changed my judgments into wickedness more than the nations, and my statutes more than the countries that are round about her: for they have refused my judgments and my statutes, they have not walked in them.***

7 *Therefore thus saith the Lord God: Because ye multiplied more than the nations that are round about you, and have not walked in my statutes, neither have kept my judgments, neither have done according to the judgments of the nations that are round about you.*

8 *Therefore thus saith the Lord God: **Behold, I, even I, am against thee, and will execute judgments in the midst of thee in the sight of the nations.***

9 ***And I will do in thee that which I have not done,** and whereunto I will not do any more the like, **because of all thine abominations.***

It may be difficult to accept that the very opposite of God's blessings would befall us **if we would NOT hearken** unto the voice of the Lord our God. Yet the Lord actually used 53 verses to tell us of the consequences (Deuteronomy 28:16-68).

Thus we read in verse 37 the shocking statement that we would be a **byword** among all nations wherever the Lord would lead us. According to Jeremiah 24:9, we'd be *a **reproach,** and a **proverb,** a **taunt** and a **curse,*** and according to Ezekiel 22:4, "... ***a reproach to the heathen and a mocking to all countries.***"

I was really startled, as you may be, when I read Deuteronomy 28:65-69. I became painfully aware that God knew all about **AUSCHWITZ** already about 3,500 years ago. Does this description sound familiar?

And among these nations you shall find no ease, neither shall the sole of your foot have rest; but the Lord will give you there a *trembling heart and failing eyes and sorrow of mind: and **your*** ***life shall hang in doubt before you; and you shall fear day*** ***and night,*** *and **shall have no assurance of your life.*** *In the* *morning you shall say **if only it were evening,** and in the* *evening you shall say, **if only it were morning!** — because of* *the fear of your hearts and the sights your eyes will see.*

Another truth of God's Word is that He not only punishes sin, as He has promised, and as we have read above. But He many times used, or permitted Israel's enemies to carry out this punishment. Then, and I can only cite it from our Bible, though I don't fully comprehend it, our God dealt in turn with that nation for having assailed His beloved people.

He used the Assyrians (Isaiah 10:5,6), the Philistines and the Amorites (Judges 10:6-10), even the Chaldeans (Isaiah 47:4-11), with whom He then dealt stringently evidently because they overstepped their bounds. He dealt also with another nation with which He was "sore displeased" (Zechariah 1:14,15) because they "helped forward the affliction" of His people.

Could it have been that GOD THE ALMIGHTY, in a strikingly similar way, saw fit to use Hitler and Nazi Germany, and then dealt with that nation, just as He did with those other nations of the past? Consider what happened to Germany: 12,000,000 war casualties; most of its cities and villages laid in ruins, and the nation (until recently) split in two.

But it is not only my people, Israel, that have forsaken the Lord. You and I have been equally guilty of being self-willed, and have followed our own sinful hearts, even as did our ancestors from the time of creation: *"And God saw that the wickedness of man was great in the earth, and* *that every imagination of the thoughts of his heart was only evil* *continually"* (Genesis 6:5). Or as our prophet, Jeremiah, wrote (chapter 17, verse 9): *"The heart is deceitful above all things, and desperately* *wicked: who can know it?"* And the answer in verse 10: *"I, the Lord, search* *the heart, I try the reins, even to give every man according to his ways,* *and according to the fruit of his doings."*

As our Lord has done on a **national basis** concerning Israel, so also has He done on an **individual basis** concerning the sins of each one of us, but with one **wonderful exception.** Here again, I am not speaking from my limited human understanding, but according to His own eternal and unfailing Word, the Bible.

Just think of it. God has transferred our sins, yours and mine, onto **SOMEONE ELSE Who had none and then punished HIM in our place.** But, and this is a solemn, critical **BUT,** this marvelous liberating transaction will only be credited to us for righteousness **if we** **appropriate it,** that is, if we **BY Faith** receive this YESHUA (Jesus) Who was willing to die for you and for me.

Here is what my Tenach tells me:

He was born of a Virgin
ISAIAH, Chapter 7

10 *Moreover the Lord spake again unto Ahaz, saying,*

11 *Ask thee a sign of the Lord thy God; ask it either in the depth, or in the height above.*

12 *But Ahaz said, I will not ask, neither will I tempt the Lord.*

13 *And he said, Hear ye now, O house of David: Is it a small thing for you to weary men, but will ye weary my God also?*

14 *Therefore the Lord himself shall give you a sign; Behold,* **a virgin shall conceive, and bear a son, and shall call his name Immanuel.**

He was born in Bethlehem
MICAH, Chapter 5

Birth of Christ Foretold: His Kingdom

1 *Now gather thyself in troops, O daughter of troops: he hath laid siege against us: they shall smite the judge of Israel with a rod upon the cheek.*

2 **But thou, Bethlehem Ephratah, though thou be little among the thousands of Judah, yet out of thee shall he come forth unto me that is to be ruler in Israel;** *whose goings forth have been from of old, from everlasting.*

3 *Therefore will he give them up, until the time that she which travaileth hath brought forth: then the remnant of his brethren shall return unto the children of Israel.*

4 *And he shall stand and feed in the strength of the Lord, in the majesty of the name of the Lord his God; and they shall abide: for now shall he be great unto the ends of the earth.*

He is "The Prince of Peace"
ISAIAH, Chapter 9

Prophecy of the Prince of Peace

1 *Nevertheless the dimness shall not be such as was in her vexation, when at the first he lightly afflicted the land of Zebulun and the land of Naphtali, and* afterward did more grievously afflict her by the way of the sea, beyond Jordan, in Galilee of the nations.

2 *The people that walked in darkness have seen a great light: they that dwell in the land of the shadow of death, upon them hath the light shines.*

3 *Thou hast multiplied the nation, and not increased the joy: they joy before thee according to the joy in harvest, and as men rejoice when they divide the spoil.*

4 *For thou hast broken the yoke of his burden, and the staff of his shoulder, the rod of his oppressor, as in the day of Midian.*

5 *For every battle of the warrior is with confused noise, and garments rolled in blood; but this shall be with burning and fuel of fire.*

6 **For unto us a child is born, unto us a son is given: and the government shall be upon his shoulder: and his name shall be called** *Wonderful, Counsellor, The mighty God, The everlasting Father,* **The Prince of Peace.**

7 *Of the increase of his government and peace there shall be no end, upon the throne of David, and upon his kingdom, to order it, and to establish it with judgment and with justice from henceforth even for ever. The zeal of the Lord of hosts will perform this.*

He Bore Our Sins
ISAIAH, Chapter 53

Isaiah Foretells Christ's Sufferings

1 *Who hath believed our report? and to whom is the arm of the Lord revealed?*

2 *For he shall grow up before him as a tender plant, and as a root out of a dry ground: he hath no form nor comeliness; and when we shall see him, there is no beauty that we should desire him.*

3 *He is despised and rejected of men; a man of sorrows, and acquainted with grief: and we hid as it were our faces from him; he was despised, and we esteemed him not.*

4 *Surely he hath borne our griefs, and carried our sorrows; yet we did esteem him stricken,* **smitten of God, and afflicted.**

5 *But he was wounded for our transgressions,* **he was bruised for our iniquities:** *the chastisement of our peace was upon him; and with his stripes we are healed.*

6 *All we like sheep have gone astray; we have turned every one to his own way; and* **the Lord hath laid on him the iniquity of us all.**

7 *He was oppressed, and he was afflicted, yet he opened not his mouth; he is brought as a lamb to the slaughter, and as a sheep before her shearers is dumb, so he openeth not his mouth.*

8 *He was taken from prison and from judgment: and who shall declare his generation? for he was cut off out of the land of the living;* **for the transgression of my people was he stricken.**

9 *And he made his grave with the wicked, and with the rich in his death; because he had done no violence, neither was any deceit in his mouth.*

10 *Yet* **it pleased the Lord to bruise him;** *he hath put him to grief:* **when thou shalt make his soul an offering for sin,** *he shall see his seed, he shall prolong his days, and the pleasure of the Lord shall prosper in his hand.*

11 *He shall see of the travail of his soul, and shall be satisfied : by his knowledge shall my righteous servant justify many; for he shall bear their iniquities.*

12 *Therefore will I divide him a portion with the great, and he shall divide the spoil with the strong; because* **he hath poured out his soul unto death:** *and he was numbered with the transgressors; and he bare the sin of many, and made intercession for the transgressors.*

If you would like to get in touch with Mr. Baum, you may contact him at:

Wilhelm Baum
11520 West 51st Terrace
Shawnee, KS 66203
Telephone number: 913 / 268-9080
Fax number: 913 / 268-4096